THE
CULTURE of
THE SACRED

THE
CULTURE OF
THE SACRED

Exploring the Anthropology of Religion

Michael V. Angrosino
University of South Florida

WAVELAND
PRESS, INC.
Long Grove, Illinois

For information about this book, contact:
  Waveland Press, Inc.
  4180 IL Route 83, Suite 101
  Long Grove, IL 60047-9580
  (847) 634-0081
  info@waveland.com
  www.waveland.com

Cover photograph: © The Palma Collection/Photodisc/PictureQuest

10-digit ISBN 1-57766-293-8
13-digit ISBN 978-1-57766-293-8

Printed in the United States of America

8   7   6   5   4

Contents

List of Illustrations ix
Preface xi
Acknowledgments xv

1 **Overview and Basic Concepts** 1
    The Culture Concept 4
    What Is Religion? 6
    Other Perspectives 10
    Looking Ahead 11
    Key Concepts 11
    Research Explorations 12
    Case Study "Fortress without Walls: A Black Community
    after Slavery" by Sydney Nathans 13
        Questions for Discussion 21
        Suggested Readings or Other Resources 22

2 **Prehistoric Religion** 25
    Learning to Look at the Past 27
    The Cultural Context of Prehistoric Religion 28
    Evidence? 29

Magic?   31
Key Concepts   32
Research Explorations   33

Case Study   "Like Water for Chocolate: Feasting and
Political Ritual among the Late Classic Maya
at Xunantunich, Belize" by Lisa J. LeCount   35

Questions for Discussion   61
Suggested Readings or Other Resources   61

3   The Ideological Component of the Sacred   **63**

Belief as a System   65
Cosmology   67
How Does Someone Become Religious?   70
Dimensions of Belief   72
Kinds of Religious Experience   73
Key Concepts   73
Research Explorations   74

Case Study   " 'I Refuse to Doubt': An Inuit Healer
Finds a Listener" by Edith Turner   75

Questions for Discussion   89
Suggested Readings or Other Resources   90

4   The Ritual Component of the Sacred   **91**

How Anthropologists Observe Rituals   94
Types of Ritual   95
Ritual Practitioners   102
Functions of Ritual   105
Key Concepts   105
Research Explorations   106

Case Study   "Ethnometaphysics of Iroquois Ritual"
by Elizabeth Tooker   107

Questions for Discussion   118
Suggested Readings or Other Resources   118

5 The Mythological Component of the Sacred   **121**

    Why People Share Myths   124
    The Analysis of Myth   125
    Myths as Social Actions   129
    Key Concepts   130
    Research Explorations   130

    Case Study   "Gilgamesh and Christ: Two Contradictory Models of Man in Search of a Better World" by Miles Richardson   133

       Questions for Discussion   143
       Suggested Readings or Other Resources   143

6 The Ethical and Moral Components of the Sacred   **145**

    Sources of Morality   148
    Virtue   149
    Thou Shalt Not . . .   152
    Knowing What Is "Right"   153
    Key Concepts   153
    Research Explorations   153

    Case Study   "The Navaho View of Life" by Clyde Kluckhohn and Dorothea Leighton   155

       Questions for Discussion   171
       Suggested Readings or Other Resources   171

7 The Environment of the Sacred   **173**

    Making the Supernatural Seem Real   175
    Natural Space as Sacred Environment   176
    Creating Sacred Space   177
    The Intersection of Sacred and Profane   181
    Key Concepts   181
    Research Explorations   182

    Case Study   "Religion and Place in Southern Appalachia" by Richard Humphrey   185

       Questions for Discussion   198
       Suggested Readings or Other Resources   198

8   Religion in an Age of Globalization   **199**

Religion and Sociocultural Change   202
Religion in Pluralistic, Secular Societies   203
Confronting the Challenges of the Modern World   206
How Religion Endures   209
Key Concepts   209
Research Explorations   209

Case Study   "Civil Religion Redux" by Michael V. Angrosino   211

Questions for Discussion   233
Suggested Readings or Other Resources   233

Appendix: Questions for Review   235

Index   243

Illustrations

Old monk with young novices, Burma   2

Offering to the gods, Cancun, Mexico   26

Totem poles, Sitka National Historic Park, Alaska   64

Priest's hands elevating gilt chalice at Mass, England   92

Statue of Neptune, Crete, Greece   122

State of Maitreya Buddha, Ladakh, India   146

Taj Mahal, Agra, India   174

Lincoln Memorial, Washington, DC   200

Preface

Regardless of one's personal views on matters of faith, it is clear that religion has played a major—in some ways a decisive—role for good or ill in world history. In the particular history of our own culture, the Renaissance and Enlightenment periods shifted the attention of Western philosophers in a secular, humanistic direction, although interest in religion by no means evaporated. Modern social scientists are keenly aware of the fact that religion has not faded away under the onslaught of secularism—a fate predicted by both scholars and laypeople early in the twentieth century. If anything, the role of religion in the modern world has taken on even greater significance; as this book is being written, no serious person can help but ponder the enduring role of religion as an element in political, economic, and social affairs in Westernized industrial democracies as well as in more tradition-minded polities. At the moment, we are preoccupied with religion as an element in crisis: Islamic fundamentalism and its challenge to the West; the ongoing and seemingly everlasting conflict in the Middle East; sectarian divisions in Northern Ireland, India, Indonesia, and the former Yugoslavia. But it would be a mistake to think that religion is only a source of discord and strife. It also remains for much of the world's population what it has been throughout human history—a source of security, identity, purpose, meaning, values.

One indicator of the importance of religion is the number of academic disciplines that have studied it. Philosophy, theology, religious studies, psychology, anthropology, and sociology have all made significant contributions to our understanding, as have more recent cross-disciplinary intellectual traditions such as women's studies, ethnic studies, oral history, and folklore.

This book, however, focuses on the contributions of anthropology. From the very beginning of anthropology as a distinct academic discipline in the second half of the nineteenth century, anthropologists have pondered the nature of religion as a human institution. Anthropologists nowadays are not as interested as their predecessors in pinpointing the absolute origins of religion, preferring to study the process of religion as an ongoing element in human culture. But there is a continuity of interest in and a tradition of inquiry about religion that characterizes the discipline of anthropology. In a recent issue of *Anthropology News* (43[3], 2002, p. 52), the monthly newsletter of the American Anthropological Association, the highly regarded scholar Edith Turner goes a step further. She writes that religion "comprises a far bigger field of investigation than we have seen before." In her essay, Turner suggests that religion is not simply a matter of dry statistics or objective analyses of value-neutral processes; one cannot—should not—study religion in the same way one studies subsistence techniques or political organizations. One must, she insists, be open to the "beauty" and "attraction" of religion, not in the sense of becoming proselytizing believers but in the sense of fully appreciating why so many people *are* believers even in the face of so many countervailing social and cultural trends that would, in a purely rational world, seem to make religion irrelevant.

Turner points out that "to reach actual religion itself, we will need to feel its beauty and treat it as a living part of human life, which it is, and much the best way to understand it and to be able to write about it is to experience it." In other words, she calls students of anthropology to "practice being open to the intimations of religion" by participating—"doing things with people"—and not simply reading about them.

This text is designed to give beginning students the sort of experience Turner is calling for. It is best used as a primary text in undergraduate survey courses on the anthropology of religion, although it might also be suitable as a supplementary text in survey courses in cultural anthropology that cover religion among other topics. The book is organized around two very basic elements—*culture* and *religion*—both seen as *holistic systems* composed of interrelated elements. It is geared to a pedagogy of "active learning," or "learning by doing." Following an orienting essay that defines and illustrates the key concepts of a chapter, there will be one or more suggested "research explorations"—activities that even students without extensive prior background can carry out locally under their instructors' supervision. The aim is to help students realize that religion is not an abstraction found only in faraway or exotic cultures, but a living force in their own communities as well.

Each chapter also includes a case study essay in which a recognized scholar illustrates the concepts developed in that chapter in terms of his or her own research. Each case study essay will conclude with several questions which the course instructor can use either as a basis for in-class discussion or as student writing assignments.

This plan is designed to integrate in-class lectures, student research, professional research, and critical discussion into a package based on common themes and teaching approaches. To that end, the style is geared toward ready comprehension; there will be a minimum of scholarly jargon, and that which is unavoidable will be clearly explained. This text is not a scholarly monograph, and specialists in the anthropology of religion may rightly find that it omits some topics, overemphasizes others, or simplifies some of the complex controversies of concern to academics. Nevertheless, the book is offered as a pedagogical tool—a synthesis of substantive material, theory, and research methods suitable for the beginner, which I hope will encourage students to enter into a dialogue with their instructors, with professionals in the field, with each other—and, perhaps most important, with the representatives of religious groups and institutions in their own communities.

It will not be possible for every student in every class to do all the research explorations in a single semester. The instructor will need to select those that are most appropriate to local conditions, as well as those that best complement his/her own emphases. Similarly the choice of discussion/essay questions to be assigned will be determined by the instructor's plan for examinations and other assignments. But it is hoped that there is a sufficient range of ideas to suit a broad constituency of both students and instructors.

Each chapter also contains some suggested readings and video resources. These entries are in no way intended to be complete scholarly bibliographies—they are highly selective and deliberately brief. They are items that even the beginning student might find valuable, although the instructor is encouraged to add items to the list that represent his/her perspectives on the themes discussed in any given chapter and to point the student in the direction of pertinent media resources available locally.

Acknowledgments

I gratefully acknowledge the support and good counsel provided by Thomas Curtin, the Anthropology Editor of Waveland Press. He has carefully guided my previous efforts for Waveland, and his enthusiasm for this current project played a large part in encouraging me to translate the material from classroom to textbook.

This book is the result of more than two decades of teaching a survey course in the anthropology of religion, and the content and thematic emphases of the text owe much to the input of my students over the years. I would like to mention in particular Jeanne Cavalcante, James Torres, Robin Stokes, and Marjorie Kellner-Wright, all of whom provided very useful feedback on the essays and exercises found herein. I also acknowledge the clerical and editorial assistance of Petra LeClair.

A particular vote of thanks goes to Cassandra Workman, who was my graduate assistant during the 2002–2003 academic year. Her contributions to the class and to the research informing the book were especially valuable to me.

Finally, I offer my profound thanks to Patricia Sorrells who has for so many years helped me ask the right questions about matters of religion and spirituality.

1

Overview and Basic Concepts

featuring

"Fortress without Walls: A Black Community after Slavery"
by Sydney Nathans

When I first began studying anthropology nearly four decades ago, there was a widespread perception that human beings, the subject matter of the discipline of anthropology, were clearly different from even their nearest primate relatives. Humans, we were taught, were the only animals who made and used tools; they alone were capable of using abstract language; and only they had religion. We now know that tool use is found not only among primates, but even in other mammalian species—although they could almost certainly survive very efficiently without tools. Chimps and gorillas have been taught to use symbolic forms of language—although there is no evidence that they spontaneously do so outside of laboratory settings.[1] There have even been suggestions that experiences of a suspiciously religious-like quality may occur in nonhuman primates—but how frequent or intense they may be is open to discussion.

Nevertheless, even if we are no longer quite so special as we once thought we were, we still believe that the material objects humans make and use, the way we communicate, and the way we attempt to find or attribute meaning to the things we do all come together in ways that are consistent, patterned, and traditional, as opposed to being transitory, incidental to survival, or taught by outsiders under controlled circumstances. It is surely no accident that all human groups that we know of have made and used tools, communicated in symbolic, abstract language, and sought to find meaning and order in the midst of the superficially chaotic and random circumstances of nature. In this sense, we might say that tool traditions, language, and religion are human universals, not because these practices will be the same at all times and in all places, but because in one form or another they are features of human communities, both in the past and in our own time.

Our special focus in this text will be on the third of those supposed human universals—**religion**. Several years ago, there was a great stir in the popular media about the discovery of a supposedly "lost" tribe, the Tasaday, who lived in a remote part of the Philippines. The Tasaday were said to be so primitive that they did not even have a religion; however, in a documentary shown widely on American television, the narrator said that the reason the Tasaday remained isolated was because they would not leave the land in which their ancestors had been buried, for to do so would be to offend the ancestors' spirits. It was later demonstrated that the Tasaday were a hoax, but the episode is instructive: even when people try to make up a society without religion, they cannot really conceive of one. The belief that the ancestors continue to have a spiritual connection with both the land and the people who continue to live on it may not seem to be analogous to singing hymns in a church or saying prayers in a mosque or offering sacrifices in a temple, but it is (as we shall see in the chapters to follow) every bit as religious.

In any case, the ties that bind religion to tool use (and the material elements of survival in general) and to other forms of symbolic expression are very strong and we cannot isolate religion as an autonomous phenomenon and still be true to the way in which it operates as a human universal. We therefore begin our exploration of religion by contextualizing it within the concept of *culture*.

THE CULTURE CONCEPT

Culture is the most important conceptual contribution of anthropology to the discourse of the social sciences. It has been at the core of the perspective by which anthropologists investigate the world since the very beginnings of anthropology as a distinct academic discipline late in the nineteenth century. It would be convenient if all anthropologists could agree on a single definition of culture, but in fact there is an enormous (and, for the beginning student, an often frustrating) diversity of opinion about what culture is and is not. We can begin to sort things out by setting aside the everyday connotation of the term "culture" as highbrow or elite affectation. We also need to go beyond the slightly more sophisticated but still restrictive tendency to think of culture as a list of traits that characterize "exotic" people. Culture is indeed a way of thinking about a total way of life, but it is something characteristic of *all* human groups, not just ones that are sufficiently different from us as to be noticeable.

A good place to start, then, would be with the definition proposed by Sir Edward Tylor, a British scholar who was one of the founders of the modern discipline of anthropology. On the very first page of his landmark 1871 treatise *Primitive Culture*[2] he proposed the following: "Culture or civilization, taken in its wide ethnographic sense, is that complex whole which includes knowledge, belief, art, morals, law, custom, and any other capabilities and habits acquired by man as a member of society." Tylor's wording is in some ways out of date (e.g., we no longer think of "civilization" as a synonym for "culture"; "man" would be more accurately rendered as "humans"), and anthropologists over the years have given varying emphases to the several parts of this very sweeping definition. But almost all would agree that there are three basic elements proposed by Tylor that in one way or another constitute a core anthropological consensus about culture.

First, culture is a *complex whole*. To use a more modern word, it is a *system*, which means that it is an entity composed of multiple parts that operate in relation to one another. Culture, therefore, is not adequately described by a mere list of traits without reference to the way they fit together. By analogy, one could lay out on a table every part of an automobile engine, but one would not in the end have a functioning car. It is necessary to see how the parts hook up with one another before we could begin to understand how a car actually works. So any attempt to deal with culture merely by listing characteristics or component parts is doomed to fail—our approach to culture must be grounded in a kind of systems model.

By convention, the elements in the system of culture (as found in the chapter headings of the typical introductory textbook in anthropology) may include: subsistence (how does a group obtain the materials necessary for its survival?); economy (how are goods and services distributed?); politics (how are decisions made and which members of the group are authorized to enforce decisions?); kinship (how are people related to one another?); language (how are ideas expressed and communicated within the group and across the generations?); art (how are ideas symbolized for both educational and entertainment purposes?); and, of course, religion (how do people find meaning and order in existence?). But we cannot truly understand any one of those elements without also understanding that it *is* by nature part of a larger system. It influences the other elements just as it in turn is influenced by them. So if we want to take an anthropological perspective on religion, we must always refer back to the cultural context from which it comes: in any given society, how do the things we identify as "religion" relate to the subsistence, economics, politics, kinship, and art, of that group?

The second important feature of Tylor's definition is that culture is "acquired," or *learned*. Some of what humans make and do, and some aspects of the ways in which they think are probably genetically programmed; but in the study of culture we are concerned with that part of our lives that is not prewired. It is important to remember that because the system we are calling culture is learned, it can—in part or in whole—be relearned (modified) or even unlearned. Culture is not destiny; it is not a gigantic Xerox machine that churns out endless replicas of itself. Because individuals vary in their capacities to learn, not all people who live in a given community know exactly the same things. Moreover, they have different interest in and skill at passing along what they know to others. There is thus a fair amount of variation within the community, even if by convention we say that the members of the community share a common culture.

The third factor flows logically from this latter idea. We acquire our knowledge as members of society. Culture is therefore always a group phenomenon. Even taking individual variations into account, we can still discern patterns or general tendencies that characterize a given community, and they are the stuff of an anthropologist's cultural analysis. There are probably things we all learn to make, do, or think about that for one reason or another we choose to keep to ourselves; in that case, we cannot speak of culture. Material production, interpersonal relations, and ideations only become cultural when they are shared within a more or less cohesive group.

So to summarize: culture is a system of learned and shared material productions, interpersonal relations, and ideas about what those productions and relations mean. Different schools of anthropological theory will emphasize one or another of those elements, but most would agree that to one degree or another, culture includes them all.

WHAT IS RELIGION?

We have included religion in the system of culture—positioning it as one element that influences many others and that is in turn influenced by them. But we have not yet come to grips with a pressing problem: what *is* religion? Like culture, religion is a word we use all the time, and it has likewise accumulated a number of everyday connotations. We all think we know what is meant whenever anyone speaks of religion, but pinning down a definition is a bit of a trick. Must "religion" always be about a supreme, creator deity? A Buddhist might beg to differ. Must it always deal with the "supernatural"? The prevalence of "civil religion" in modern societies argues otherwise. Does it necessarily have to do with spiritual beings or forces? Not if one admits that the faith of a committed atheist or rationalist can be just as compelling as that of any other kind of believer.

Most definitions of religion do, in fact, rely on concepts of divinity or the supernatural or the spiritual. But while these concepts may arguably cover *most* expressions of religion, they also omit significant elements that an anthropologist—interested always in placing religion within the system of culture—might want to explore or address. So for purposes of our discussion, we will use a definition proposed by the contemporary American anthropologist Clifford Geertz:

> A religion is a system of symbols which acts to establish powerful, pervasive, and long-lasting moods and motivations in [human beings] by formulating conceptions of a general order of existence and clothing these conceptions with such an aura of factuality that the moods and motivations seem uniquely realistic.[3]

No gods, no spirits, no supernatural forces—a very peculiar definition at first glance. Let's take a closer look and see what Geertz has in mind, and how his definition might help us explore the phenomenon of religion in human culture.

First, we see right away that Geertz is using a system model. Like culture of which it is a part, religion is itself a system. (Think, perhaps, of the moon circling the earth—a small system—even as the earth circles the sun as part of a larger planetary system.) But in this case, the system is composed of symbols. **Symbols** are things that signify something other than (or in addition to) themselves. For example, in a cartoon a dark cloud over a person's head is a shorthand, symbolic way of telling us that the person is in a bad mood. If we lived in a purely "me Tarzan, you Jane" sort of world where we could just point to things and have everyone understand exactly what we meant we would have no need of symbols. But human beings move in a world defined not only by concrete, material objects, but also by emotions, values, ideas. Human language, which has the capacity for nearly infinite expansion, as well as a capacity for abstraction, allows us to talk about these strongly held, but difficult-to-express notions. But language is more than words; it includes gestures and objects used in a meaningful, symbolic way. In the wake of September 11, 2001, for example, people in the United States found themselves swept by many potent feelings and wanted in some way to express a sense of renewed patriotism. But instead of going into a complicated explanation of what they were feeling, or about what the concept "patriotism" may have meant to them, they simply flew the flag. The flag itself does not explain anything, but it is a universally recognized symbol of national unity and pride. It is certainly true that there might be as many different interpretations of patriotism as there are citizens of the nation; but the symbol averages them all out and provides a rallying point that in this case provided a sense of common purpose in the face of crisis.

Some people think that calling something a symbol implies that it is unreal and hence unimportant. But of course the flag is real, just as the feeling of patriotism that it symbolizes is real. Calling something a symbol is not a means to undercut its significance; it is a way to express powerful and complex emotions and ideas in a concise and direct fashion. We must keep in mind, however, that the implied meanings of a symbol are usually culture-specific. We are respectful of the flags of other nations (as at the Olympics, for example), but they certainly do not evoke the same feelings (positive or negative) that our own flag does. In any case, religion deals with matters of great, transcendent importance and complexity. The language of symbols is our best way to make sense of those matters.

Second, the system of symbols is not simply a list any more than culture is simply a compendium of traits. A system implies a process, an action—it *does* something. In this case, the system acts to establish *moods* and *motivations*. By "moods" we mean feelings or states of mind. In and of themselves, they may or may not be important. But Geertz pairs them with "motivations"—impulses to further action. So the system of symbols Geertz calls religion instills a mind-set in people that makes them feel a certain way, and then impels them to do something about it. Moreover, those moods and motivations are not simple and transitory: they are *powerful*—they cannot be ignored; they are *pervasive*—they are shared widely throughout the group; and they are *long-lasting*—they influence peoples' behaviors and ideas over the course of time.[4]

How, we might well ask, can something as apparently insubstantial as a "system of symbols" establish moods and impel people to collective action? By *formulating conceptions of a general order of existence.* In other words, the main action of a religion is to explain everything. Doing so need not imply that religions have a tendency to be simplistic or reductionist. To the contrary, most religious systems are highly complex. But whether they are simple or complicated, they must all provide explanations for the way things are, for how things got to be the way they are, for how we are supposed to react given the way things are, and for what we can expect in the future. Human beings usually cannot "live in the moment" or "go with the flow," despite the advice of well-meaning self-help gurus. We like to feel that we are in control, and a knowledgeable understanding of the way things work gives us the impression that we are in control. This is not to say that our desire for control and mastery is necessarily positive or mentally healthy; it is just a description of the way most people in most societies seem to function.

Of course, anyone can say anything, and history is replete with misguided people who thought they had "*the* answer," only to be rejected as delusional. Therefore, in order for the system of symbols to be effective, its conceptions of a general order of existence must be *clothed in an aura of factuality.* That is, they must be expressed in whatever symbolic language the members of a particular culture will find most convincing. For example, our society gives an honored place to science, and we tend to be most impressed by arguments that come clothed in the trappings of science. It is no accident that Biblical fundamentalists prefer to present themselves as "creation scientists" when addressing the general American public. We are a people who love to dress up even sports and entertainment with statistics and the language of probability. Over-the-counter health and beauty products generally sell better if someone wearing a white coat is delivering the commercial pitch. We therefore tend to be most impressed when religion and science seem to mesh: the field of Biblical archaeology, for example, provides concrete, scientific evidence for the people and events described in sacred scripture. But it stands to reason that in other cultures, the "clothing" of religious discourse would be different. In traditional India, for example, the highest honor would have been accorded to the ascetic mystic; the pronouncements of such a seeker-after-truth, delivered after heroic fasts or other bodily mortifications, would carry much more weight than the explanations of someone who came in the guise of a rationalistic scientist.

When the conceptions of a general order of existence come clothed in an aura of factuality that makes them convincing to the culture at large, the moods and motivations that the people experience come to seem *uniquely realistic.* In other words, the true believers cannot really fathom how anyone could think or behave in ways other than their own. Their perspective, they believe, is not simply one option out of many equally plausible options; it is the *only* reasonable, enlightened choice. Our democratic heritage teaches us to be tolerant of people regardless of "race, creed, or national origin," but we really do have a hard time with the "creed" part. During the Cold War, most Americans could not bring themselves to think that people might honestly be attracted to communism; people were believed to become communists only through brainwashing or some other kind of coercion. By the same token, in the old Soviet Union, political dissidents were routinely incarcerated in mental hospitals, on the theory that anyone who did not accept the principles of communism had to be insane.

In the current post–9/11 crisis, we are honestly confused about "Why do they [Muslims] hate us?" as if to say that because we are so manifestly right, anyone who opposes us must by definition be either stupid or evil. "They," for their part, feel just the same—that their perspective is inherently better, more logical, more spiritual, more truthful than anyone else's. When we are dealing with claims to explain everything and provide a grounding for all behavior, and when we come to be convinced that those claims represent absolute truth (or else why would we believe them?), then it is very difficult for us to imagine any other way of looking at things.

Anthropologists have always insisted on the principle of *cultural relativism* as a key element in their analysis of culture; anthropologists study cultures objectively, understanding that other people's ways of life are neither better nor worse than theirs—just different, because they are adapted to different circumstances. But of course that principle is an element of Western, rationalistic, humanistic philosophy; we take it (although we should know better) as if it were a universal principle and are surprised when we encounter people in other parts of the world who are just as ethnocentric (i.e., convinced of the superiority of their own way of life) as the most narrow-minded American. In any case, we should not be surprised at the lesson of history: conflicts rooted in religious or other ideologies are often more intractable and passionately fought than those resulting simply from economic or political rivalries. The upside of religion is that it lifts our minds and hearts above the mundane and the merely physical; the downside may be that it breeds in us a tendency to convince ourselves of the absolute truth of this or that idea.

It should be clear by now that Geertz's definition gets at the dynamic of religion, rather than a specific description of its component parts. It certainly encompasses all the traditional elements (divinities, spirits, supernatural forces) even though it does not name them explicitly. But it also encompasses other kinds of symbol systems, such as political/economic ideologies (democracy, communism) or even sports fandom. Please note that even conclusions such as "There is no God," "Nothing has any meaning," "Everything is random," or "Everything is chaos" are all statements of a general order—they purport to explain things and they all suggest that they are insights into some sort of universal truth. None of them can be proven with empirical finality any more than statements such as "There is a creator God" or "A personalized supernatural force guides the universe." All such statements must, at some point, be accepted on the level of faith. Even the statement "Nothing can be true unless it is empirically provable" is based on unchallengeable presuppositions that are taken to be true. So if we follow Geertz's definition, we would have to say that atheism and chaos theory are just as "religious" as Christianity and Islam or any other more conventionally defined system.

Including these seemingly nontraditional elements does not water down the concept of religion; rather, the notion of religion is enhanced when we are allowed to see a common dynamic at work in all sorts of cultural settings. When we say that religion is "universal," we certainly do not mean that everyone in every culture believes in God and attends church on Sunday. What we do mean is that in all cultures there is a tendency to adhere to systems of symbols that establish powerful, pervasive, and long-lasting moods and motivations by formulating conceptions of a general order of existence, and by clothing those conceptions in such an aura of factuality that the moods and motivations come to seem uniquely realistic.

For purposes of our discussion, we will refer to religion as a cultural *domain* which we will label **the sacred**.[5] "Sacred" is often used in contrast with "profane," which in this context means beliefs or behaviors relative to the material, physical world. The domain of the sacred, on the other hand, is concerned with beliefs or behaviors relative to the sphere of existence that enhances, illuminates, or transcends the material world of the five senses.

OTHER PERSPECTIVES

This text is grounded in the anthropological perspective on religion—a dynamic, systematic analysis of the cultural context of symbol systems. The discipline of anthropology, particularly as it is practiced in most universities in the United States, is a compound discipline that includes, but is certainly not limited to cultural anthropology (sometimes called "ethnology"), which is the description and analysis of living cultures. It also includes archaeology, the description and analysis of cultures of the past that are known to us primarily through their material remains. It also involves physical or biological anthropology, the study of human population genetics and the processes of evolution. And finally, it entails the study of linguistics—not the learning of any one particular language, but the analysis of how language, the basic human communication system, works.

What links these four traditional subfields is, of course, the concept of culture, as even biological anthropologists (as opposed to other kinds of biologists) must always strive to see the role of learned, shared behaviors and ideas in the physical adaptation and evolution of the species. The anthropological approach must therefore be *comparative*, as manifestations of culture at all times and in all places must be taken into consideration when making generalizations about patterns or trends in human behavior. Religion, a part of culture, is thus not only to be found in living societies, but also in societies of the past. It is to be understood in terms of how humans communicate. And it must be seen as an element in the ongoing survival of the species.

Another point of linkage among the four subfields is the emphasis on **fieldwork**. Anthropology is based on naturalistic inquiry, as opposed to experiments carried out under controlled clinical or laboratory conditions. Anthropologists prefer to do their research out among the people (or their remains), a more time-consuming approach than is typical in an experimental design, but one more apt to immerse the researcher in the insider's point of view. Rather than reading *about* religion, for example, anthropologists want to experience it for themselves in cultural context.

Because of the multidisciplinary, comparative, and relativistic nature of the discipline of anthropology, the anthropological study of religion is a **holistic** endeavor. By comparison, *theologians* study single religious traditions rather than religions in comparative focus; they often approach that single tradition from the standpoint of the believer. *Philosophers*, like theologians, are concerned with the "great questions" posed by the major religious traditions, but they approach them from a more skeptical, rationalistic point of view. *Psychologists* tend to focus on religion as experience and as a factor in such processes as child-rearing and group identity. *Sociologists* are particularly interested in the relationship between religion and large-scale social movements. The interdisciplinary field of *comparative religion* (sometimes called "religious studies") makes use of the insights of all these disciplines in addition to anthropology (although it has not generally embraced the biological aspects of the latter); it does, however, have the disadvantage of seeming to isolate religion by making it the exclusive unit of analysis.

LOOKING AHEAD

With these basic principles in mind, we will proceed to our anthropological overview of religion, beginning with a consideration of what we know, or can infer, about the origins of religion and about religion in societies without written traditions. We will then look at religion in living cultures, examining in turn the main elements in the domain of the sacred: belief, ritual, mythology, ethics/laws/ values, and the physical environment in which those factors are enacted. We will conclude with an examination of the role of religion in the modern world, asking what place remains for the domain of the sacred in the face of the challenges of globalization and secularization.

In each of the chapters you will find first a set of exercises ("Research Explorations") that will allow you, under your instructor's supervision, to do your own anthropological research (including, in some cases, on-site fieldwork) on some aspect of religion. Each chapter also contains an article by a professional anthropologist whose research illustrates the main themes of that chapter. Some questions to guide essays or class discussions accompany each of these articles. Finally, each chapter will end with some suggestions for follow-up readings or other resources for study.

It has sometimes been the practice of anthropologists of religion to make categorical distinctions between "primal" religions (those that are typical of nonliterate societies) and the "world" religions (those associated with large, complex societies and a written tradition) or between "magic" and "religion." In this text, we will follow the lead suggested by Geertz's definition. When we study belief, for example, we will use examples from many different types of religious systems. For us, the critical issue will be the interrelationships among the elements in the domain of the sacred, rather than in the differentiation of one "type" of religion from any other.

KEY CONCEPTS

Be sure you can define the following terms, and give at least one illustrative example of each:

- culture
- holism
- the sacred
- fieldwork
- religion
- symbol

RESEARCH EXPLORATIONS

1. Construct an overview map of religion in your local community. Begin with the local Yellow Pages, but also check such sources as Web sites, chamber of commerce or other civic guidebooks, the religion pages of the local newspapers. List all the religious institutions in the area; the list will certainly include places of worship (churches, chapels, temples, mosques, synagogues, meeting houses, etc.), but might also include such institutions as schools, museums, health care facilities, ethnic associations, book stores, and so forth that operate with some sort of religious affiliation. Plot the locations of these institutions on a map of your community. Collect as much information as is publicly available about the institutions (e.g., number of members, regular meeting times, services available, people in leadership roles). Compile your findings into a concise table. These data can form the basis for some of the exercises suggested in later chapters that will ask you to visit some of these institutions in person, make detailed on-site observations, and conduct interviews.

2. Select two or three of the religious institutions that seem to be most prominent in your community, based on the research conducted in Exercise 1. Do some background research from published sources about the basic beliefs and practices of the religious traditions with which these institutions are affiliated. Summarize your findings either in an essay, or in some sort of visual display (e.g., poster, Web page) or in-class presentation.

Notes

[1] There is a body of opinion that asserts that dolphins are capable of sophisticated, quasi-linguistic communication, but as we have not yet cracked the code, it is difficult to say what dolphin "language" might be like.

[2] Tylor, Edward Burnett. 1871. *Primitive Culture*. London: John Murray, p. 1.

[3] Geertz, Clifford. 1973. *The Interpretation of Cultures*. New York: Basic Books, p. 90.

[4] The ideas of a person suffering from schizophrenia are certainly powerful and long-lasting, but they are not pervasive, and hence neither truly religious nor truly cultural—unless that person happens to live in a culture that accepts nonnormative utterances and experiences as evidence of supernatural power (see chapter 4).

[5] The concept of the domain of the sacred, which is composed of dimensions such as belief, ritual, mythology, and so forth—a concept that underlies a good part of the organization of this text—derives from the work of Ninian Smart. See in particular his monograph *Dimensions of the Sacred: An Anatomy of the World's Beliefs* (Berkeley: University of California Press, 1996).

Case Study

"Fortress without Walls: A Black Community after Slavery"

by Sydney Nathans

Nathans' article gives us an interesting, historically rich example of how a community came into existence and continues to define its identity in terms of its religious principles. Paul Cameron, North Carolina's wealthiest slave owner, sent a group of slaves to a plantation in Alabama. More than one hundred years after the end of slavery, descendents of Cameron's slaves still work and live on or near that Alabama plantation. Nathans found that attachment to the land and adherence to a common religious tradition formed those people into a cohesive community and accounted for the continuity of the group.

This inquiry started with a single document. It was a slave register and had on it 109 names of men, women, and children who in 1844 were sent from one of the largest estates in North Carolina to a newly purchased cotton plantation in Alabama. Both plantations belonged to Paul Cameron, North Carolina's largest slaveholder and wealthiest man by 1860. Famous in its time, the North Carolina plantation has become for historians a unique source of study, because the owners' century-long correspondence and records—as well as their homes, outbuildings, and slave quarters—have been preserved.[1] Paul Cameron's Alabama land had a different fate. Sold off in parcels after 1870, the land and the community of people on it "disappeared" from the historical record. In 1978, I asked myself, Is it possible to locate that land, to find the descendants of the people sent to it, and above all, to recover the story of that community of black immigrants in slavery and freedom? I began with the list of 109 people, almost all identified by first names only. After a summer of research in North Carolina and Alabama I determined the exact location of the old plantation, in Hale County, Alabama, discovered the church and school that the black freedmen had

Reprinted by permission of the Southern Anthropological Society from *Holding on to the Land and the Lord: Kinship, Ritual, Land Tenure, and Social Policy in the Rural South,* ed. Robert L. Hall and Carol B. Stack (Proceedings #15, 1982), pp. 55–65.

established on it, and found descendants rich with memory of their history from the time of the 1844 migration down to the present. A remarkable story began to unfold.

It was soon evident that the black community in Alabama was marked by notable continuity. One of the few last names given in the original Cameron slave register of 1844 was also listed in the local telephone directory and carved on the cornerstone in front of the community church. Names of individuals residing in the locality in the 1870s—names found in the deed books and mortgage records and in the 1870 manuscript census—were also painted on mailboxes throughout the settlement. The church and the school, mentioned in a letter from the overseer to the plantation owner in 1872, stood in almost the same spot described by the overseer a century before. Here were descendants of families forced to migrate to Alabama in slavery times who had fashioned a community for themselves and held onto it for more than a century. How had they done it? What kind of world had they created?

Land and religion, it became clear, were central to the maintenance of this black settlement over time. Paul Cameron had sold his Alabama plantation to black people. "All black, no white," was how one descendant put it, and with one exception the names in the deed record books bore her out: all black, no white. Cameron had sold off his land to blacks who had put no money down and paid off their debt in bales of cotton over a five-year period. By 1884, each of the black landowners on this plantation possessed considerably more than "forty acres and a mule." Most had more than a hundred acres, and owned mules, oxen, and cattle to boot.[2]

Yet if land provided the economic wherewithal for individuals, religion provided spiritual resources that were essential to the coherence of the community for more than a century. The complementary role of land and religion can be suggested by brief encapsulations of the experiences of members of three generations in the settlement's history since emancipation. For the first generation, the focus is on Paul Hargress, a former slave who obtained land and made it the basis of several family business partnerships. For the second generation, attention shifts to Forrest Hargress, who dedicated much of his life to sustaining a religious community in the settlement. For the third generation, the inquiry turns to the experience of individuals who left and returned to the community in the twentieth century, and explores the function of the settlement in a time of massive out-migration.

Carrie Davis was a child when she knew Paul Hargress early in the twentieth century. She recalls him as "a huge of a man," with a thick, long gray moustache that curved down on each side toward his shoulders. He had a "high, fine voice." And that voice often told of how it was when he came out to Alabama as a slave. The other slaves, he often repeated, walked their way out from North Carolina, perhaps linked by a chain. Not Paul Hargress. He came out on a coach with Paul Cameron himself. Together they crossed the Blue Ridge Mountains, separate from the rest of the work force. When Cameron left Paul Hargress behind on his Alabama plantation, he gave Paul Hargress a small bag of gold.[3] There is no corroboration for the story. But what the story seemed to suggest was fascinating: that Paul Hargress viewed himself as a trusted man, a cut above the others, a man who saw himself as much a partner of the master as his slave.

When freedom came, Paul, his brother Jim, and at least four other former slaves took the name Hargress—the name of the family they had belonged to before the

Camerons obtained title to them sometime in the 1830s. Along with another group of Cameron's former slaves who took the name Cameron—which for some later became Cannon—the family groups continued to live on and work the plantation.[4] After a tempestuous three years from 1865 to 1868, in which the freedmen signaled in various ways that they felt claims on the land, displayed a strong interest in the assertions of radical Republican politicians that they *deserved* the land, and made it clear that *they* would decide how much labor their families would contribute to work on the plantation, they seemed to reach a modus vivendi with the beleaguered overseer, who had managed the plantation continuously since 1859.[5]

In 1868, Paul and Jim Hargress and Sandy Cameron became supervisors of three squads of laborers who worked the plantation and brought the land they plowed back to prewar levels of productivity. Freedmen elsewhere in Alabama and the South often rebelled against working the land in a manner so reminiscent of slavery days. Perhaps the postwar role was made easier for the three squad leaders by the probability that they had been slave drivers before emancipation.[6] Despite the best effort of the labor force, the plantation did not flourish. Poor weather and worms, not poor labor, cut down the cotton crop of 1868. The prior departure from the estate of perhaps the bulk of the labor force meant that broomsedge began to encroach on the uncultivated portion of the plantation, giving the land an unkempt look to neighbors.[7] The repeated poor crops and reports of continued political instability led Paul Cameron to consider by 1870 the sale of his land.

As numerous historians have discerned from the written record, many former slaves chose after freedom to stay on or near the homeplace. On Cameron's Alabama land, as on other plantations, ties of kin and community were of major importance in that decision. The clearest evidence of a commitment to continue the community begun in slavery came in 1872, when white overseer Wilson O'Berry suggested to Paul Cameron that they set aside an acre of land for the creation of a church and a school. The savvy overseer gave his reasons: "I want to know if you will let me have one acre of land . . . it is for the Purpus of building of a negroe church also for a school house. It will be a neighborhood busyness and you will see my reasons for it. It is to manage to ceep [*sic*] hands in the neighborhood. In the neighborhood where farmers have done this they invarybly can get a plenty of hands." But in the final sentence of his letter he revealed that the idea and the initiative for the school and the church had come from the black families on the plantation: "They will pay for it [in] cash."[8] Cameron did not accept the offer, deciding instead to try to sell off his land. But families constructed a brush-arbor church on the acre anyhow, on the very spot designated in the overseer's letter.

Paul and Jim Hargress were able to buy 120 acres of Paul Cameron's land in the mid-1870s, and a family partnership began. Paul, Jim, and Squire Hargress, along with other members of the family, worked the land. They used the crops, the tools, the farm animals, and the land itself as the basis for cash advances from local merchants. The mortgage deed records show that for a time they prospered. Without children of his own, Paul needed farm laborers. Without land, Paul's brother-in-law's family and Paul's other relatives needed a place to work. A family partnership evolved.[9]

No evidence indicates that Paul Hargress, like Nate Shaw in Theodore Rosengarten's *All God's Dangers* (1974), sought to use his land or his family for "striving," for getting ahead. For him, for Sandy Cameron, and for others in the first generation of freedom, all effort seemed directed instead at getting and holding onto their foothold in the Alabama earth. The goal of "getting by," to use a phrase I heard numerous times in interviews, will come as no surprise to students of post-plantation and peasant societies. Paul Hargress never bought any land in addition to his purchase of the 1870s; his quantity of mules and tools and credit remained stable from year to year. Security and independence seemed to be what he sought and what hard labor wrested for him.

Independence and security for Paul Hargress became harder to maintain in the twentieth century. Widowed, aging, and childless at the turn of the century, this "huge of a man" nonetheless might have continued to make his land pay had he not been "cut down" one night in the early 1900s. An ice storm froze Hale County. Paul Hargress's poorly insulated cabin, with openings in the roof and with crevices in the floor big enough for a quarter to drop through, did not hold what heat there was. His leg froze and had to be amputated. Two in the community who were not blood-kin "adopted" "Unc Paul" and looked after him. He seemed to resent the fact that those closer to him by bloodline showed insufficient concern. "Family? I don't know any family!" he once despaired angrily.[10] But he did have blood-kin close by, and one last time linked their interest with his land in a family business partnership. He deeded off his land in eleven equal parcels to his nine blood-kin and the two "adopted" kin who cared for him, contingent on their agreeing to pay him ten dollars cash each October and agreeing further to pay one-eleventh each of his burial costs and his outstanding debts upon his death.[11] Paul Hargress thus contracted with his kin for them to provide his pension and his burial insurance. They—many farm laborers living and working on nearby estates—moved onto "Unc Paul's" land and built cabins there. Unc Paul's final partnership created for the next generation a measure of independence and security of their own. It was a smaller foothold than Paul Hargress had possessed. But in the twentieth century, as the life of one of the next generation would reveal, even a small foothold provided a measure of independence and was better than no foothold at all.

The sack of gold? Rumor had it—after Paul Hargress's death in 1918—that he had buried it under the cherry tree in front of his house. People in the community today can still recall hearing the sounds of searchers scraping and digging at night for the buried treasure. The digging went on for weeks—until the cherry tree collapsed into a gaping hole. No one knows if the gold was ever found after Paul Hargress's death. But in his life, the gold had served as an emblem of aspirations for this "huge of a man": partnership, independence, and holding onto what he had.[12]

Ned Forrest Hargress was one of the adopted kin who early in the twentieth century assumed the duties of "son" to Paul Hargress and who looked after Paul Hargress until his death in 1918. In one way Forrest Hargress's background was exceptional. According to family tradition, he was the son of Dorothy, a cook on the Alabama plantation, and of a Confederate officer who had forced himself on her while his troops were encamped near the plantation during the final days of the Civil War.[13] In many other ways, Forrest Hargress's long life—which began in 1866 and ended a century later during the months of civil rights demonstrations in his hometown of Greensboro, Alabama—typified the lives of the black community's second generation in freedom.[14] He married the daughter of a member of the original community, Betty Cameron. He and his wife inherited thirty acres owned by his father-in-law, Sandy Cameron, and he acquired an additional eighteen acres in return for his aid to Paul Hargress.

Ned Forrest Hargress's inheritance—a white father, fifty acres of land—gave him and his family a measure of independence during his lifetime. But neither proved sufficient to permit him complete autonomy, or to support his family of twelve children. Like so many, he had to labor for others—but for others, not under them. Insulted by one employer when he came on a Saturday morning, hat in hand, to ask for some molasses—"Can't you niggers let a man read his newspaper on his porch in peace?"—he could put on his hat and reply, "Cap'n Earl, my daddy was as white as you are!" and stalk away. With enough land for a "house seat" of his own, he could take off a Monday from work when he wanted to, and if challenged by his employer—"Where you goin' with that mule and wagon, Forrest?"—retort, "I'se goin' to town just like you are Cap'n Jim."[15] And he could get away with it. But for income and perhaps also for "influence" with a white patron in the county, he hired out his labor in addition to tending to his own land and crops.

But though his white father and his property-holdings were doubtless factors in Forrest Hargress's independence, when I talked to one resident about this, he brought me up short. I told my source—who had known Hargress for fifty years—that everything I had heard made Forrest Hargress sound like a pretty independent man. "Oh, I don't know that he was so independent. He was a *Christian* man."[16] As I listened more, it became clear that Forrest Hargress did not spend the bulk of his time trying to get along with or rebuff challenges from white folks. Nor did he spend all his energies just trying to make a living or get a bit ahead, though he did go to the field most days and though he did energetically supplement his income by making and selling work-baskets and by running a molasses mill and small candy and grocery store.[17] Much of his energy and effort went into being a Christian and into making his community a *Christian* community.

For Forrest Hargress and for his generation, it was not only land, not only family networks, but also the vibrant religious life of the community that gave the settlement its strength and longevity. After 1900, their church was no longer a brush-arbor construction in the woods but a weatherboard building with green shutters on the outside. Inside, it had a large chandelier holding dozens of candles.[18] Members of the community—which included forty to fifty families who worked adjacent lands as tenants, as well as the families of landowners—gathered in church for much of the day on Sunday, into the night every Wednesday, and for a full week at revival time. On all occasions, the church was always described to me as "full to overflowing." Revivals were special occasions, when the congregation swelled with prayers for the unbaptized, who sat on the mourners' bench while others prayed and wept for their souls, until the spirit came and they "confessed religion." When the baptisms occurred, it was again a collective event for the entire community. All would come out for the processional through the settlement from the church to the waters of Little Prairie Creek. When a member of the community died or suddenly took ill, a bell near the church pealed loudly—it was called "toning the bell"—and the entire settlement poured in from the field or out of their homes to learn who had fallen and to give aid. Repeatedly people used the same phrase to describe the sheer density of the people in the settlement and their density on religious occasions especially: "There was so many folks you couldn't stir 'em with a stick.[19] Such stories of the past and the still-intense spirituality of the church service today suggest the presence of a powerful religious culture, a fortress without walls, that over the generations has sustained the community's way of life.

Yet there were flourishing elements of culture in the community that were distinctly outside the pale of religion. The community had its own stores, its own baseball team, its own brass bands that played into the night, its own gambling dens. Sacred and secular cultures might contest each other loudly, as when the strains of the brass bands and the parties they announced could be heard mixing with religious singing from a church-sponsored picnic called the "Festival in the Wilderness." Or the sacred and the profane might contest covertly when a church member and family man would hire a "rambling man" to buy a ticket to the church picnic for his "outside woman."[20] In this community, as on the plantation of slavery days and as in the communities of other working people in the nineteenth and early twentieth centuries, the sacred, the secular, and the profane, the churched and the unchurched, coexisted in close physical proximity.[21]

In this setting, what did Christian men like Forrest Hargress do? As best they could, they policed the settlement, seeking to maintain a code of moral strictness. If Forrest Hargress came upon a game of craps, the gamblers scattered at the sight of him. If he identified some of the sinners as church members, they were reported. If a churchman was overheard to swear "Well, I'll be goddamned"—as one was when he discovered that his unwed daughter had given birth to a child—he lost his membership in the church. Parents were strict with their children, disciplining them heavily and often. And *any* adult in the community was entitled to punish physically the misbehavior of *any* child in the settlement. If the child complained of the whipping to his parents, he got thrashed again at home.[22] Yet along with the code of strictness went leniency, the obligation to forgive, and the mechanisms for redemption. Parents and children were urged to forgive each other their offenses. Those ostracized from church for misbehavior could appear before the preacher or the congregation to "beg pardon," and receive it promptly. Even the men "called to preach"—the holiest calling in the settlement—were expected to "go slack" and need redeeming forgiveness.[23]

How did this mixture of moral strictness and ready forgiveness help maintain the community? The strictness was not just rural black Puritanism. It was not, as H. L. Mencken might have put it, the fear by a righteous few that somewhere, someone in the settlement might be happy. Moral strictness was a means to autonomy. That autonomy was partly spiritual, the peace and strength that comes from walking right with God. But the autonomy was also worldly. As one mother told her children, they had better *"behave,"* for she did not have and would not seek "influence" with a white man to save them if they got into trouble.[24] Yet the close proximity of the sacred and profane in the settlement heightened the chances for lapses. The Christian men and women and the church stood ready always to forgive and reclaim the faithful. Moral strictness, forgiveness, and day-to-day generosity helped to cement together the second-generation families of the community. Their qualities were embodied in Forrest Hargress, "a Christian man."

The role of the home settlement for many in the third generation since emancipation has been different from what it was for their forebears. Most have gone out into the world; most of those still in the settlement today have come home again. For many in the third generation, wide-ranging migration became a necessity. The sheer press of people on the land, and natural disasters such as the boll weevil and the flood of 1916, increased pressure to leave. But many were lured away, especially by the increased employment of blacks in industry and in the coalmines of Alabama. For some, migration was the alternative to economic strangulation. For others, it offered an escape from intense family strain or—for a young man—the chance to "ramble" and "to be a man!"[25]

Many of the third generation who inhabit the community today have come back from the larger world. One couple hastened back from living in Bessemer, Alabama, a mining city, after lightning struck a trolley they were in. They took it as an omen, and two weeks after their return in 1919 an explosion in the mine killed dozens of the husband's friends. Another member of the community, forced during the Depression to seek work elsewhere, was cut up one night in a knife fight. He returned home in 1937 and has spent most of his time there since, vigorous but bound to a wheelchair. One woman, after twenty-five years of labor in Detroit and New York, bought herself a bright red trailer and returned home to "go fishin'." Another woman recalled that one year she and her husband moved onto a white man's land to "try and get ahead." All they got was debt, and the next year moved back to stay.[26] The outside world for many seemed to be the same—high hopes but harsh realities, a devil with a crooked smile and a snaggle-toothed grin.

What does the home place mean to those of the third generation who reside there today? James Lyles is such a man. In striking ways, he embodies the values of his forebears. Like Paul Hargress, he owns a portion of the original Alabama plantation and has a deep attachment to it. Like Ned Forrest Hargress, he lacks a "literary education" but is a deeply Christian man and lives by "the Master Book." Like so many of his own generation, he has migrated out into the world and returned home from it. James Lyles left first in 1916, a young man eager to get free of home and to ramble. He worked in the mines, first in Bessemer, then in West Virginia. He was called back by a premonition, by a visit from the spirit telling him his mother was ill. He returned; she was; he stayed. After he married and began a family, he went out a second time to the mines in the 1930s—the only way, during the Great Depression, that he could support a large family and keep from losing his home place to creditors. By 1944, he had earned enough to reclaim the land from debt and his sons were old enough to contribute their labor to the farm. He returned home again and for good.[27]

James Lyles knows that many young people think differently than he does about the home settlement. He knows that most are now off to Birmingham and Detroit and the West Coast. He knows that though they come back temporarily—for family reunions, for church homecomings, sometimes for July 4th or Christmas—many believe they will never return. He knows that some of the current generations are even ready to sell out their portion of the home settlement from which they came. He thinks they are wrong. What will happen in the city when people find they cannot eat, or cannot work, and need a home again?

So James Lyles is holding on to his inheritance, to the sanctuary for three generations, to what he calls the "plant bed" in which so many seeds have taken root and flourished. When they need to, James Lyles's children and grandchildren will have a place to come home again.[28] In holding on to the land and the Lord, James Lyles carries on a long tradition.

Notes

[1] Herbert Gutman in *his The Black Family in Slavery and Freedom* (1976) and George McDaniel in oral interviews have delineated the genealogies and family relationships of the Bennehan-Cameron black families in North Carolina. The Cameron's North Carolina plantation, Stagville, just north of Durham, is now a state historic site and a Center for the Study of Historical Preservation.

[2] Interview with Alice Hargress, August 1978, Hale County, Alabama. Confirmation of the oral testimony came through tracing the sale of the Cameron estate in the deed books of Hale County, which are located in the Office of the Probate Judge, Greensboro, Alabama. Sixteen individuals bought Cameron's land from 1872 to 1889; through other written and oral sources, I have identified fifteen as black. Cameron authorized the sale of his lands through a local lawyer who acted as his agent. Sales commenced in 1872; all but 200 acres were sold by 1885. Cameron tried to sell in tracts ranging from 80 to 240 acres. Only one black landowner, Sandy Cameron, came to own a very small tract. His 30 acres represented all he could hold on to after he failed to meet the payments on the 160 acres he had originally contracted to purchase.

The Cameron correspondence suggests that Cameron first sought a single purchaser for the entire 1,600-acre plantation. No buyer made an adequate offer. Both an Alabama landowner and his son-in-law informed him that the only way to get his price was to sell the land in smaller tracts. Every purchaser paid at least the minimum of $8 per acre that Cameron required; most paid $10 per acre for the land. A. G. Jones (Greensboro) to Paul Cameron, 6 October 1869; George P. Collins to Cameron, 7 December, 11 December, 1869, in Cameron Family Papers, Southern Historical Collection, University of North Carolina (hereafter abbreviated SHC).

[3] Interview with Carrie Hargress Davis, August 1979; interviews with Louis Rainey, August 1978 and July 1979.

[4] To avoid confusion in the paper, I use here the name Hargress. The name in fact varied over time in the places it was written down. The name first appeared in the 1844 register of slaves sent to Alabama, where "Jim Hargis" was one of several slaves listed with a surname. In the 1866 manuscript census for Alabama, there is a York Hogis listed. The postwar plantation overseer referred in 1868 to Jim and Paul Hargrove. The names in the manuscript census, the deed books, and the mortgage records also vary, from Hargess in the 1880s to Hargress in 1918. It seems probable that Paul and Jim and the other members of the families who took the name Hargis/Hargress derived the name from that of a business partner of Duncan Cameron, who sold or transferred his slaves to Cameron in the 1830s.

[5] Wilson O'Berry to Paul Cameron, 11 August 1867, Cameron Family Papers, SHC.

[6] O'Berry to Cameron, 6 April 1868, Cameron Family Papers, SHC. In this letter, the overseer reported: "The negroes are working well and have been all of the year, and behave themselves well. I have the best lot of hands in Hale Co. . . . Jim Hargrove is at the head of one squad Paul at the head of another and Wesley at the head of the other one. . . . [Wesley] is a very industrious boy . . . he does not mind whipping them no more than he did in slavery time. Sandy works his 4 hands besides himself and have planted a good crop." The terms of agreement between the overseer and the squad leaders are not revealed in the letters. Because O'Berry rented the entire postwar plantation from Cameron, and then made his own terms with the "hands," he was under no obligation to reveal the labor contract to the owner.

[7] O'Berry to Cameron, 17 June, 13 September 1868; George P. Collins (Greensboro) to Cameron, 11 December 1869, Cameron Family Papers, SHC.

[8] O'Berry to Cameron, 16 May 1872, Cameron Family Papers, SHC.

[9] Hale County, Deed Record Book X, pp. 614–15. The indenture between Cameron and Paul and James Hargress was originally made on 27 March 1876. They paid $8 per acre for 80 acres of land. Paul Hargress made a second purchase of 20 acres in 1884, for which he paid $10 per acre. Hale County, Deed Record Book K, p. 480.

[10] Interview with Louis Rainey, August 1978 and July 1979.

[11] Hale County, Deed Book X, pp. 616–17 (1912); Deed Book Y, pp. 2, 27, 83, 151, 213, 275, 449 (1912–13).

[12] Interview with Louis Rainey, August 1979.

[13] Interviews with Louis Rainey, August 1978, July 1979; interview with Betty Hargress Washington, August 1978.

14 His children give the date for Forrest Hargress's birth as 1 January 1866. The family Bible lists him as having been born on 1 January 1865, but the year is crossed out and "1866" is written over it. The *Greensboro Watchman,* which refused to carry news accounts of the 1965 voter-registration demonstrations in Selma, ran a front-page obituary column about Forrest Hargress upon his death in June 1965.

15 Interviews in August 1978 and July–August 1979, with Louis Rainey, Betty Hargress Washington, Angeline Hargress Banks, and Alice Hargress.

16 Interview with Louis Rainey, August 1978.

17 Interviews with Minnie Hargress Williams and Angeline Hargress Banks, August 1978; interview with Robert Cabbil, July 1979.

18 Interviews with Betty Hargress Washington, August 1978; interview with Louis Rainey, July 1979.

19 Interviews with Elijah Banks, August 1978 and August 1979; interviews with Robert Cabbil, July and August 1979; interview with Carrie Hargress Davis, August 1979.

20 Interviews with Louis Rainey, July and August 1979.

21 For a discussion of the world of the "rough and respectable" among working people of Victorian England, see Thompson 1973 and 1975. For the spiritual and the sinful on the plantation, see Epstein 1977. Kennedy 1973 presents an illuminating discussion of a quite different pattern of sexual mores, religious norms, and population practices among a society of small landowners and peasant proprietors.

22 Interviews with Louis Rainey, Joel Wallace, James and Lillie Mae Cannon, August 1979.

23 Interviews with Carrie Hargress Davis and with Joel Wallace, August 1979.

24 Interview with Alice Hargress, August 1978.

25 Interview with Elijah Banks, August 1979.

26 Interviews with Angeline Hargress Banks, Elijah Banks, Louis Rainey, and Alice Hargress, August 1979.

27 Interview with James Lyles, August 1979.

28 Interview with James Lyles, August 1979.

References

Epstein, Dena J., 1977. *Sinful Tunes and Spirituals: Black Folk Music to the Civil War* (New York: Oxford University Press).

Gutman, Herbert, 1976. *The Black Family in Slavery and Freedom* (New York: Pantheon Books).

Kennedy, Robert E., Jr., 1973. *The Irish: Emigration, Marriage, and Fertility* (Berkeley: University of California Press).

Rosengarten, Theodore, 1974. All *God's Dangers: The Life of Nate Shaw* (New York: Alfred A. Knopf).

Thompson, Paul R., 1973. Voices from Within. In *The Victorian City: Images and Realities,* H. J. Dyos and Michael Wolff, eds. (London: Routledge and Kegan Paul), 1:59–80.

———, 1975. *The Edwardians: The Re-Making of British Society* (Bloomington: Indiana University Press).

QUESTIONS FOR DISCUSSION

1. How was Nathans able to explain three generations of people remaining in a community?

2. What role did religion play in the community?

3. In what ways is the community described by Nathans similar to other rural communities? What forces in addition to religion may account for the continuity of community?

4. How does religion influence other aspects of life in the community? How is religion influenced by other factors (e.g., economics, politics)?

Suggested Readings or Other Resources

Some General Texts in the Anthropology of Religion

Bowen, John R. 1998. *Religions in Practice: An Approach to the Anthropology of Religion*. Boston: Allyn & Bacon.
Child, Alice B., and Irvin L. Child. 1993. *Religion and Magic in the Life of Traditional Peoples*. Englewood Cliffs, NJ: Prentice Hall.
Collins, John J. 1978. *Primitive Religion*. Totowa, NJ: Littlefield, Adams.
Klass, Morton. 1995. *Ordered Universes: Approaches to the Anthropology of Religion*. Boulder, CO: Westview.
Malefijt, Annemarie de Waal. 1989. *Religion and Culture: An Introduction to Anthropology of Religion*. Prospect Heights, IL: Waveland.
Molloy, Michael. 1999. *Experiencing the World's Religions*. Mountain View, CA: Mayfield.
Norbeck, Edward. [1974] 1988. *Religion in Human Life: Anthropological Views*. Prospect Heights, IL: Waveland Press.
Pandian, Jacob. 1991. *Culture, Religion, and the Sacred Self: A Critical Introduction to the Anthropological Study of Religion*. Englewood Cliffs, NJ: Prentice Hall.
Smart, Ninian. 2000. *Worldviews: Crosscultural Explorations of Human Beliefs*. Upper Saddle River, NJ: Prentice Hall.
Wallace, Anthony F.C. 1966. *Religion: An Anthropological View*. New York: Random House.

Readers in the Anthropology of Religion

Bowen, John R., ed. 1998. *Religion in Culture and Society*. Boston: Allyn & Bacon.
Hicks, David, ed. 1999. *Ritual and Belief: Readings in the Anthropology of Religion*. Boston: McGraw-Hill.
Kiev, Ari, ed. 1964. *Magic, Faith, and Healing*. New York: Free Press.
Klass, Morton, and Maxine K. Weisgrau, eds. 1999. *Across the Boundaries of Belief: Contemporary Issues in the Anthropology of Religion*. Boulder, CO: Westview.
Lambek, Michael, ed. 2002. *A Reader in the Anthropology of Religion*. London: Blackwell.
Lehmann, Arthur C., and James E. Myers, eds. 2001. *Magic, Witchcraft, and Religion: An Anthropological Study of the Supernatural*, 5th ed. Mountain View, CA: Mayfield.
Lessa, William A., and Evon Z. Vogt, eds. 1979. *Reader in Comparative Religion*, 4th ed. New York: Harper & Row.
Middleton, John, ed. 1967. *Gods and Rituals: Readings in Religious Beliefs and Practices*. Garden City, NY: Natural History Press.
———. 1967. *Myth and Cosmos: Readings in Mythology and Symbolism*. Garden City, NY: Natural History Press.
Scupin, Raymond, ed. 2000. *Religion and Culture: An Anthropological Focus*. Upper Saddle River, NJ: Prentice Hall.

Encyclopedias and Dictionaries

Alexander, Pat, ed. 1994. *Handbook to the World's Religions*. Grand Rapids, MI: Eerdmans.
Hinnells, John R., ed. 1991. *A Handbook of Living Religions*. London: Penguin Books.
Levinson, David, ed. 1996. *Religion: A Cross Cultural Dictionary*. New York: Oxford.
Swatos, William H., ed. *Encyclopedia of Religion and Society*. 1998. Walnut Creek, CA: AltaMira.

On-Line Resources

For information about the Anthropology of Religion section of the American Anthropological Association, go to the A.A.A. home page (www.aaanet.org) and follow the link to section and interest groups and then to the religion group. The latter has a number of useful links of its own to: academic organizations; museums and foundations; religions, religious practices, and texts; issues; folklore; archaeology and religion; history and religion; cultural and social groups; world regions; materials for social science educators (K–12); discussion groups and on-line services; on-line bibliography; journals; and funding sources and educational resources.

www.historychannel.com includes explanations of many religious traditions.

Video

How Beliefs and Values Define a Culture (Insight Media, Inc.) is a 24-minute video that provides an overview of the issues discussed specifically in this chapter and more generally throughout this text.

Note: Insight Media is an excellent source of video materials dealing with religion in general, and with specific religious traditions.

2

Prehistoric Religion

featuring

**"Like Water for Chocolate:
Feasting and Political Ritual among the
Late Classic Maya at Xunantunich, Belize"
by Lisa J. LeCount**

Early anthropologists were very interested in the origins of religion, asking questions such as "When did religion arise?" "What were the most basic forms of that first religion?" Although this intellectual quest resulted in a few works of lasting significance, most notably Émile Durkheim's *The Elementary Forms of the Religious Life*,[1] it also resulted in a great deal of fruitless speculation. Moreover, modern anthropologists realize that it is futile to think in terms of a single point of origin; beliefs and behaviors that *in retrospect* we might label "religious" were probably developed many times and in many places. There was no single "primal religion" from which all others evolved.

Following the traces of those suggestive beliefs and behaviors involves us with the methods of **archaeology**, which help us reconstruct the cultures of the past when we no longer have the luxury of interviewing living practitioners of those cultures. It must be kept in mind, however, that while archaeology is very good at identifying *what* happened in the past and *how* artifacts were produced, it cannot be equally informative when it comes to the question of *why* people did something or made something—the very questions that are at the heart of the religious impulse. An archaeologist can identify a site that *seems* to be a deliberate burial, and we can make **inferences** that the people who buried that body had certain ideas about the value of the individual and his or her relationship to the survivors—and perhaps (although this is more of a stretch) about some sort of afterlife. But we cannot be at all certain that those people had ideas that fit into more modern categories of religion.

With these very important cautions in mind, however, we can attempt to discern the elements out of which our "system of symbols" eventually coalesced.

LEARNING TO LOOK AT THE PAST

Archaeologists deal with a wide variety of material remains such as tools, shelters, storage vessels, clothing, items of adornment, and so on. Those that might have a religious significance (in addition to a purely utilitarian one) are those that are (or seem to be): (1) associated with burial places; (2) offerings (left in a particular, artificial order, rather than randomly discarded); (3) representations of figures not found in nature; (4) constructions such as altars or pillars.

Such remains are typically analyzed by **analogy**. In other words, we interpret prehistoric culture by reference to living cultures that we can know directly. For example, a smoothed, flat stone bearing the traces of burning suggests an altar on which votive lights have been placed because that is what such a thing would probably mean in the cultures with which we are familiar. But in the end, such an assumption is guesswork. We cannot be sure that our analogy is even a good approximation of (let alone a perfect match for) what prehistoric people were doing and thinking. For example, the famous Inca site of Machu Picchu has been characterized as a sacred place since it was first excavated early in the twentieth century. Since that time, it has been widely assumed that Machu Picchu was the mythological birthplace and last stronghold of the Incas. That interpretation was based on the presence of numerous temple-like structures. Contemporary archaeologists, however, are no longer so sure; some of them suggest that the site was a mountain retreat for one of the Inca emperors and his court. Since the Inca emperor was a kind of high priest, he would have been expected to carry out some religious ceremonies even while on vacation, hence the prominence of the temples. Modern research suggests that Machu Picchu was not an enduring sacred place at all but a site abandoned after only a few decades in a time of political and economic dislocation. We must therefore be very cautious when we try to "read" the necessarily fragmentary and ambiguous evidence of the past. We rely on trained archaeologists to give us highly educated guesses, but at this point in the history of the discipline, our scientific methodology cannot give us documentary proof beyond a reasonable doubt.

THE CULTURAL CONTEXT OF PREHISTORIC RELIGION

Whatever religion may have been like in the millennia before written history, we can be certain that it was organized around the needs and perspectives of hunters, gatherers, and foragers, for such were the prevailing subsistence strategies for much of human history. We know (again from analogy) that **hunting and gathering** societies tend to be organized into small units with a low population density (as opposed to agrarian communities, which can support densely packed populations in a relatively small area). Moreover, such societies must be mobile, as they need to follow the game or other food supplies. The basic hunting-gathering unit would have been some family (kin) group. The people would have had a very intimate knowledge of the weather and topography, and all the other natural forces that enabled them to survive. It is not unreasonable to assume that they would have done everything they could think of to ensure the cooperation of those natural forces in their quest for survival.

The earliest hominids (the date of whose advent in eastern or southern Africa is being pushed further back in time as new finds are unearthed) were distinguished by their stone tools. While other animals can make and use tools, only the hominids seem to have had a **tool tradition**—tools were widely shared, consistently passed along from generation to generation, and essential to survival. We assume some degree of food sharing in these populations and probably some sort of sexual division of labor. If they attached any religious significance to their tools, their social relationships, or to the larger quest for survival, we have little or no way of knowing. Other than the stone tools and the bones of the hominids, nothing else survives to tell us what their lives may have been like. It is generally assumed that while they, like nonhuman primates, might have had fleeting religious "ideas," they did not develop them into a consistent religious "tradition" in the way that they integrated the tools into an ongoing cultural pattern.

EVIDENCE?

The first bit of archaeological information that might lend some support—albeit fragile—to the emergence of religion as a consistent cultural pattern comes from the Homo erectus populations of about one million years B.C.E., particularly those who lived in the caves of what is now China. Those caves yielded evidence that human skulls were broken in a careful and consistent way at the foramen magnum (the large hole at the base of the skull where the spinal cord attaches to the brain). It would seem that through this enlarged opening, the brain could be extracted and eaten. Since there were apparently other, ample food resources in the area, we can assume that eating human brains was done for "ritual" rather than nutritional purposes. We also can assume that only the brains of the dead were consumed; members of the group were probably not murdered for the express purpose of eating their brains. This conclusion is based on the analogy with those modern societies that practice **ritual cannibalism**, usually upon the death of a member of a group; eating that person's brain was a way of incorporating the dead person's power (spirit?) into the living survivors. But of course, we cannot know for sure. It is certainly possible that Homo erectus developed a taste for brains as a delicacy to enhance a more substantial meal (much as we might eat an hors d'oeuvre prior to a "real" meal) and that their actions reflected something that merely pleased their palates rather than satisfied some loftier ideal.

We are on somewhat more solid ground when we analyze the remains of the Neanderthal people (approximately 100,000 years B.C.E.). There is an ongoing and seemingly endless debate as to whether the **Neanderthals** are or are not Homo sapiens. Even if they are not (the prevailing opinion as of this writing), they almost certainly had a brain capacity roughly within the range of Homo sapiens. And with the advent of that more or less modern human brain apparently comes the ability to think abstractly. Hence the evidence of seemingly religious behavior among the Neanderthals, while not to be taken without several grains of salt, is certainly more compelling than that for "ritual cannibalism" among the Homo erectus.

The Neanderthals' "religiosity" is marked in their burial practices. Earlier hominids did not pay any apparent attention to the dead, but at several sites the Neanderthals carefully placed the corpses in prepared graves, often decorated with "gifts" (items the person might have used in life) or ornamental materials. By analogy, it might be suggested that the gifts, which archaeologists refer to as **grave goods**, are items designed to serve the person in the afterlife—although the nature of their ideas about that afterlife are, of course, unknown to us. Neanderthal graves are also strewn with flowers (which are not preserved, although their pollen is fossilized); some have pointed out that this may have been nothing more than a pragmatic early effort at deodorizing a decided stench at the site, although it is difficult not to think that among the Neanderthals, as among more modern people, flowers are a symbol of life. In a similar way, we see the Neanderthal graves stained by red ochre powder, which is still a widespread symbol of life, red being the color of blood.

Certain cave sites associated with the Neanderthals contain the remains of bears, apparently carefully placed (although some skeptics believe that the remains are of cave bears who died natural deaths and were interred by falling rock). This evidence has given rise to the assumption that the Neanderthals were devotees of a **bear cult**, which was practiced until recent times among various peoples of the Arctic and sub-Arctic. (The Neanderthals lived during the last glacial advance, and their environment, particularly in Europe, was that of a cold tundra.) The bear makes a logical symbol: not only is it a very large animal, but it is the only one in such an environment that can stand up and move about on two legs and thus seem like some sort of giant human. More important, the bear's most notable characteristic is its annual hibernation. So the bear, this man-like creature that seems to die but then returns to life on a regular basis, is not an improbable focus for a religious cult. Although such speculation may be logical, we simply have no way of knowing if the Neanderthals actually made deliberate shrines of the bears' caves, or if they engaged in the sort of sophisticated symbolic reasoning represented by more modern practitioners of the bear cult.

The Neanderthals were replaced by anatomically modern Homo sapiens populations, big-game hunters on the broad grasslands that succeeded the sub-Arctic tundra once the glaciers finally retreated. Most experts agree that these people probably did have a concept of the afterlife, given the material elaboration of the grave goods associated with their burials. They also seemed very interested in representing and interacting with the abstract concept of fertility. For example, one of the most characteristic material remains of their era are the so-called **Venus figurines**. These objects obviously long pre-date the Roman goddess Venus, but they are certainly representations of human females, albeit with striking distortions: the head, arms, and legs are much reduced, while the breasts, hips, buttocks, and private parts are greatly exaggerated. Since the artists of that era elsewhere demonstrated their ability to create accurate, naturalistic representations of animals, and since it is highly unlikely that the women of that period actually looked like the figurines, the distortions must have been deliberate. Our best guess is therefore that the figurines represent fertility, growth, fruitfulness. Some analysts have jumped to the conclusion that the Venuses are depictions of the hypothetical "mother goddess." We cannot rule out that possibility, but neither can we accept it beyond doubt. As is always the case with prehistoric remains, we can see perfectly well *what* was being produced, but we are on very shaky ground when we begin to make assumptions about what the producers were thinking in the act of creation.

The other great artistic achievements of these late Stone Age people were the engravings and paintings on the walls of caves, the most famous of which are at Lascaux in France.[2] The drawings mostly depict animals, specifically the animals the people would have hunted. The figures are not only beautifully drawn, but they are anatomically accurate; many of them are depicted as pregnant, yet another example of the people's interest in fertility.

The conjunction of fertility and artistic representation raises a matter of great importance to the student of religion, because the Venus figurines and the cave paintings have both been seen as evidence of *magic*. Given the importance of this topic in the history of anthropological studies of religion, we need to consider this matter in a bit more detail.

MAGIC?

Anthropologists long argued over the relationship between magic and religion; for a long time, the prevailing opinion was that magic was an early manifestation of religion, the latter term being reserved for the supposedly more elevated forms of belief and worship associated with literate cultures. We now understand, however, that "magic" is an element in all religions, although it seems to be most prominent in the religious traditions associated with nonliterate people. **Magic** may best be defined in operational terms: it involves the manipulation of physical objects to achieve supernatural ends. The term "magic" implies no disrespect, although it might seem a pejorative word because of its connotations in our culture of chicanery and show-business trickery.

In nonliterate societies where magic is especially prominent, it functions in the context of a philosophical idea that Tylor (who gave us our definition of "culture" elaborated in chapter 1) named **animism**, from the Latin (*anima*: "soul" or "spirit"). It reflects the belief, prevalent in nonliterate religious traditions, that all living things have souls. Moreover, it is believed that all souls share a common spiritual essence, such that all living things—people, animals, and plants—are linked at the spiritual level. This belief at the heart of non-Western notions about the ecology and about the need to treat all living things with respect and care. Since all of life is connected in spirit, it makes sense to conclude that anything that touches or affects life in one place at one time will reverberate throughout that interconnected web to touch and affect things elsewhere. Drawing a picture of a living thing (using the natural objects of paint and the stone wall of a cave) sets up a sympathetic vibration throughout the web of life, a ripple that will eventually touch the real animals whose portraits are being drawn. The animals (vibrant in their fertility) will themselves be physically drawn to the area where their images have been traced. Hence the artist serves the hunter (he may even have been a hunter, or she may have been the wife of a hunter) by making magic to insure the abundance of the herds on which the people depended.[3]

Because early humans were hunters necessarily concerned with fertility, and because they lived in such intimate connection with the animals on whom they depended, the underlying assumptions of animism must have been very early additions to the human way of looking at and explaining the world. Tylor, in fact, believed that animism was the first and most basic form of religion. In his own time, that conclusion was challenged by those who saw a related idea as even more basic: **animatism**, the belief in an impersonal spiritual force that is external to material things but can enter into (and hence "animate") them. It is pointless to argue which of these ideas is older or more fundamental; it seems clear that both figure into most religious traditions—old and new—and we will in fact encounter them in various aspects throughout the rest of this book.

In any case, the magical/animistic interpretation of late Stone Age art, like every other interpretation of prehistoric religion, has not gone unchallenged. Some experts, for example, suggest that the art was purely decorative (although the paintings, executed in the dark recesses of more or less inaccessible caves, would seem to argue against this idea). Others agree that it did, indeed, serve a religious function but refuse to go so far as to say what that religion was all about. The most we can say is that in living cultures that we can document directly there is a connection between the making of art and the making of magic; the question is whether the people of the late Stone Age are sufficiently like more modern people for us to conclude that they had the same ideas in mind.

KEY CONCEPTS

Be sure you can define the following terms, and give at least one illustrative example of each:

- analogy
- animatism
- animism
- archaeology
- bear cult

- grave goods
- hunting and gathering
- inference
- magic

- Neanderthals
- ritual cannibalism
- tool tradition
- Venus figurines

RESEARCH EXPLORATIONS

1. Select one Old World (Africa, Europe, Asia) and one New World (the Americas) religion known mainly through the archaeological record. Compare and contrast them, using concepts developed in this chapter. Pay particular attention to the potential limitations of archaeological inference when dealing with nonmaterial aspects of culture. Your report may take the form of an analytical essay, or some sort of visual display.

2. Visit an archaeological site in your vicinity (with the permission and guidance of the archaeologist in charge, of course). Ask the archaeologist how he/she makes inferences about nonmaterial culture and about how he/she believes such cultural elements as religion might have been integrated into the life of the people who inhabited that site. Write a brief essay or prepare a brief talk for in-class presentation about your findings.

3. Visit a museum that features exhibits about one or more prehistoric cultures (or a historical cultures known primarily through the archaeological record). What sorts of evidence have been used to reconstruct the religious aspects of life? Draw up a list of questions you would like to ask the museum curator about how he/she planned and carried out the display(s) to convey information about religion. Conduct that interview if possible, and summarize your findings in a brief report.

4. Compare and contrast a traditional natural history or art museum with a museum operated under the auspices of a Native American tribal organization. What are the differences in thematic emphasis? How do their display styles differ? How do their treatments of traditional religious beliefs and practices differ? Write up your findings in an analytical essay or prepare a brief talk for in-class presentation.

Notes

[1] Durkheim, Émile. 1915. *The Elementary Forms of the Religious Life*, tr. Joseph Swain. London: George Allen & Unwin.

[2] Because the weather and the increasingly polluted atmosphere were threatening to erode the precious paintings, the cave of Lascaux has been closed to all but carefully monitored scientists.

[3] One particularly provocative painting depicts what appears to be a human with the head of a deer. It has been assumed that it is a picture of the magic-making artist wearing an antlered headdress in the act of painting.

"Like Water for Chocolate: Feasting and Political Ritual among the Late Classic Maya at Xunantunich, Belize"

by
Lisa J. LeCount

Although we know something about the Maya civilization from historical sources, we recognize that those sources (written by the Spanish conquerors) are apt to be biased. So for more detailed information about that civilization, we rely on the archaeological record. This article is based on a common archaeological technique, the analysis of pottery. LeCount uses evidence from Mayan pottery to reconstruct the rituals and symbols involved in food consumption, which is a ritual with religious significance that is also seen as a marker of civil and social competition. Social hierarchy is thus not simply an economic matter, but one that reflects larger ideologies of cosmic order.

Anthropologists have long recognized that feasting encompasses a complex dialectic that defines and reifies an individual's position within the social, economic, and political order.[1] Feasting integrates and differentiates group members by providing the public backdrop for the construction and reproduction of social relations. Sponsoring a feast can benefit a host by creating obligations for future payments in kind, often with interest. Provisioning abundant food and drink at public gatherings bolsters partisan loyalty and crafts a strong group image critical in maintaining civil power. The prominent position of feasting, as a setting for the negotiation of social and political relations, derives both from the symbolic associations of superiority and inferiority when food is given and received and from the economic realities of food production and distribution (Wiessner 1996:6).

For archaeologists, the problem lies not only in grasping the anthropological significance of feasting but also in grappling with the issues of recognizing its ancient signatures and differentiating among feasting's many roles in past societies.[2] While some feasts differ quantitatively from daily commensal meals, even within modern complex societies they may remain qualitatively similar (Goody 1982:78; Mennell 1996:32). Not surprisingly, archaeologists have found that feasting may best be identified in ancient societies that adopted specialty festival foods and serving vessels or maintained ritualized banquet locations that are highly visible and ascertainable in the archaeological record. Dietler calls such high cuisine and styles of consumption a "diacritical feasting pattern" (1996:98) and suggests that they are symbolic devices for naturalizing concepts of ranked differences in social status. As exclusionary events, diacritical feasts are hosted by the wealthy and powerful members of society, and company is limited to those who command social and economic attention.

Diacritical feasts stand in opposition to the many kinds of inclusionary affairs in which hosts attempt to promote solidarity and equality by widely casting invitations to community members and supporters. Dietler's (1996:92–97) patron-role feasts, in which food is redistributed between a centralized authority and a supporting populace, and entrepreneurial feasts, in which food exchange is used as a means to incur indebtedness, are good examples of inclusionary feasts, as are Hayden's (1995:27) work party, solicitation, and reciprocal feasts. Although the purpose of inclusionary feasts can be significantly different, they generally attempt to create support by providing abundant amounts of commonly consumed foods. Inclusionary feasts can be very similar to daily commensal meals regarding the types of food and drink served and the style of consumption; however, they may be more public in nature and larger in scale.

The broad dichotomy between exclusionary and inclusionary feasts that I have just described does not adequately explain the intricacies of ancient feasting and the difficulties of finding feasting patterns in the archaeological record. It does, however, allow archaeologists to explore the commingled and not necessarily linear relationships among feasting patterns, social status, and political ritual. The basic assumption that underlies this view is that specialized serving paraphernalia, much like the foods they are intended to hold and display, are political currency, and as such they are used by individuals to create and maintain power. Although underutilized, this is not a new approach. Dietler (1996) traces political interaction between European Bronze Age societies using wine drinking and storage vessels, and Brumfiel (1995) examines changes in Aztec women's status by charting patterns of food preparation using vessel forms. This study goes one step further, however, placing feasting patterns into recent models that show how political competition stimulates the production and distribution of prestige goods.[3]

The Late Classic Maya serve as an excellent case study to investigate the linkage between feasting patterns and political competition because evidence for these behaviors is readily available. Based on ethnographic and ethnohistoric data, Maya feasts are partitioned into two, often overlapping components: the private religious aspect that is centered around family, gods, and ancestors and the public festival aspect that is more political in nature. This distinction is recognizable in the archaeological record through specific vessel forms that were used to serve sacred and festival foods. Comparison of ceramic assemblages across two sets of contexts—elite versus common and public versus private—at the Late Classic Maya center of Xunantunich, Belize, illustrates subtle variation in diacritical feasting patterns. The conclusion suggests factors that may underlie the political significance of eating tamales and drinking chocolate among the ancient Maya.

DIACRITICAL FEASTING PATTERNS AND POLITICAL RITUAL

Diacritical feasting patterns are not universal across complex societies; nor do they assume a standard pattern. Goody (1982:99) and Mennell (1996:32) link elaboration and differentiation in the manners of feasting to highly stratified, hierarchical societies such as Han-period China, classical Rome, or Renaissance Italy. They suggest that in these literate societies, innovations in cuisine and styles of consumption were prompted by the escalating levels of social and political competition in the upper stratum of society and the emulation of courtly eating by the lower stratum. Haute cuisine is characterized by the utilization of prohibitively expensive or exotic items, technologically advanced methods of food preparation, and, oftentimes, privileged or guarded information concerning recipes. Not only is the food exquisite, the service and ambiance are too. Haute cuisine is served on the finest possible tableware, and its outstanding, if not utterly audacious, display denotes class and privilege.

Not all state-level societies, however, are characterized by diacritical feasting to mark social status. In his classic study of world cuisine, Goody (1982) found that nineteenth-century rulers of African kingdoms neither consumed haute cuisine nor owned special serving vessels. He suggests that consumption patterns are related to differences in sociopolitical organization and the means of production (1982:213). Intensification of agriculture and the emergence of cultural hierarchies in Eurasian societies led to innovations and differentiation in food and styles of consumption. In African societies where the political hierarchy was based on divine rule, festival foods were used as framing devices, in Dietler's terms (1996:99), which establish the ritual significance of events. As symbolic cues, special foods, such as beer for the Gonja of northern Ghana or wedding cakes for Americans, are essential components of ceremonies that mark the completion or consummation of ritual action. Participants greatly anticipate these foods, and the weight of tradition demands serving them. In general, they are time consuming or expensive to make but are not so costly that they could not be eaten at daily meals. More importantly, festival foods are not restricted to the elite class, nor are they regarded as haute cuisine that marks status, although some people attempt to impress others with the size and grandeur of their feasts. Presumably, the stability of social hierarchy and the relatively limited number of noble rivals for political office in African hieratic societies did not encourage the innovation of high styles of food and serving vessels.

Goody's observations conform to recent political economy models that attempt to understand the role prestige goods play in creating and maintaining political power. Such models are based on three fundamental propositions first outlined by Douglas and Isherwood (1979:62) and summarized by Brumfiel (1987a:676). Consumption functions to classify people; therefore, it provides an effective means for validating social status. Consumption itself is inherently competitive, thereby making prestige good display and exchange a means for airing conflicting claims to political positions or social status. Consequently, the distribution of prestige goods varies depending on the openness of competition, and it is sensitive to changes in political structure. Based on these propositions, Brumfiel concludes that consumption of prestige goods should flourish in competitive political situations and languish in structured contexts when social and political rights are rigidly defined and relatively uncontested.

This large and growing body of theory suggests that variation in the distribution of prestige goods reflects ancient political strategies. Exclusionary strategies, such as diacritical feasting, are associated with what Blanton and colleagues (1996:5) call network-based political economies in which privileged individuals attempt to monopolize rights to social standing and political offices but also contend with powerful peers for such positions. In such competitive situations, ostentatious consumption and exchange are effective methods to recruit support and to craft a strong image (Cannadine 1985; Hayden 1995). In order to gain influence, competitors stimulate production of prestige goods for use in rival exchange networks. Luxury items, however, may devalue rapidly if they can be imitated using less expensive raw materials or more efficient technologies. To keep a competitive edge, novel items or new fashions must be devised, ultimately inflating the production and diversity of prestige goods. This escalating process can be seen in the shift from medieval cookery to haute cuisine in seventeenth- and eighteenth-century Europe when it would have been physically impossible for the nobility to eat quantitatively more than they already consumed at feasts. Increased demands on chefs to create elaborate meals and service began in the city-courts of Renaissance Italy and quickly spread to the noble houses of France. Later, the burgeoning bourgeoisie of England who could afford such fineries readily adopted the customs of royalty (Mennell 1996:33).

Blanton and colleagues (1996:7) suggest that in corporate political organizations in which collective representation and power sharing form the underpinning of governance, production of prestige goods should be reduced overall with a greater equity in wealth distributions. Leaders emphasize solidarity and interdependence between social and political groups, and rituals center around broad themes such as fertility and renewal. Goody (1982:207) makes the case that in many African states, marriage ties cut across social strata, and there is a strong emphasis on cultural homogeneity rather than class. For Goody, however, the more inclusive nature of African feasting is based not just on social relations but also in the relations of production. Swidden agriculture limits possibilities for monopolizing land and agricultural products and has an equalizing effect on diet. Feasting among the Gonja of northern Ghana is therefore characterized by the consumption of large quantities of common foods such as beer or beef by the entire village. Nevertheless, the political primacy of the chief and his role in maintaining cosmological order are highlighted during communal feasts through protecting or hiding his eating (Goody 1982:77).

It is clear from this discussion that distinguishing between diacritical feasts that demarcate social class and the diacritical use of festival foods that signal ritual events relies on demonstrating both the differentiation and the contextualization of feasting patterns. It is also apparent that although serving paraphernalia may easily be viewed as prestige goods and their distribution may be operationalized to fit recent models, festival foods may not be. Festival foods range from commonly available dishes to exotic meals and, therefore, do not conform to typical definitions of prestige goods that emphasize the restricted nature of their distribution. Archaeologists must consider the context and ritual of eating in order to understand how ordinary food is transformed into festival fare.

THE LATE AND TERMINAL CLASSIC MAYA OF XUNANTUNICH, BELIZE

Xunantunich is a medium-sized center located atop a high ridge overlooking the Mopan River just three kilometers east of the modern-day Guatemala–Belize border and less than 20 kilometers away from the large Classic Maya state of Naranjo (figure 1). The site grew in size and architectural grandeur during the Hats' Chaak phase (670–780 C.E.) of the Late Classic period, when much of the architecture visible today was built.[4] The political climax and collapse of the polity occurred during the Terminal Classic in the early portion of the Tsak' phase (780–850 C.E.) when Xunantunich's ruler proclaimed paramount authority in the upper Belize Valley by dedicating three public monuments and modifying major civic architecture.[5] After 850 C.E., the site appears to have gone through a period of decline and diminution until it was abandoned sometime in the tenth century.

Xunantunich is situated on the eastern periphery of the central Petén, where large, centralized states such as those centered at Tikal and Caracol are located. Small kingdoms like Xunantunich are often characterized as decentralized polities with political structures redundantly organized across centers and dependencies.[6] As such, integration was relatively weak both horizontally between factions of the same political rank and social standing and vertically among ruling nobility, subordinate elites, and their supporting populace. Elite lineages monopolized rights to social standing and political office, yet individuals competed against intrafactional challengers for specific positions. At the top of the political hierarchy the hereditary ruler assigned administrative offices to members within his own noble lineage and other closely related ranked lineages. Secondary elites in turn replicated this kingly model by forming loyal factions of their own complete with collaborators from lower ranked groups. Support for political ambitions depended on maintaining close relations with lineage members and persuading distant kin and foreign allies, often of equal rank, to join forces. Internal competition for kingship, tribute, and regional power is documented in historical inscriptions that describe intra- and interpolity warfare (Stuart 1993:332–336), social conflict (Fash 1991:175), and the rapid succession of rulers (Pohl and Pohl 1994:149).

Public feasting realized the delicate task of simultaneously demonstrating group inclusion of the commoner masses while celebrating elite prerogatives. Private negotiations, meanwhile, could fully engage exclusive strategies such as diacritical displays of prestige items, particularly specialty foods among the elite. Consideration of archaeological context is thus essential to understanding the political ramifications of ancient feasting. In order to elucidate feasting patterns, pottery samples are derived from five contexts that crosscut elite and commoner households and public and private spaces at the regional center of Xunantunich. Architecture is considered the most reliable indicator of status among the Maya; therefore, the sizes of households and their locations in the community are used to suggest ancient social status. The archaeological contexts and inferences concerning the function of civic space and the status of households are described below.

Structure A-6 (known as El Castillo) was the primary focus of ritual and civic life in the community (figure 2). Encircling the roof of this multiplatformed, multistoried complex was an impressive plaster frieze, which still can easily be seen across the upper Belize Valley today. The frieze widely publicized a program of political legitimization by depicting acts of creation and ancestor worship (Fields 1994). Material from El Castillo derives from Structure A-26, a six-room palace structure with four doorways opening from the north and a single branching entrance to the south. Situated on the southern medial terrace, its restricted and private location would have insured that activities occurring inside were limited to resident elite individuals and to those visitors with official business.

Structure A-11, located at the far northern end of the compound, is generally considered to have been the royal residence. It consisted of a lower and upper gallery of rooms that mirrored in the architectural layout and sculptural design the two-story building topping El Castillo (Yaeger 1997:34). The remaining sides of the compound were formed around Plaza A-II by the addition of an *audiencia*, Structure A-13, and

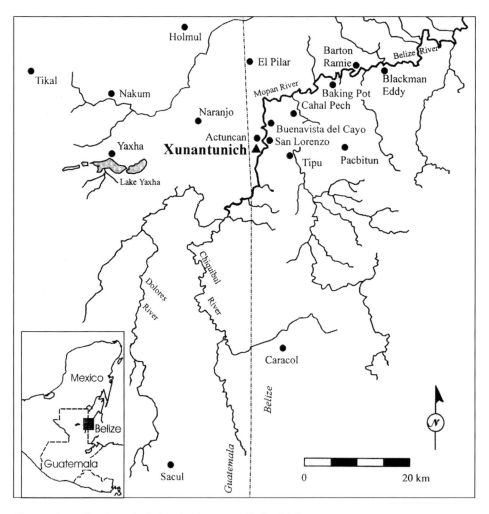

Figure 1.   Classic period sites in the upper Belize Valley.

two palace structures, Structures A-10 and A-12. Ceramics from Group A derive from Structures A-23, A-24, and A-25, a set of three low platforms interpreted as a service area for the royal residence (Jamison and Wolff 1994; LeCount 1996). Staircases connected the ancillary group to Structure A-12, and the alleyways between the two architectural groups contained the highest volume of utilitarian and highly decorated pottery at the site. I presume that this material was associated with private activity inside the royal compound and those public events sponsored by the royal family.

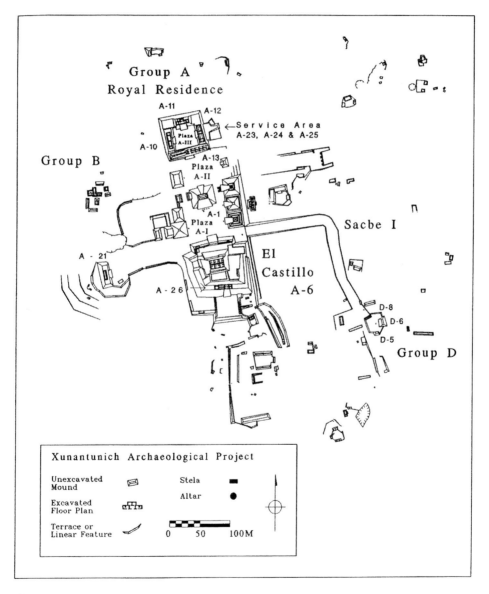

Figure 2.   Classic period architecture of Xunantunich, Belize. Map prepared by Angela Keller and modified by the author.

Group D, a nonroyal residential group, was located on the southeast periphery of the site and linked to the civic core by *sacbeob,* or raised causeways. Braswell (1998:30) suggests that the complex was the home of a nonroyal elite group because small pyramids (like Structure D-6) have been interpreted as ancestor shrines and because range structures, like those found around the central platform, have been interpreted as elite dwellings. Two uncarved stelae, which may have portrayed painted images of lineage leaders and possibly described their genealogical background, also attest to the elite status of the Group D occupants. Extensive excavations at 12 of the 14 mounds recovered occupation and midden material associated with domestic and ritual activities (Braswell 1998).

San Lorenzo, situated 1.5 kilometers northeast of Xunantunich, is a spatially discrete settlement cluster composed of seven patio groups *(plazuelas)* and nine mounds without patios (mound clusters). The site sits on a set of ancient alluvial terraces overlooking the Mopan River and its rich floodplains (figure 3). Yaeger (2000) proposes that the community was composed of a group of related patrilineages not dissimilar to the *pet kahob* hamlets mentioned in colonial period documents (Marcus 1983) or to the kin groups that exist in many contemporary Maya communities (e.g., the *sna* of Zinacantan [Vogt 1983] or the *aldea* of Chiquimula [Wisdom 1940]). Variation in the sizes of San Lorenzo households and their locations in the community can be linked to two ranked social statuses within the presumed commoner stratum.

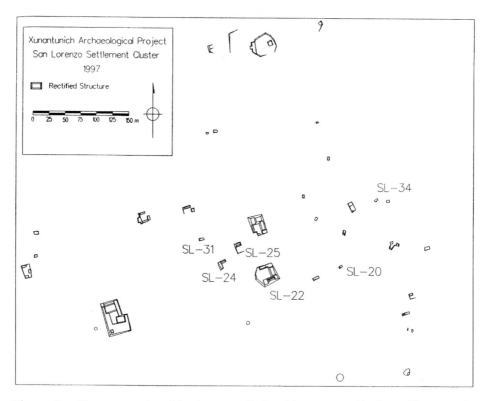

Figure 3.   The community of San Lorenzo, Belize. Map prepared by Jason Yaeger and modified by the author.

Plazuelas are interpreted as homes to the descendants of the first families who founded the community and established control over local resources. Lineage heads that lived at these households held the highest social status and greatest authority within the community. Mound clusters were the residences of new families related by real or fictive ties to the founding families. Over time, gradual growth and fissioning processes related to the domestic developmental cycle created a community composed of several intermarrying localized patrilineages (Goody 1958). This developmental model is confirmed by ceramic analysis that dates initial construction of many plazuelas to the early portion of the Late Classic while mound clusters were built later. By the Terminal Classic mound clusters were already abandoned, but some plazuelas underwent at least one further episode of architectural modification. Data derive from six residences: three plazuela groups (SL-22, SL-24, and SL-25) and three mound clusters (SL-20, SL-31, and SL-34) that received extensive horizontal stripping of the last occupation surfaces to recover Late and Terminal Classic artifactual material (Yaeger 2000).

FOOD AND RITUAL AMONG THE MAYA

Cuisine is a rapidly changing aspect of culture (Mintz 1985:122) and, like other forms of material culture, cannot be expected to remain stable. This is especially true for the Maya who, during the 1,000 years between the Late Classic period and the ethnographic present, lost substantial portions of their once complex society. It is apparent through a comparison of ethnographies and ethnohistories that ancient Maya feasting was more competitive, larger in scale, and broader in scope. This pattern is to be expected given that the sixteenth-century Yucatec Maya, like their Classic ancestors, lived in more hierarchical organized societies than modern groups. But, although scale and styles of consumption have clearly changed, examining the postcontact feasting literature may help to elucidate basic ritual patterns, such as the distinction between ritual and festival fare and the context of rituals, which can be used to create hypotheses about ancient Maya feasting.

PATTERNS OF MODERN MAYA FEASTING

Eating and drinking, processions and prayers, and offerings and sacrifices compose the basic set of recurring rituals that are combined to form a modern Maya ceremony (Vogt 1993:30). The replication of these ritual segments symbolically reproduces the key propositions concerning the nature of life and universe for the Maya. Rituals commence with relatively private sacramental meals that establish sacred connections between individuals and ancestors or gods. They end in public festivals where feasts become stages to materialize social status and arrange political matters. These two core ritual segments—the first private and highly religious, the second more public and celebratory—have remained relatively stable despite Spanish intervention (Vogt 1993:192).

The sacramental aspect of Maya feasts can be divided into three parts: the invitation to gods or ancestors to receive offerings, the actual delivery of consecrated foods, and the subsequent dining on the food blessed for the gods (Bunzel 1952:226; Redfield and Rojas 1934:140; Wisdom 1940:305). Food is not merely eaten in commemoration of saints, gods, or the dead; rather, it is sacrificed and transformed into a sacred element, much like the sacrament of the Eucharist among Christians.

The small-scale, relatively private nature of sacramental meals is illustrated in the modern Yucatec Maya Cha-Chaac ceremony, where a series of consecrated foods marks ceremonial activities and ritual time. Rain ceremonies demand three full days of ritual activities (Redfield and Rojas 1934:140). On the first day, ritual specialists, called *h-men,* erect an altar a slight distance from the public plaza where men of the village will congregate and partake in the ceremony. On the second day, ritualists arrange food on a mesa and offer the sacred meal to the gods at dawn, noon, three o'clock in the afternoon, seven in the evening, and twice again before two in the morning (figure 4). After each offering a drink is distributed to men "some distance from the altar, keeping complete silence so as not to interrupt the feasting of the gods" (Redfield and Rojas 1934:142). After the gods are satiated, sanctified foods are consumed by ritual participants, and a small rack is constructed to hold minor food offerings. Throughout the ritual an endless array of modest portions of sacred food is

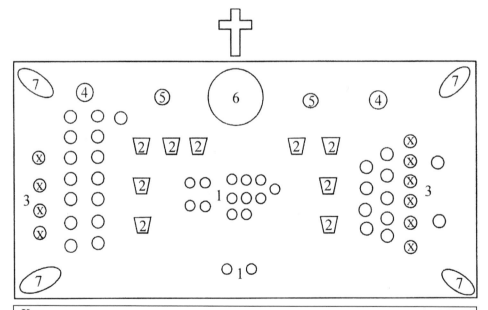

Key:

1. Thirteen *homa* (small bowls) and two shallow gourd dishes of *balché*
2. Nine pails of soup
3. Thirty-six *yal-uah* (ritual bread stuff); those marked with a cross contain chicken meat
4. Two *bolontz-uah* (ritual bread stuff)
5. Two *noh-uah* (ritual bread stuff)
6. One *holche-uah* (ritual bread stuff)
7. Four *yaxche-uah* (ritual bread stuff)

Figure 4. Illustration of ritual mesa for Cha-chaac ceremony demonstrating prescribed arrangement of food offerings. Redrafted from Redfield and Villa Rojas 1934: n. 14.

presented to the gods in small individual bowls, later to be consumed a short distance from the shrine by participants.

More public festivals generally occur after the highly religious portion of the ritual ends. Although festivals are appropriately held on either holy or auspicious days and are imbued with high religious meanings, essentially they are a time for renewing friendships, engaging in sport and profit, and indulging in food and drink. Families celebrate marriages (Wisdom 1940:300), funerals (Bunzel 1952:153; Wisdom 1940:305), first fruit ceremonies (Redfield and Rojas 1934:144), *novenas* or village festivals (Redfield and Rojas 1934:150), and days of the dead (Redfield and Rojas 1934:202–203) by hosting public fêtes. The male head of the household organizes the feast while women collaborate with female kinfolk to prepare the foods. Every family puts aside extra food and drink, striving to provide the best fiesta they can, for such public displays reflect the prosperity of the household. Community-based festivals such as saints' days and cargo ceremonies are more elaborate and incorporate greater numbers of people; however, their organization and structure are similar to those of household fêtes (Vogt 1990:127). The final day of community-wide festivals can feature markets, bullfights, fireworks, masked dances, and, of course, eating and heavy drinking (Bunzel 1959:192; Redfield and Rojas 1934:153–154; Wisdom 1940:433–436). Ultimately the responsibility of providing for the festival lies with the principal organizers and a great deal of the food is purchased by them.[7] In order to defray expenses, organizers may solicit food from community members and sponsor dances (Bunzel 1952:169, 255). In general, however, organizers absorb most of the cost themselves, as this is one of the primary responsibilities and prestige-enhancing characteristics of the office.

Although lowland and highland Maya vary substantially in their repertoire of ritual cuisine, both groups make a distinction between sacramental foods and festival fare (Bunzel 1959:45; Redfield and Villa Rojas 1934:128; Wisdom 1940:387). Among the Yucatec Maya, a modern population closely related to ancient southern lowland groups, sacramental meals center around *zaca,* a maize gruel in which chicken may be added to make *kol;* balché, a fermented honey and tree bark drink; and *tuti-uah*, a variety of baked breads (table 1). Tuti-uah are offered as consecrated food to the gods and are an essential ingredient in zaca. Many small containers of zaca, balché, and kol are placed on the altar or sacrificial mesa (Redfield and Villa Rojas 1934:141, 145). According to Redfield and Villa Rojas (1934:128–129), maize-based foods are suitable for gods, not simply because they are traditionally correct but because they evoke rain-giving functions of the gods and signify purity and divinity.

Festival foods also include maize-based foods and meat, though the dishes are distinct in style of preparation and ingredients. Festival foods common at Yucatec Maya celebrations include tamales, *relleno negro,* tortillas, *atole,* boiled chicken, roasted pigs, chocolate, and rum. These foods are considered "hot" rather than "cold," like sacred fare. Foods, like plants, diseases, and lands, therefore belong to one of two fundamental states (hot or cold), a distinction the Yucatec Maya associate with the duality of nature (Redfield and Villa Rojas 1934:130).

Cacao is consumed more often at social and political events than at religious meals. As a drink, the highland Quiché serve a special atole containing cocoa butter and *sapuyul,* and new *alcaldes* are toasted with chocolate during the Ceremony of the

Table 1.   Modern Yucatec Maya cuisine

Name	Preparation
Atole	Lime-soaked maize is ground and boiled in water, sometimes with sugar or honey.
Pinole	Toasted maize with cinnamon and other spices is ground, boiled like coffee, and sometimes beaten with cacao.
Tortillas	Lime-soaked maize is ground, shaped into cakes, and toasted on a *comal* (griddle).
Pozole	Coarsely ground, cooked maize meal mixed with cold water.
Beans	Boiled.
Meat	Boiled.
Tamales	*Nixtamal* is strained and cooked till thick, mixed with lard and meat, wrapped in banana leaves, and steamed in chicken broth.
Relleno negro	Chicken soup with maize meal dumplings, heavily spiced with roasted peppers.
Zaca	Ground, cooked corn (without lime) stirred into cold water.
Balché	Lonchocarpus tree bark is pounded, placed in a jar with water and honey, and left for three days to ferment.
Kol (yach)	Chicken soup seasoned and thickened with cornmeal bread *(uah)* baked in a *pib* (earthen oven).
Tuti-uah	Seven types of cornmeal breads made with ground squash seeds baked in a pib.
Chocolate	Cacao powder and water are beaten up in a wooden vessel with a wooden beater and sweetened with either sugar or honey; milk is not used.

Source: Redfield and Villa Rojas 1934:37–41.

Surrender of Office (Bunzel 1952:41, 228–247). The Chord mix chocolate into unsweetened atole, a drink they call *chilate,* but they never sacrifice or offer it to the gods (Wisdom 1940:387). Among the lowland Yucatec Maya, chocolate is consumed at weddings, baptisms, and other Catholic rites but not during traditional rites (Redfield and Villa Rojas 1934:192). Cacao beans, however, are considered sacred, and the Quiché offer them to honored participants (Bunzel 1952:44). Bunzel (1952:44) suggests that cacao still retains its ancient role as money in highland society, for seeds are the first gift offered in negotiations for marriage and the last gift exchanged at the conclusion of initiation ceremonies. Similarly, the highland Zinacantecos trade in cacao beans, yet there is no mention of chocolate as a ritual food. For modern Maya, chocolate drinks are consumed by high-ranking officials or honored individuals in more private rituals in which toasting cements social and political relations.

Reconstructing Ancient Maya Feasts

A review of sixteenth-century Yucatec rituals observed by Bishop Deigo de Landa clearly documents the broad scope and scale and differentiated nature of post-contact Maya feasting. Especially relevant are the descriptions of diacritical meals not seen in the ethnographic literature. In addition to the private/public, small-scale/large-scale dimensions explored in the previous ethnographic section, the following ethnohistoric section exams the inclusive versus exclusive nature of Maya feasting. All these lines of evidence are then used to reconstruct Classic Maya feasts.

At small-scale family rites, such as Pocam and Ihcil Ix Chel, Maya families celebrated life passages and personal health by hosting feasts. At larger rites, communities placated gods that governed bees, plants, or animals with food offerings at shrines. Tozzer (1941:163) suggests that the altars were temporary affairs erected at the time of the ritual and that few, if any, ceremonies took place in civic buildings. At the end of these rituals, participants "all ate the gifts and the food, which they had brought, and drank until they were sacks of wine" (Tozzer 1941:154). Annual ceremonies to deities such as Chac, god of rain, and Itzamna, high god of the Yucatec Maya, ended in communal festivals to help ensure a good year of rains (Tozzer 1941:163). Large-scale calendrical and political ceremonies involved many days of commensal feasting. Tonalamatl, which occurred every 65 or 260 days and marked *tun* (year) and *katun* (20-year) endings, lasted for three days with perfumings, offerings, and movable feasts attended by lords and priests of lesser villages (Tozzer 1941:162). Five days of dancing, sacrifices, ceremonies, and feasts surrounded the festival for the cyclical departure of Kukulcan, a preternatural ruler of Chichén Itzá. The celebration culminated in separate village festivals that lasted until the month of Pop.

The distinction between inclusive, communal fêtes and competitive, diacritical feasts was clearly recognized by Bishop Landa. Presumably, this dichotomy extended back into the Classic period, for throughout this large period of time the Maya were organized into competing states. Bishop Landa stated that the sixteenth-century Yucatec Maya had two types of feasts:

> The first, which is that of the nobles and of the principal people, obliges each one of the invited guests to give another similar feast. And to each guest they give a roasted fowl, bread and drink of cacao in abundance; and at the end of the repast, they were accustomed to give a manta to each to wear, and a little stand and vessel, as beautiful as possible. And if one of the guests should die, his household or his relations are obliged to repay the invitation. The second way of giving feasts was used among kinsfolk when they marry their children or celebrate the memory of the deeds of their ancestors, and this does not oblige the guests to give a feast in return, except if a hundred persons have invited an Indian to a feast, he also invites them all when he gives a banquet or marries his children. They have strong friendship and they remember for a long time these invitations, although they are far apart from one another. (Tozzer 1941:921)

Based on this passage, feasting appears to have been widespread across social groups and not confined to the elite class. Both commoner and elite lineage heads were expected to host festivals that marked group members' rites of passages and commemorated important ancestors. McAnany (1995:8) suggests that feasting, like other Maya rituals centered around ancestor worship, legitimized status and rights to lands and property through repetitive social performances and oral history. Among elites, household feasts were competitive and diacritical. Nobles and principal lords sponsored festivals where they provided lavish meals and exchanged prestige items such as cloth and pottery vessels with guests. These obligations were the responsibility of the lineage head, possibly even those from less privileged ranks, whose duty it was to uphold the social honor of the family.

Ancient festival foods described by Landa—"roasted fowl, bread and drink of cacao in abundance"—are remarkably similar to those still being served among the Maya today. Bread, in this situation, refers to tamales. Taube (1989), working with epigraphic and iconographic data, suggests that tamales, *wa* or *wah* (*uah* as cited in the ethnographic literature), were the main daily and ritual food in the central Maya lowlands. At least three different types of tamales have been identified through hieroglyphic texts: curled, notched, and loaf shaped (Taube 1989:42). Presumably these various kinds differed in the context of consumption much like the tamale varieties made today by the modern Maya who prepare some types solely for religious ceremonies while they consume others in festival and secular contexts. Eating meat, specifically deer, peccary, turkey, and dog, was largely confined to public festivals in the sixteenth century, a pattern that according to Pohl and Feldman (1982:302) has Classic period precedents. Sacred foods also appear to have remained remarkably stable, although some new foods, most notably coffee and wheat bread, have been added to the list of foods consumed at contemporary Maya sacramental meals. The continued distinction between ancient sacred and festival foods exists partly because these meals symbolize the essential oppositions between individuality and communality that characterize Maya daily and spiritual life (Vogt 1993:42).

In contrast, everyday fare appears to have changed substantially since the early historic period, and it is thus the most difficult aspect of the cuisine to reconstruct in the archaeological past, especially given the simple nature of food preparation and the lack of prehispanic textual information concerning daily life. What we do know is that tortillas were not commonly eaten in the central lowlands until the Postclassic (Taube 1989), although they may have been introduced to ancient elites by the Late or Terminal Classic, for *comals* appear in the archaeological record at large lowland sites (Ashmore 1981; Brainerd 1958; Harrison 1970; Hendon 1987; Pendergast 1979; Smith 1971), including Xunantunich (LeCount 1996:255), at this time. Comals are generally associated with tortilla preparation, although they can be used to toast cacao or other seeds and nuts (Hendon 1987:350). Because elite diets contained greater amounts of meat than did commoner fare (Pohl 1990:167), it can be speculated that elites ate other festival items such as tamales and chocolate on a more regular basis also. The ancient commoner diet, however, was probably very similar to that consumed by the contemporary Maya whose daily diet relies heavily on tortillas, atole, beans, and chile. These food items are cooked by boiling or toasting with little additional elaboration in preparation or ingredients. Tamale making, conversely, requires labor-intensive preparation. Today women prepare tamales on Sundays or for special occasions, especially Christmas, Easter, and birthdays. Likewise, in the past tamales may have been considered a festival food, a pattern also suggested by Brumfiel (1995:239) for the Aztec. Daily food for the Classic Maya most likely consisted of simple atole and *pinole.*

ARCHAEOLOGICAL MARKERS OF FEASTING

Variation in feasting patterns among the ancient Maya of Xunantunich may be documented by the kinds of pottery vessel forms found in formal assemblages. Cooking and preparation pots are less specific indicators of feasting than serving ware because Maya cuisine, whether it was daily, sacred, or festival foods, essentially involved the same set of cooking techniques: soaking, mixing, boiling, and toasting.[8] Such fundamental tasks could have been adequately accomplished in most open-mouthed jars and large bowls. Serving items, on the other hand, function predominantly in the public domain and are more likely to convey household wealth and status (Smith 1987:312). The display aspect of serving ware makes it a more sensitive marker of diacritical feasting patterns.

The ancient Maya appear to have distinguished among vessel forms and favored particular styles to serve ritual foods. Hieroglyphic texts along the rims of Classic period pictorial vessels make reference to pre-Columbian Maya functional categories (Houston et al. 1989; Reents-Budet 1994; Taube 1989). Some pottery vessels display hieroglyphs around the rim in a format called the Primary Standard Sequence (PSS), an elaborate name tag that generally includes the method of surface decoration, the name of the vessel type, its contents, as well as the social status of the owner. Based on this epigraphic data, Houston, Stuart, and Taube translate an emic classification of vessel types identifying vases as drinking vessels for cacao and plates and dishes as platters to serve tamales. Small bowls likely contained more aqueous foods such as atole that the Maya wished to keep cool (Houston et al. 1989:722). This hypothesis is supported by substantial independent data. Pictorial scenes on Classic period vessels depict elite individuals seated on palace benches with vases in hand and platters stacked with *wah* (figure 5),[9] and often they are shown offering food or gifts to guests or dignitaries. Close examination of these vessels reveals heavy wear patterns on their surfaces; there-

Figure 5.   Late Classic polychrome painted cylinder vase depicting the offering of food and drink at the court of the Lords of Xibalbá. Rollout photograph, copyright Justin Kerr 1976, file no. K504.

fore, it can be assumed that their primary function involved repeated use (Reents-Budet 1994:75), even those items found in burial contexts. Finally, chemical analyses of organic residues found on the interior of vases from an elite tomb at Rio Azul (Stuart 1988) lend support to the proposal that vases were containers for chocolate drinking.

Characterization of ancient vessel forms is based on rim sherds given that archaeological types are defined by a ratio of vessel height to maximum diameter (table 2). Five primary formal categories are defined: plates, dishes, bowls, vases, and jars. Plates and dishes are lumped into a single category called platters because the ancient Maya appear not to have distinguished functionally between the two etically derived forms. Bowls are divided secondarily into large (mean rim diameter = 30 centimeters) and small forms (mean rim diameter = 18 centimeters), for the Maya used them, unlike plates and dishes, for distinctly different purposes (LeCount 1996:251). Rims, rather than body sherds, were used for analysis because they exhibit the critical attributes that define forms. Rims were refit before analysis resulting in counts of the maximum number of vessels per deposit. In an attempt to control for brokenness and completeness, only those rim sherds from refuse deposits qualified for analysis. For this analysis, it is assumed that all vessels of similar form have similar primary functions, even though some vessels lack intricately decorated surfaces.

The context of consumption may be as important as the material remains of meals in distinguishing ancient feasting patterns. Evidence for diacritical feasting among the ancient Maya may be documented by the kinds of vessel forms found in public and private contexts. Diacritical feasting to mark social status should be more prevalent in private contexts where sumptuous foods and splendid tableware would have been reserved for honored guests. Here elites could fully engage in the exclusive strategy of diacritical feasting without alienating valuable supporters. If Xunantunich elites engaged in diacritical feasting, high frequencies of vases and platters should be restricted to civic or elite households. If, however, formal assemblages across the site appear fairly homogenous with relatively similar frequencies of vessel types, then it could be suggested that feasting in the Late and Terminal Classic periods at Xunantunich was more inclusive. Both elite rulers and commoner lineage leaders may have presided over feasts, supplying sacred maize gruel in small bowls, serving tamales on platters, and distributing chocolate in vases. Such inclusive events would have emphasized commonality rather than differentiation by serving customary foods in appropriately autochthonous vessels.

Table 2. Vessel form categories

Primary Form	Formal Description
Plate	Height is less than one-fifth its maximum diameter.
Dish	Height is more than one-fifth but less than one-third its maximum diameter.
Bowl	Height is more than one-third but no more than its maximum diameter; orifice may be restricted (a rimmed bowl) or unrestricted.
Jar	Height is greater than maximum diameter, and it has a neck.
Vase	Height is greater than maximum diameter with a neck very narrow in comparison with its height and width.

Source: Sabloff 1975:227.

Archaeological samples derive from single component excavation lots found in primary contexts such as middens, floors, and occupation debris and not from fill or collapse material. Single-component deposits are critical for analytical comparisons because they represent a discrete archaeological time frame and do not introduce temporal error. The use of primary contexts, rather than secondary deposits, increases the likelihood that the assemblage was the product of specific activities and not the result of commingling materials from many different activities. Such strict sampling criteria resulted in small sample sizes for commoner habitations; however, I argue these samples best represent ancient assemblages. Continued excavations at San Lorenzo (Yaeger 2000) and Chan Nóohol (Robin 1999) have yielded larger samples for plazuela and small mound groups associated with the greater Xunantunich polity. These studies report highly comparable data sets with those presented here and indicate the power of my small samples to draw conclusions concerning the larger population of commoner households.

ANALYSIS AND DISCUSSION

Analysis of pottery forms delineates the existence of a diverse set of pottery assemblages that reflect significant variation in household feasting and important differences between public and private rituals (table 3). The prerequisite domestic assemblage can be reconstructed by viewing the relative frequencies of forms at San Lorenzo mound clusters. These small, commoner families presumably owned the most basic set of cooking and serving ware. Comparison of the relative frequency of primary forms using the mound cluster assemblage as a base line illustrates the complexity of feasting in Late Classic Maya society.

Small bowls, proposed as individual food containers, exhibit distributions that appear to be heavily conditioned by social status. The highest relative frequencies of small bowls are found within elite assemblages. Such forms make up 8 percent of the assemblage associated with royal service area at Group A. El Castillo and Group D assemblages contain between 5 and 6 percent. Small bowls found on El Castillo may also be indicative of cloistered sacramental ceremonies performed there by priests dur-

Table 3. Relative frequency of forms within ritual and household ceramic assemblages.

	El Castillo		Group A		Group D		*Plazuelas*		Mount Clusters	
	n	%	*n*	%	*n*	%	*n*	%	*n*	%
Platters	18	6.64	50	5.57	16	6.84	5	3.94	0	0.00
Vases	37	13.65	39	4.34	2	0.85	1	0.79	1	1.33
Small bowls	13	4.80	76	8.46	15	6.41	1	0.79	2	2.67
Large bowls	90	33.21	324	36.08	139	59.40	58	45.67	44	58.67
Jars	113	41.70	409	45.55	62	26.50	62	48.82	28	37.33
Total rims	271		898		234		127		75	

Note: Derived from rims recovered from occupation contexts of the Hats' Chaak and early facet of the Tsak' phases.
X^2 = 129.376, *df* = 16, *p* = .001.

ing calendric events or possibly royal family ancestor worship. Their presence in elite households can also be used to suggest that individuals may have extended the contexts in which they could mark status. This pattern lends evidence to infer that elites used small bowls for both daily dining and sacred rituals. Commoner households, however, contained very few small bowls constituting less than 3 percent of the formal assemblages at plazuelas and mound clusters. Based on these data, it could be argued that sacramental rituals rarely occurred at commoner households; however, this negates ethnohistoric and ethnographic reports that clearly indicate that such ceremonies did take place among less privileged families. I suggest that commoners offered sacramental foods to gods in small gourds just as they do today.

Plates and dishes, proposed as serving platters for tamales, are surprisingly consistent across assemblages, whether contexts are public or private, elite or common. Relative frequencies within elite assemblages at El Castillo, Group A, and Group D cluster tightly between 6 and 7 percent. Similarly, platters constitute 4 percent of the assemblage associated with large commoner households living at plazuelas. Only small families living at mound clusters had no such serving items. Small families may have participated in household rituals at the home of the lineage patriarch who was responsible for arranging food and providing tableware for feasts, thus they did not need to acquire serving vessels until their obligations increased. This basic assemblage is also characteristic of rural households at hinterland communities in the upper Belize Valley (Robin 1999). Residents living at mound clusters may have lacked service ware because it was costly to obtain. Based on the widespread distribution of these platters, it can be suggested that serving tamales appears to have been an accepted practice that occurred at small family-based festivals, large public ceremonies, and private functions during Late Classic times.

Vases, proposed as drinking containers for chocolate, exhibit much more complex patterning. The highest relative frequency is found on El Castillo with nearly 14 percent of the assemblage composed of such forms. Fewer are found in the service area of the royal residence where they constitute less than 5 percent of the formal assemblage. Household assemblages found at Group D, plazuelas, and mound clusters all contain very low relative frequencies of vases, constituting 1 percent of the formal assemblage. Patterning indicates that chocolate drinking, like tamale eating, was customary at Maya rituals, yet it was more commonly associated with elite events.

Based on these data, I suggest that chocolate drinking was a highly charged political ritual among the Late Classic Maya, a critical act that consolidated political allegiance and cemented civic agreements between individuals, both elite and common. The highest frequency of vases at Xunantunich is found in elite, nonresidential locations removed from public space. Structure A-26, situated on the southern medial terrace of El Castillo, is visually and spatially isolated from the communal plazas. Here, elite men would have gathered in secluded rooms to conduct affairs of state or lineage. At the royal service center vases may also have been associated with private events, as most were recovered from Structure A-25. Of the three platforms that form the royal service area, Structure A-25 is farthest from Plaza A-II. I have argued previously that the presence of vases at this structure could be interpreted as marking the preparation of chocolate drinks for consumption at large festivals in Plaza A-II (LeCount 1996:268). Nevertheless, it is also reasonable to assume that this preparation may have been for private consumption by royalty and their guests in palace structures within the royal compound itself. The consistent, yet extremely low frequencies of vases across households, even those of the least privileged, attests to the fact that all lineage heads may have owned at least one vase.

This archaeological pattern appears analogous to that described in the ethnographic literature, which documents chocolate drinking associated with rituals involving civil functions, such as the installation of new *alcaldes* (mayors) or marriage arrangements. Generally, these rituals are performed in private houses or offices, a pattern confirmed at Xunantunich and also seen depicted on Classic period pottery.[10] According to Vogt (1993:35), a drink must accompany any kind of crucial transaction among the modern Maya of Zinacantan men.

The scenario above leads to the conclusion that chocolate drinking was a relatively private, possibly one-on-one activity between men in power. Houston et al. (1989) have long argued that the PSS found along the rim of pottery vessels makes proprietary statements that identify not only the owner of the vessel but his or her social status as well. Further, scenes painted on Classic vases may have depicted important historical events that occurred during an individual's lifetime (Chase 1985). Vases, particularly those prominently displaying name and rank, could therefore be considered inalienable possessions (Weiner 1992) that materialized an individual's rank at ritual events.

SUMMARY AND CONCLUSIONS

I have attempted to identify variation in ancient feasting patterns and link it to political rituals that maintain power in Late and Terminal Classic society. Interpreting the archaeological patterning from five contexts that cut across private, civic, elite, and common contexts at the Late and Terminal Classic Maya site of Xunantunich is challenging because the distribution of forms is not arranged into neatly defined sets of serving vessels. My approach to this complexity is to view individual vessel forms separately because I assume that each type informs us about specific ritual foods and their role in the religious, social, and political aspects of ancient feasting. Sacramental meals appear to be the most difficult aspect to investigate, for small bowls, the archaeological marker used to identify offerings of sacred food, also could have functioned as individual serving containers for elite secular dining. Commoners may have substituted perishable gourds for small bowls, a pattern seen today in modern Maya rituals. Celebratory feasting, in contrast, is more visible in the Maya archaeological record. The wide distribution of plates and vases lends evidence to suggest that most elite and large commoner households sponsored lineage-based feasts where tamales and at least a small amount of chocolate were consumed. Although headmen might have owned at least one chocolate drinking vessel, the high concentration of vases in Structure A-26 on El Castillo and elevated levels found in Group A indicate that drinking may have taken on special significance.

The political significance of chocolate has long been noted by Mesoamericanists, especially epigraphers such as Houston et al. (1989), whose reading of ethnohistorical and Classic period texts has shown that chocolate drinks were integral to dynastic ceremonies and to affirming important social contracts. The Xunantunich data, which focus on excavation materials, add yet another line of evidence to support this interpretation. But what makes chocolate different than other Maya drinks, such as *balché* or *chicha* (maize beer), as a locus of value (Netting 1964)? The significance of chocolate stems partly from its prominent place in the origin myth of the Maya, the Popol Vuh, in which gods created humans from maize and chocolate found in the Mountain of Sustenance. Chocolate, however, is unlike maize in the ways it is raised and processed (Coe and Coe 1996:42). Cacao trees are difficult to grow and require year-round moisture and specific soil conditions, such as those found in the Sosconusco area on the Pacific coast or the Gulf Coast plain. Cacao beans themselves also demand extensive processing which limited coca production until 1815, when a Dutch chemist invented a process for the manufacture of powdered chocolate with a low fat content. Therefore, ancient people could not have been fed chocolate, unlike beer, chicha, or other beverages made from high-yielding crops at entrepreneurial feasts, work parties, or patron-role festivals. Presumably, the restricted nature of cacao farming allowed Maya elites at some point in the distant past to seize control of its means of production and/or distribution. Such high-value and cosmologically significant prestige goods often served as political currencies (Earle 1991:7). For the ancient Maya, cacao condensed religious, economic, and social meaning into a single material referent and, as a drink, was the symbolic cue for the consummation of political rituals.

It could be argued that such strict interpretations of vessel functions are misleading. Elaborately painted and inscribed vases and plates could have functioned primarily as tribute items. Substantial archaeological evidence shows that some highly decorated vase styles were exchanged over long distances and did act as social currency (Reents-Budet 1994). Text along the rim of cylinder vases describe how these vessels were gifts from paramount leaders to lesser elites at smaller sites, presumably to establish or maintain social and political relations (Ball 1993; Houston et al. 1992; Schele and Mathews 1991). Other researchers suggest that cylinder vases, plates, and dishes might have also functioned for other less utilitarian and more prestigious purposes. Justin Kerr (personal communication, 1999) believes cylinder vases were containers for sacred offerings. He cites the text on vase no. K504 (see figure 5) that reads "In the vessel are the seeds of the genitals" as evidence that the vase held corn kernels for the gods of the underworld. Coe (1978:11) has long argued that all pictorial vases are funerary in nature. When such forms are viewed solely as luxury objects, then it is clear from the Xunantunich data that vases and small bowls may have moved about society in limited elite circles. However, it is also evident that all forms were found widely distributed, albeit in small frequencies, at the site. I have concluded elsewhere (LeCount 1999) that pottery as a prestige item was a less specific indicator of ancient social status than other exclusive status markers, a conclusion elaborated below.

If the functional interpretation of vessels presented in this article is accepted, what can be gleaned from the archaeological record concerning the nature of feasting and its role as a marker of ancient political strategies among Late Classic Maya at Xunantunich? According to the model, when political bureaucracies are deeply stratified and the scale of competition is great, emulation and imitation of feasting patterns should lead to the innovation of haute cuisine and specialty serving vessels. On the other hand, when levels of power are relatively shallow and competition is restricted to a few elite lineages, feasting patterns should be less differentiated. At Xunantunich, little evidence exists for diacritical feasting to mark social status. Formal assemblages differed only in the quantity of primary forms, a pattern characteristic of inclusive feasting where public displays of generosity and hospitality extended across broad sectors of society. Although elite households clearly owned a greater amount of serving vessels and more highly decorated pieces, commoners also possessed vases and platters and probably served the same basic fare at festivals. In fact, there is more variation in formal assemblages within social classes than between them. Studies elsewhere within the Maya area confirm that glyph and figural serving vases were found in moderate-sized plazuela groups (Beaudry 1987; Hansen et al. 1991), nonroyal tombs (Chase 1985), and domestic trash piles (Fry 1979), illustrating how prevalent decorated serving ware had become in the Classic period.

Based on these data, it can be suggested that Late Classic Maya lacked a sufficiently complex, civil hierarchy that would have promoted truly high styles of food consumption. The relative simplicity of Classic Maya feasting is in stark contrast to that of the far more hierarchically organized Postclassic Aztec. According to conquistador Díaz del Castillo (1956:209–210), the daily cuisine of Motecuhzoma II consisted of 30 different dishes set on a low table with tablecloths of white fabric and napkins. He was attended by four women who erected a gold-gilded screen in front of him so that his dining was not seen by others. Sumptuary laws also restricted drinking of cacao and eating of exotic foods to nobles. Diacritical feasting among the Maya was clearly less developed, thus adding one more piece of information supporting the relatively decentralized nature of Late Classic Maya at small provincial centers.

Notes

[1] See Douglas 1966; Feeley-Harnik 1985; Goody 1982; Hocart 1970; Mennell 1996; Mintz 1985; Lévi-Strauss 1969; Richards 1960; Wiessner and Schiefenhovel 1996; and Young 1971.

[2] See Blitz 1993; Brumfiel 1995; Clark and Blake 1994; Dietler 1990, 1996; Hastorf and Johannessen 1993; Hayden 1990, 1995, 1996; and Welch and Scary 1995.

[3] See Anderson 1994; Blanton et al. 1996; Brumfiel 1987b, 1994; DeMarrais et al. 1996; Brumfiel and Earle 1987; LeCount 1999; and Peregine 1991.

[4] Xunantunich ceramic complex names have recently changed (LeCount et al. n.d.). The previous phase names of Late Classic I, Late Classic II, and Terminal Classic have been changed to Samal, Hats' Chaak, and Tsak', respectively.

[5] See Ashmore 1996; Ashmore and Leventhal 1993; LeCount et al. n.d.; Leventhal et al. 1993; and Leventhal and LeCount 1997.

[6] For debates on the nature of Maya political organization and social integration, see Chase and Chase 1996; Culbert 1991; Demarest 1992; Freidel 1992; Hendon 1991; Pohl and Pohl 1994; Marcus 1993; Sabloff 1986; Sanders 1989; and Stuart 1993.

[7] Organizers are the *cargador* (Redfield and Rojas 1934:157), the *mayordomo* (Wisdom 1940:450), and the *cofradia* (Bunzel 1952:165). At the festival of Santiago, a group of about 50 Chorti women are appointed by the mayordomos to cook festival foods in large ovens and fireplaces located in the cofradia courtyard (Wisdom 1940:450). Most foodstuffs are contributed by individual families, but a great deal is purchased by mayordomos.

[8] Cooking sacred meals, with the exception of tuti-uah, is similar to preparing everyday foods. Although tuti-uah is painstakingly prepared by men, who layer maize dough with various special ingredients, wrap the cake in leaves, and bake it in an earth oven or *pib* (Love 1989; Taube 1989), little archaeological evidence would remain to signal its preparation.

[9] See Coe 1978: fig. 7; Coe 1994; Kerr 1990: file no. 2573, 1992: file nos. 3813, 1599, 1728, 1775; Reents-Budet 1994: figs. 1.25, 2.20, 3.2; and Taube 1989: fig. 7.

[10] Scenes on Classic period vases depict elite men sitting on palace benches and offering drinks, sometimes in conjunction with food, other times solely extending cylinders of foaming chocolate to guests. For scenes in which drinking is divorced from eating, see Culbert 1993: fig. 75; Kerr 1989: file nos. 1563, 3827; and Reents-Budet 1994: figs. 1.6, 3.14c.

References Cited

Anderson, D., 1994. Factional Competition and the Political Evolution of Mississippian Chiefdoms in the Southeastern United States. In *Factional Competition and Political Development in the New World*, E. M. Brumfiel and J. W. Fox, eds. (Cambridge: Cambridge University Press), pp. 61–76.

Ashmore, W., 1981. Precolumbian Occupation at Quirigua, Guatemala: Settlement Patterns in a Classic Maya Center. Ph.D. dissertation, Department of Anthropology, University of Pennsylvania.

———, 1996. Settlement Archaeology at Xunantunich, 1996. In *Xunantunich Archaeological Project: 1996 Field Season*, R. M. Leventhal, ed. (On file, Institute of Archaeology, University of California, Los Angeles, and Belmopan, Belize), pp. 17–27.

Ashmore, W., and R. Leventhal, 1993. Xunantunich Reconsidered. Paper presented at the Belize Conference, University of North Florida, Jacksonville, March.

Ball, Joseph, 1993. Pottery, Potters, Palaces, and Polities: Some Socioeconomic and Political Implications of Late Classic Maya Ceramic Industries. In *Lowland Maya Civilization in the Eighth Century A.D.*, J. A. Sabloff and J. S. Henderson, eds. (Washington, DC: Dumbarton Oaks Research Library and Collection), pp. 243–272.

Beaudry, M., 1987. Interregional Exchange, Social Status, and Painted Ceramics: The Copan Valley Case. In *Interactions on the Southeast Mesoamerican Frontier*. E. J. Robinson, ed. (BAR International Series, 327. Oxford: British Archaeological Reports), pp. 227–246.

Blanton, R., G. Feinman, S. Kowalewski, and P. Peregrine, 1996. A Dual-Processual Theory for the Evolution of Mesoamerican Civilization. *Current Anthropology* 37:1–14.

Blitz, J. H., 1993. Big Pots for Big Shots: Feasting and Storage in a Mississippian Community. *American Antiquity* 58(1): 80–95.

Brainerd, G., 1958. The Archaeological Ceramics of the Yucatan. *Anthropological Records, 19* (Norman: University of Oklahoma Press).

Braswell, J., 1998. Archaeological Investigations at Group D, Xunantunich, Belize. Ph.D. dissertation, Department of Anthropology, Tulane University.

Brumfiel, E. M., 1987a. Consumption and Politics at Aztec Huexotla. *American Anthropologist* 89:676–686.

———, 1987b. Elite and Utilitarian Crafts in the Aztec State. In *Specialization, Exchange, and Complex Societies*, E. M. Brumfiel and T. K. Earle, eds. (Cambridge: Cambridge University Press), pp. 102–118.

———, 1994. Factional Competition and Political Development in the New World: An Introduction. In *Factional Competition and Political Development in the New World*, E. M. Brumfiel and J. W. Fox, eds. (Cambridge: Cambridge University Press), pp. 1–14.

———, 1995. Weaving and Cooking: Women's Production in Aztec Mexico. In *Engendering Archaeology: Women and Prehistory*, J. M. Gero and M. W. Conkey, eds. (Oxford: Blackwell), pp. 224–254.

Brumfiel, E. M., and T. K. Earle, 1987. Specialization, Exchange, and Complex Societies: An Introduction. In *Specialization, Exchange, and Complex Societies*, E. M. Brumfiel and T. K. Earle, eds. (Cambridge: Cambridge University Press), pp. 1–9.

Bunzel, R., 1952. Chichicastenango, a Guatemalan Village. *American Ethnological Society Publication, 22.* (Locust Valley, NY: American Ethnological Society).

Cannadine, D., 1985. Splendor Out of Court: Royal Spectacle and Pageantry in Modern Britain, c. 1820–1977. In *Rites of Power: Symbolism, Ritual, and Politics since the Middle Ages,* S. Wilentz, ed. (Philadelphia: University of Pennsylvania Press), pp. 206–243.

Chase, A., 1985. Contextual Implications of Pictorial Vases from Tayasal, Petén. In *Fourth Palenque Round Table, 1980,* M. G. Robertson and E. P. Benson, eds. (San Francisco: Pre-Columbian Art Research Institute), pp.193–210.

Chase, A., and D. Chase, 1996. More than Kin and King: Centralized Political Organization among the Late Classic Maya. *Current Anthropology* 37(5): 803–830.

Clark, J., and W. Blake, 1994. The Power of Prestige: Competitive Generosity and the Emergence of Rank Societies in Lowland Mesoamerica. In *Factional Competition and Political Development in the New World,* E. M. Brumfiel and J. W. Fox, eds. (Cambridge: Cambridge University Press), pp. 17–30.

Coe, M., 1978. *Lords of the Underworld: Masterpieces of Classic Maya Ceramics* (Princeton: The Art Museum, Princeton University Press).

Coe, S., 1994. *America's First Cuisines* (Austin: University of Texas Press).

Coe, S., and M. Coe, 1996. *The True History of Chocolate* (London: Thames and Hudson).

Culbert, T., 1991. Maya Political History and Elite Interaction: A Summary View. In *Classic Maya Political History,* T. Culbert, ed. (Cambridge: Cambridge University Press), pp. 311–346.

———, 1993. The Ceramics of Tikal: Vessels from the Burials, Caches and Problematical Deposits. *Tikal Report, 25, part A,* W. Coe and W. Haviland, series eds. University Museum Monograph, 81. (Philadelphia: University Museum, University of Pennsylvania).

Demarest, A. A., 1992. Ideology in Ancient Maya Cultural Evolution: The Dynamics of Galactic Polities. In *Ideology and Pre-Columbian Civilizations,* A. A. Demarest and G. W. Conrad, eds. (Seattle: University of Washington Press), pp. 135–158.

DeMarrais, E., L. Castillo, and T. Earle, 1996. Ideology, Materialization, and Power Strategies. *Current Anthropology* 37:15–31.

Díaz del Castillo, Bernal, 1956. *The Discovery and Conquest of Mexico* (New York: Farrar, Straus and Cudahy).

Dietler, M., 1990. Driven by Drink: The Role of Drinking in the Political Economy and the Case of Early Iron Age France. *Journal of Anthropological Archaeology* 9:352–406.

———, 1996. Feasts and Commensal Politics in the Political Economy: Food, Power, and Status in Prehistoric Europe. In *Food and the Status Quest: An Interdisciplinary Perspective,* Polly Wiessner and Wulf Schiefenhovel, eds. (Providence, RI: Berghahn Books), pp. 86–126.

Douglas, M., 1966. *Purity and Danger* (London: Routledge and Kegan Paul).

Douglas, M., and B. Isherwood, 1979. *The World of Goods* (New York: Basic Books).

Earle, Timothy, 1991. The Evolution of Chiefdoms. In *Chiefdoms: Power, Economy, and Ideology,* Timothy Earle, ed. (Cambridge: Cambridge University Press), pp. 1–15.

Fash, W., 1991. *Scribes, Warriors and Kings* (London: Thames and Hudson).

Feeley-Harnik, G., 1985. Issues in Divine Kingship. *Annual Review of Anthropology* 14:273–313.

Fields, V., 1994. The Royal Charter at Xunantunich. In *Xunantunich Archaeological Project: 1994 Field Season,* R. M. Leventhal, ed. (On file, Institute of Archaeology, University of California, Los Angeles, and Belmopan, Belize), pp. 65–74.

Freidel, D., 1992. Ideology in Ancient Maya Cultural Evolution. In *Ideology and Pre-Columbian Civilizations*, A. A. Demarest and G. W. Conrad, eds. (Seattle: University of Washington Press), pp. 115–134.

Fry, R., 1979. The Economies of Pottery at Tikal, Guatemala: Models of Exchange for Serving Vessels. *American Antiquity* 44(3): 494–512.

Goody, J., 1958. *The Development Cycle in Domestic Groups* (Cambridge: Cambridge University Press).

———, 1982. *Cuisine, Cooking, and Class: A Study in Comparative Sociology* (Cambridge: Cambridge University Press).

Hansen, R., R. Bishop, and F. Fahsen, 1991. Notes on Maya Codex-Style Ceramics from Nakbe, Péten, Guatemala. *Ancient Mesoamerica* 2:225–243.

Harrison, P. D., 1970. The Central Acropolis, Tikal, Guatemala: A Preliminary Study of the Functions of Its Structural Components during the Late Classic Period. Ph.D. dissertation, Department of Anthropology, University of Pennsylvania.

Hastorf, C., and S. Johannessen, 1993. Prehispanic Political Change and the Role of Maize in the Central Andes of Peru. *American Anthropologist* 95:115–138.

Hayden, B., 1990. Nimods, Piscators, Pluckers, and Platers: The Emergence of Food Production. *Journal of Anthropological Archaeology* 9:31–69.

———, 1995. Pathways to Power: Principles for Creating Socioeconomic Inequalities. In *Foundations of Social Inequality*, T. D. Price and G. M. Feinman, eds. (New York: Plenum Press), pp. 15–86.

———, 1996. Feasting in Prehistoric and Traditional Societies. In *Food and the Status Quest: An Interdisciplinary Perspective*, Polly Wiessner and Wulf Schiefenhovel, eds. (Providence, RI: Berghahn Books), pp. 127–148.

Hendon, J., 1987. The Uses of Maya Structures: A Study of Architecture and Artifact Distribution at Sepulturas, Copan, Honduras. Ph.D. dissertation, Department of Anthropology, Harvard University.

———, 1991. Status and Power in Classic Maya Society: An Archaeological Study. *American Anthropologist* 93:894–918.

Hocart, A., 1970. *Kings and Councillors: An Essay in the Comparative Anatomy of Human Society* (Chicago: University of Chicago Press).

Houston, S., D. Stuart, and K. Taube, 1989. Folk Classification of Classic Maya Pottery. *American Antiquity* 91:720–726.

———, 1992. Image and Text on the "Jauncy Vase." In *The Maya Vase Book: A Corpus of Rollout Photographs of Maya Vases*, vol. 3, J. Kerr, ed. (New York: Kerr Associates), pp. 499–512.

Jamison, T., and G. Wolff, 1994. Excavations in and around Plaza A-I and Plaza A-II. In *Xunantunich Archaeological Project: 1994 Field Season*, R. M. Leventhal, ed. (On file, Institute of Archaeology, University of California, Los Angeles, and Belmopan, Belize), pp. 25–47.

Kerr, J., 1989. *The Maya Vase Book: A Corpus of Rollout Photographs of Maya Vases*, vol. 1 (New York: Kerr Associates).

———, 1990. *The Maya Vase Book: A Corpus of Rollout Photographs of Maya Vases*, vol. 2 (New York: Kerr Associates).

———, 1992. *The Maya Vase Book: A Corpus of Rollout Photographs of Maya Vases*, vol. 3 (New York: Kerr Associates).

LeCount, L., 1996. Pottery and Power: Feasting, Gifting, and Displaying Wealth among the Late and Terminal Classic Lowland Maya. Ph.D. dissertation, Department of Anthropology, University of California, Los Angeles.

———, 1999. Polychrome Pottery and Political Strategies in Late and Terminal Classic Maya Society. *Latin American Antiquity* 10(3): 239–258.

LeCount, L., R. Leventhal, J. Yaeger, and W. Ashmore, n.d. Dating the Rise and Fall of Xunantunich, Belize: A Late and Terminal Classic Lowland Maya Secondary Center. Unpublished MS.

Leventhal, R., and L. LeCount, 1997. The Terminal Classic Social and Political Organization of Ancient Xunantunich. Paper presented at the 62nd Annual Meeting of the Society for American Archaeology, Nashville, March.

Leventhal, R., S. Zeleznik, T. Jamison, L. LeCount, J. McGovern, J. Sanchez, and A. Keller, 1993. Xunantunich: A Late and Terminal Classic Center in the Belize River Valley. Paper presented at Palenque Mesa Redonda, Palenque, Mexico, May.

Lévi-Strauss, C., 1969. *The Raw and the Cooked*, J. Weightman and D. Weightman, trans. (New York: Harper and Row).

Love, B., 1989. Yucatec Sacred Breads through Time. In *Word and Image in Maya Culture: Explorations in Language, Writing, and Representation*, W. Hanks and D. Rice, eds. (Salt Lake City: University of Utah Press), pp. 336–350.

Marcus, J., 1983. Lowland Maya Archaeology at the Crossroads. *American Antiquity* 48(3): 454–488.

———, 1993. Ancient Maya Political Organization. In *Lowland Maya Civilization in the Eighth Century A.D.*, J. A. Sabloff and J. S. Henderson, eds. (Washington, DC: Dumbarton Oaks), pp. 111–184.

McAnany, P., 1995. *Living with the Ancestors: Kinship to Kingship in Ancient Maya Society* (Austin: University of Texas Press).

Mennell, S., 1996. *All Manners of Food: Eating and Taste in England and France from the Middle Ages to the Present, 2nd edition* (Urbana: University of Illinois Press).

Mintz, S., 1985. *Sweetness and Power: The Place of Sugar in Modern History* (New York: Penguin Books).

Netting, R. McC., 1964. Beer as a Locus of Value among the West African Koyfar. *American Anthropologist* 66:375–384.

Pendergast, D., 1979. *Excavations at Altun Ha, Belize, 1964–1970*, vol. 3. (Toronto: Royal Ontario Museum).

Peregrine, P., 1991. Some Political Aspects of Craft Specialization. *World Archaeology* 23:1–11.

Pohl, M., 1990. The Ethnozoology of the Maya: Faunal Remains from Five Sites in Péten, Guatemala. In *Excavations at Seibal, Department of Péten, Guatemala*, Gordon R. Willey, ed., *Memoirs of the Peabody Museum of Archaeology and Ethnology*, 17(3), (Cambridge, MA: Peabody Museum, Harvard University), pp. 143–174.

Pohl, M., and L. Feldman, 1982. The Traditional Role of Women and Animals in Lowland Maya Economy. In *Maya Subsistence: Studies in Memory of Dennis E. Puleston*, K. Flannery, ed. (New York: Academic Press), pp. 295–312.

Pohl, M., and J. Pohl, 1994. Cycles of Conflict: Political Factionalism in the Maya Lowlands. In *Factional Competition and Political Development in the New World*, E. M. Brumfiel and J. W. Fox, eds. (Cambridge: Cambridge University Press), pp. 1–14.

Redfield, R., and A. Villa Rojas, 1934. *Chan Kom: A Maya Village*, Carnegie Institution of Washington, 448 (Washington, DC: Carnegie Institution of Washington).

Reents-Budet, D., 1994. *Painting the Maya Universe: Royal Ceramics of the Classic Period* (Durham: Duke University Press).

Richards, A., 1960[1939]. *Land, Labour and Diet in Northern Rhodesia: An Economic Study of the Bemba Tribe* (London: Oxford University Press).

Robin, C., 1999. Towards an Archaeology of Everyday Life: Ancient Maya Farmers of Chan Nóohol and Dos Chombitos Cikín. Ph.D. dissertation, Department of Anthropology, University of Pennsylvania.

Sabloff, J., 1986. Interaction among Maya polities: A Preliminary Examination. In *Peer-Polity Interaction and Socio-Political Change*, C. Renfrew and J. F. Cherry, eds. (Cambridge: Cambridge University Press), pp. 109–116.

Sanders, W., 1989. Household, Lineage, and State in Eighth-Century Copan, Honduras. In *The House of the Bacabs, Copán, Honduras*, D. Webster, ed. (Washington, DC: Dumbarton Oaks), pp. 89–105.

Schele, Linda, and P. Mathews, 1991. Royal Visits and Other Intersite Relationships among the Classic Maya. In *Classic Maya Political History*, T. P. Culbert, ed. (Cambridge: Cambridge University Press), pp. 226–252.

Smith, M., 1987. Household Possessions and Wealth in Agrarian States: Implications for Archaeology. *Journal of Anthropological Archaeology* 6(4): 297–335.

Smith, R., 1971. *The Pottery of Mayapan Including Studies of Ceramic Material from Uxmul, Kabah, and Chichén Itzá*, Papers of the Peabody Museum of Archaeology and Ethnology, 66. (Cambridge, MA: Harvard University Press).

Stuart, D., 1988. The Rio Azul Cacao Pot: Epigraphic Observations on the Function of a Maya Ceramic Vessel. *Antiquity* 62:153–157.

———, 1993. Historical Inscriptions and the Maya Collapse. In *Lowland Maya Civilization in the Eighth Century A.D.*, J. A. Sabloff and J. S. Henderson, eds. (Washington, DC: Dumbarton Oaks), pp. 321–354.

Taube, K., 1989. The Maize Tamale in Classic Maya Diet, Epigraphy, and Art. *American Antiquity* 54(1):31–51.

Tozzer, A., 1941. *Landa's Relación de las Cosas de Yucatán*. Papers of the Peabody Museum of Archaeological and Ethnology Papers, 4. (Cambridge, MA: Harvard University).

Vogt, E., 1983. Ancient and Contemporary Maya Settlement Patterns: A New Look from the Chiapas Highlands. In *Prehistoric Settlement Patterns: Essays in Honor of Gordon R. Willey*, E. Z. Vogt and R. M. Leventhal, eds. (Albuquerque: University of New Mexico Press), pp. 89–114.

———, 1990. *The Zinacantecos of Mexico: A Modern Maya Way of Life*, 2nd edition (Fort Worth: Holt, Rinehart and Winston, Inc.).

———, 1993. *Tortillas for the Gods: A Symbolic Analysis of Zinacanteco Rituals* (Norman: University of Oklahoma Press).

Weiner, A., 1992. *Inalienable Possessions: The Paradox of Keeping-while-Giving* (Berkeley: University of California Press).

Welch, P. D., and C. M. Scarry, 1995. Status-Related Variation in Foodways in the Moundville Chiefdom. *American Antiquity* 60(3): 397–120.

Wiessner, Polly, 1996. Introduction: Food, Status, Culture, and Nature. In *Food and the Status Quest: An Interdisciplinary Perspective*, Polly Wiessner and Wulf Schiefenhovel, eds. (Providence, RI: Berghahn Books), pp. 1–19.

Wiessner, Polly, and Wulf Schiefenhovel, eds., 1996. *Food and the Status Quest: An Interdisciplinary Perspective* (Providence, RI: Berghahn Books).

Wisdom, C., 1940. *The Chorti Indians of Guatemala* (Chicago: University of Chicago Press).

Yaeger, J., 1997. The 1997 Excavations of Plaza A-III and Miscellaneous Excavation and Architectural Clearing in Group A. In *Xunantunich Archaeological Project, 1997 Field Season*, R. M. Leventhal, ed. (On file, Institute of Archaeology, University of California, Los Angeles, and Belmopan, Belize), pp. 56–75.

———, 2000. Changing Patterns of Maya Community Structure and Organization at the End of the Classic Period: San Lorenzo, Cayo District, Belize. Ph.D. dissertation, Department of Anthropology, University of Pennsylvania.

Young, M., 1971. *Fighting with Food: Leadership, Values, and Social Control in a Massim Society* (Cambridge: Cambridge University Press).

Questions for Discussion

1. What, in LeCount's opinion, is the main anthropological significance of feasting? What aspect of feasting is of most interest to archaeologists?

2. What is a "political ritual"? What examples can be found in various highly stratified, hierarchical societies?

3. What are the main elements in LeCount's reconstruction of ancient Mayan feasting behavior? What potential problems does she identify when using material culture to make inferences about non-material elements such as ritual, beliefs, or political ideologies?

Suggested Readings or Other Resources

Concise Surveys of Prehistoric Religion

Hultkrantz, Åke. 1994. Religion before History. In *Handbook to the World's Religions*, ed. R. Pierce Beaver, et al. Grand Rapids, MI: Eerdmans (pp. 22–29).

Molloy, Michael. 1999. Oral Religions. In *Experiencing the World's Religions* by M. Molloy. Mountain View, CA: Mayfield (pp. 25–54).

Parrinder, Geoffrey. 1983. Prehistoric Religion. In *World Religions: From Ancient History to the Present* by G. Parrinder. New York: Facts-on-File (pp. 22–34).

Smart, Ninian. 1997. Earliest Religion. In *The World's Religions* by N. Smart. Cambridge (U.K.): Cambridge University Press (pp. 33–41).

Conceptual Works

Frazer, James G. 1922. Magic and Religion. In *The Golden Bough*, vol. 1 by J. G. Frazer. London: Macmillan.

Tylor, Edward B. 1873. Animism. In *Primitive Culture*, vol. 1, 2nd ed. by E. B. Tylor. London: John Murray.

Videos

Primal Religions (Insight Media, Inc.) is a two-volume set (60 minutes each) that explains the characteristic features of prehistoric religions and discusses the nature of their beliefs and rituals.

The World of the Goddess (Insight Media, Inc.) is a 103-minute film featuring Marija Gimbutas, a renowned archaeological expert on prehistoric religion, who discusses the culture, beliefs, and mythology of prehistoric Europe.

3

The Ideological Component of the Sacred

featuring

"'I Refuse to Doubt': An Inuit Healer Finds a Listener"
by Edith Turner

We begin our tour of the domain of the sacred with the ideology, or belief that underlies religious behavior. As Geertz's definition suggests, we must be concerned not only with content (*what* people believe—e.g., their "conceptions of a general order of existence") but with process (*how* do people get to a point at which they believe? how do they go from moods and motivations to actions?). Belief is therefore concerned not only with specific ideas, but also with the ways in which ideas come to be and then get shared and passed along to others. It's the latter part of that process that is cultural, for anthropologists do not study the unique ideations of individuals.

BELIEF AS A SYSTEM

Just as religion as a whole is a system within the larger system of culture, so belief can be thought of as a system within the domain of the sacred. There are three main elements in any belief system. First, there are **assumptions**, which are ideas or concepts that are considered so fundamental to believers that they are never questioned or challenged. For example, Christians of various denominations might disagree about matters such as how often to distribute communion at services, but they cannot disagree with the notion that Jesus Christ has divine status within a Trinity and still be considered Christian. It is irrelevant to us as anthropologists whether that proposition is right or wrong; what matters is that believers take it as a point so basic that it is a definitional part of their faith, a position from which other beliefs flow. By the same token, the Declaration of Independence, one of the foundational documents of American democracy (a religion under the terms of our definition) states explicitly that there are certain truths held to be "self-evident." In other words, proponents of democracy can (and do) disagree about many things, but they cannot deny these truths and still be said to uphold a democratic creed. The Declaration's "self-evident truths" have the same function as the assumptions of a more traditional religious belief system.

Beliefs per se are the ideas that flow logically from the foundational assumptions, although unlike the latter they can be challenged, questioned, and even changed over time. They do not change easily or frequently, but when they do change that modification does not compromise the entire system, as would be the case if a basic assumption were ever called into serious dispute. For example, scientists and philosophers *assume* that there is some sort of order in the universe (or else why bother to study it?); but ideas about the nature of that order have changed over time in the history of our own culture, and vary widely from one culture to another. The model that placed the earth at the center of the universe was replaced over time by one that saw the sun as the center of a system of which the earth was but a tiny member. As profound a change as that was, it did not undermine the basic assumption that the universe operates in an orderly fashion; it just represented a new understanding of that operation.

It would be convenient to say that new beliefs emerge when the facts make former beliefs untenable; advances in astronomy made it impossible to continue to believe in the earth-centered model. But saying so depends on an assumption in our scientific worldview: that **facts** are real things that can be collected and analyzed in an objective fashion. What if, however, the "facts" are essentially "social constructions"—in other words, they are reflections of the people who claim to see them rather than things that have an independent reality. For example, biologists and anthropologists tell us that "race" is a more or less meaningless category—humans exhibit physical variation along a continuum; they do not fall into neatly boxed categories with homogeneous members. And yet it is obvious that for many people race continues to matter. We "see" race in features like skin color and attribute all sorts of intellectual and moral qualities to people with such features. Race is certainly a social construct, a category arising out of an unspoken consensus rather than one with an objective, scientific reality. It is no less powerful a force in our society (and many others) for being constructed. Race and racism are socially true even if they are biologically false. They are facts because people act *as if* they were objectively true.

Our scientific traditions lead us to expect that we work from empirical facts and then generate increasingly abstract levels of interpretation and explanation. But it might well be the other way around. We begin with our unproven assumptions and then we "see" the facts that "prove" those assumptions because that is what we want to believe. Although the true believer may say that it is unnecessary to prove his or her assumptions—they are said to be taken on faith—people generally spend a great deal of intellectual and emotional energy in trying to make the most convincing case for their faith, marshalling as much factual evidence as they can to prove that their faith is grounded in objective truth. That process is probably of particular importance in pluralistic societies where there may be many belief systems competing for attention; it is less noticeable in small-scale traditional societies where most people share a set of beliefs and where there is no external challenge to those beliefs.

COSMOLOGY

Keep in mind that any belief system that is considered religious must ultimately tell us something about the way everything fits together—it must, in Geertz's terms, provide us with conceptions of a "general order of existence." We can refer to such conceptions as "cosmologies" because they deal with the *cosmos* (a Greek word that literally means "an orderly, harmonious, systematic universe"). Some cosmologies are mainly physical in orientation (e.g., the prevailing Western scientific model of the material universe) while others are mainly metaphysical, concerned with the question of why things are as they are (e.g., a notion of divine creation). But most cosmologies have something to say about three levels of perceived reality: the *natural* order (the world we can know through our five senses), the **supernatural** order (the world we know through extra-sensory means such as mystical contemplation), and the *social* order (the way humans are supposed to think and act once they believe themselves to live within a defined natural and supernatural order).

Ideas about the natural order typically fall into one of four categories. Some cosmologies, for example, are based on the model of *order arising out of primal chaos*, either through some impersonal self-generating creative force or through the actions of a creator **deity**. The familiar Judeo-Christian Genesis story of God creating order is an example of the latter; Hindu ideas about the origins of the material world (see below) fall into the former subdivision. Other cosmologies, such as those of the Maya of pre-Columbian Mesoamerica, are conceived in terms of an *essential order* which has always existed and which must be carefully maintained. Many animist religious traditions favor a cosmology based on the *rhythm of the seasons* (seeing all things in terms of cycles of birth, maturation, death, and rebirth). Still others stress the *equilibrium of nature*, seeing all things in a perpetual balance without much concern for origins or end-times.

Ideas about the supernatural order may deal with *impersonal powers* (see the discussion of *animatism* in chapter 2). A common name for an impersonal supernatural force is **mana** (a word of Polynesian origin not to be confused with "manna," the bread from heaven mentioned in the Bible). An inanimate article infused with mana may be referred to as a **fetish**. A human being who has been infused with mana may be so charged with supernatural power that he or she is off-limits to ordinary people. In traditional Polynesian societies, mana was usually a property of chiefs; because the mana was believed to reside in the chief's head, ordinary people had to approach him at a lower level (e.g., on their knees) so that they would not be in the direct line of the power emanating from his head. Sometimes mana gives a person the power to bestow supernatural blessings (in the Islamic world this power is referred to as **baraka**), but it can also be a way of directing harm, as is the case in the widespread belief in the "evil eye"—the power once again emanating from the region of the head. In our own time, the pop mythology of the *Star Wars* series revolves around "the Force," which seems to guide the destiny of all living things.

On the other hand, the supernatural may be embodied in *personified beings*. Those of nonhuman origin are known as *deities* or *divinities, gods* or *goddesses*; because of their great power and their distance from the world of humans, they must be approached only very carefully, through prayer and sacrifice. By contrast, those of human origin (referred to as *souls* or **ghosts**), while of lesser power than deities, are, in many cultures, more influential figures because they were once part of the living community and therefore continue to have a close association with it (for good or evil, depending on the culture) even after physical death. When the ghosts are believed to be good, offerings may be made to them in thanksgiving; when they are believed to be evil, offerings are made to appease them. When the ghosts accept the offering and in return do what people want, they may be referred to as the **grateful dead**. In some traditions there are figures of semi-divine origin (i.e., the offspring of a god and a mortal). Some of these figures, like Prometheus in Greek mythology, are **culture heroes**, believed to have given humans some important gift that belonged originally to the gods (Prometheus brought fire). Others are **tricksters** whose job it is to test mortals with riddles or other challenges in order to prove their worth. Some famous trickster figures are the coyote of Native North American mythology, Anansi the spider in West African folklore, and the Sphinx of Greek tradition.

Let us take a closer look at the interplay of these factors in one particular tradition—the belief system of classic Hinduism. Hindu philosophers have been more inclined to begin with the supernatural order than have Westerners, and they developed a metaphysical understanding of a universe in which order had been brought out of primal nothingness through creative forces inherent in the cosmos (and not necessarily personalized, as in the figure of a creator god). That order has, in some versions, been envisioned as being like a giant egg; in others it is seen as a kind of human body. In the case of an "egg" metaphysic, order is seen to evolve through a natural progression not unlike the passage of time through the day. Thus the clear yellow light of morning gives rise in the eastern part of the cosmic egg to those physical things that are believed to exhibit the greatest purity, including humans of the priestly (Brahmin) order. The stronger, brassier light of midday gives rise to things in which purity yields somewhat to physical power, including humans of the warrior and princely (Ksattriya) order. The shadowy light of afternoon gives rise to physical things of somewhat ambiguous character, including humans of the artisan and merchant (Vaisya) order. And the darkness of night gives rise in the west to things that are impure, including humans of the worker (Sudra) order. The fourfold division of this color-coded scheme is referred to as the system of *varnas*, which literally means "colors." The Portuguese who arrived in India in the early years of the age of European exploration translated "varna" as "casta," which has come into English as "caste." Given common beliefs about race in Western society, it would be easy to assume that caste is a system based on *skin* color, but that is not the case—the colors referred to are the metaphorical colors of a metaphysical system.

Nevertheless, this system certainly has important social consequences, and Hindus have devised an elaborate network of mutual rights and obligations designed to keep the less pure from "polluting" the more pure. In the Hindu way of thinking, the cosmos is not egalitarian or "fair" in ways that make sense to Westerners; it is, however, quite orderly. Indeed, the order of the cosmos is the source of all morality, for without an orderly universe, there could be no such thing as right behavior among the living things of that universe. The cosmic moral order is called **dharma**, and one implication of this belief is that people born into a particular *varna* must act in accordance with the precepts of that order; to do otherwise would be a violation of dharma that would upset not only interpersonal relations but also the proper functioning of the cosmos as a whole. At the beginning of the revered epic poem *Bhagavad-Gita* ("The Song of the Lord") the hero Arjuna is heartsick; although born into the warrior *varna* he is despondent over being involved in a battle in which many—including perhaps even kinsmen—will be slaughtered. He decides to sit out the battle, but his servant (really the god Krishna[1] in disguise) reprimands him and points out that as a Ksattriya, he is morally obligated to engage in warfare, even though doing so involves a breach of the general injunction against doing violence to living things. Krishna tells Arjuna that he cannot act as if he were a Brahmin, for the law of dharma requires that he do his bit to uphold the entire cosmic edifice. In sum, it is better to be a faithful representative of one's own *varna* than to try to live in accordance with the ways of another order, even if the latter is theoretically more pure. All actions have moral consequences, and we all pay for those consequences over the course of the eternal wheel of rebirth (the law of *karma*); the faithful discharge of one's own obligations—even if that entails acts that are, in the abstract, impure—is the best way to earn merit.

As we can see, this complex set of ideas intricately links supernatural and natural concepts in such a way as to have very definite consequences for the way people live on the social level. Westerners sometimes wonder why Indians put up with the caste system, which to them seems grossly unfair. But for the devout Hindu, any challenge to caste would be not merely a social or political act but a violation that could rend the fabric of the entire cosmic order. What looks to the Westerner like passive fatalism is, to the devout Hindu, a way of living in harmony with the creative forces of the cosmos.

The people of pre-Columbian Mesoamerica (the area of modern-day Mexico and Central America) were also apparently very concerned with the cosmic order, and they saw their own ritual cycle as a way of preserving that order. Unlike the Hindus (for whom a principal moral ideal is nonviolence), the Aztec and the Maya made human sacrifice the focus of much of their order-preserving ritual. Indeed, it seems as if a great deal of political, economic, and military energy was expended on the waging of wars for the express purpose of amassing captives who could be sacrificed. Europeans have always looked with particular horror on human sacrifice, and saw its prevalence in the great civilizations of Mesoamerica proof of the depravity of those people. The Spanish conquerors undoubtedly exaggerated the numbers of sacrifices, but those sacrifices were certainly prominent features of the public life of those societies. As far as we can now tell, however (remembering the cautions about making inference from archaeological records, as discussed in the previous chapter), the Aztec and Maya did not engage in human sacrifice out of mindless, bloody cruelty or unreasoning evil. Indeed, their rituals were highly respectful, difficult as that might be for the Westerner to appreciate. The captives were treated with honor—why would the cosmic forces be satisfied with anything less than a most noble sacrificial victim? And the whole enterprise was undertaken with a very serious purpose in mind: the preservation of the cosmic order.[2]

How Does Someone Become Religious?

It is all very well for us to outline belief systems, whether they are very familiar ones like that of American democracy, or those that, like Hinduism, may seem very foreign to many Westerners. But the larger question is: how do people come to believe such things? When the system is our own, we have a kind of gut feeling for the "self-evident" nature of its stated "truths" and assume that it takes no great effort to go along with belief. But if we take the comparative perspective of anthropology, then we must acknowledge that *every* belief system seems as self-evident to its practitioners as it seems strange and unconvincing to outsiders. Since there are obviously many, many ways in which reasonable, sensitive people throughout history and in all parts of the world have understood truth, it is clear that no one truth is universally self-evident. That being the case, what convinces people that *this* proposed truth is more worthy of belief than *that* other one?

There are four ways in which someone becomes a believer. These processes probably overlap in most cases, but we can separate them for purposes of this introductory discussion. Remember too that while the process begins with the individual believer, his or her belief must ultimately be shared and transmitted (that is, his or her belief must be persuasive to others) in order for us to consider it an element in a system of *culture*.

The first, and most apparently straightforward way in which one comes to belief is through *personal experience*. We sometimes hear, for example, of people having near-death experiences and then returning fully to life. They sometimes describe those experiences in terms featuring things like a great white light or the embrace of deceased loved ones; some have reported the sensation of floating somewhere above their own bodies lying on operating tables or in a car wreck. Regardless of the particular details, the important thing is that people have experienced something that convinces them of some truth higher, more powerful, more beautiful than the reality they began with. Some people (mystics, contemplatives) can deliberately put themselves into the sort of mind-set in which they are particularly receptive to these higher insights. Great artists caught up in the act of creation may also enter into a whole other dimension of experience. Great athletes often describe themselves as being "in the zone" when they are at the peak of their powers. Whatever happens, it cannot be taken lightly; the one who has had such an experience cannot simply say, "Well, that was fun. Now back to the mundane stuff I was doing before I was so rudely interrupted." The person who has had such an experience cannot forget it or put it aside; the experience has had some sort of life-changing impact.

It is not necessary to have an experience as spectacular as those mentioned above. Sometimes the experience is more quietly revelatory. For example, there are those who witness a beautiful sunrise and become convinced of some power greater than they had previously imagined. There are those who find transcendent truth in the simple beauty of a baby's smile. Some have such an experience when reading a book or listening to music or meeting a particularly charismatic person. It is likely that most of us, in most cultures, have many such experiences over the course of our lifetimes; but we tend to downplay them ("Oh, that was just my imagination playing tricks on me!") precisely because they don't seem to fit the pattern of what we have come to think of as normal. But the experience that pushes us over into belief is simply the one we can no longer ignore.

A second way one might become a believer is through *myth and ritual*. Both myth and ritual will be explored in greater detail in separate chapters, and we will leave definitions and descriptive details for those discussions. At this point, however, we are mainly concerned with *participation*. Simply put, myths are stories that explain how things came to be; rituals are formal public reenactments or commemorations of important events in the tradition of a community. It may be that someone who is only indifferently connected to a tradition becomes more enthusiastic the more he or she participates in story-telling or other sharing activities that draw members of a community together. Most people do not like to feel like outsiders, and if they are invited in and become active in a group's functions, they are very likely to go along with and come to accept whatever it is that the group believes, even if they are skeptical at the beginning. Coming to belief via mythical and ritual participation is usually a gradual process, requiring repeated exposure to a group, its stories, and its activities—unlike the flash of inspiration characteristic of the more direct personal experience discussed earlier. But it can, in the long run, be just as intense a conversion. Even if it begins with the simple motive of just wanting to fit in with a group, it can end up (if participation is consistent enough) with a genuine affirmation of what that group stands for.

Belief may also be engendered when one feels oneself in *harmony* with something greater than oneself. People all over the world seem to have a real need to know how things fit together; rare is the individual who is content with living in sheer chaos. An understanding of how things all fit gives people a sense of security; in Western culture that feeling often takes the form of a feeling of a perception of mastery and control, while in other cultures it may mean that one is content to be protected by some higher power or greater force. Of course, as we saw in chapter 1, not every "conception of a general order" is equally persuasive; such a statement must be "clothed in an aura of factuality" that is convincing to the potential believer. If I appeared before a room full of skeptics at a college in the United States and announced that the universe began with a "big bang," the audience's reaction might well depend on my presentation. If I appeared wearing flowing robes with aluminum foil on my head as I explained my ideas in the form of a chant and rhythmic dance, I would almost certainly not be taken as seriously as I would if I showed up in a white lab coat and covered the board with equations. The audience in neither case would necessarily understand my thesis, but in the latter case they would be prepared to give me the benefit of the doubt. Susceptible individuals might well be seduced by the occasional charismatic crank, but in order for there to be an emerging consensus about truth, ideas have to be encountered via a "prophet" (or mystic, or scientist, as the case might be) who seems plausible to a larger number.

The goal, however, is not simply acquiescing to something just because a recognized authority figure has espoused it. It is necessary for members of the audience to experience the truth of that authority figure's assertions. The general proposition that "all nature is good" might make sense to people living in a benign environment—mild weather, bounteous crops, healthy children—where they could see the truth in that statement; it might conversely be nonsense to people continually beset by calamities and disasters.

The fourth way to belief might be summarized by the familiar saying, "The truth shall set you free." It is one thing to have a personal experience that convinces one of some higher truth; but if that knowledge is burdensome or frightening, such that the person cannot or will not act on it, then it is unlikely to be the foundation for anything more than mental illness. On the other hand, if it has a *liberating* effect, then one is more apt to acknowledge it as a general truth that can and should be shared.

DIMENSIONS OF BELIEF

Once one has become an active believer one deals with that belief on several levels. Again, these levels may overlap although it is useful to separate them for definitional purposes. First, there is the *ideological* level of belief—the enthusiastic engagement with the "general order" propositions. Then, there is *intellectual* belief, the consideration of those factors that seem to flow logically from the general assumptions. It may also involve the making of choices among competing subsidiary ideas. *Emotional* belief is the way one's mood (in the sense of an overall outlook or approach to life, rather than a passing sensation) is changed in the direction of that belief. When that happens, one may engage in *ritualistic* belief—the willing participation in activities designed to confirm one in the perceptions to which one has already given emotional assent. And finally there is *consequential* belief, which occurs when one's moods lead to motivations—the believer is impelled to action justified by his or her belief.

For example, one might feel that the only way to accept the travails of everyday life is to put one's faith in an all-powerful, provident deity who has a plan that will make all things come out right in the end (ideological belief). But is that deity a wrathful judge who demands unquestioning obedience or a loving parental figure who is tolerant of our doubts and mistakes (intellectual belief)? If the former, one is very concerned with order, propriety, righteousness; if the latter, with loving responses (emotional belief). Either way, one seeks out like-minded people with whom one can share experiences and discuss common feelings and ideas (ritualistic belief). In the end, one comes to the conclusion that one must *act* in a certain way (consequential belief).

KINDS OF RELIGIOUS EXPERIENCE

However one comes to believe, he or she tends to interpret all subsequent experiences in terms of that larger perceived truth; in other words, he or she has **religious experiences** that may be **confirming** (intellectually or emotionally reinforcing the truth already embraced), **responsive** (in which one has a sense of active engagement with some higher power or transcendent force), **ecstatic** (in which one becomes as one with that higher power), or **revelatory** (in which one feels empowered to carry out some sort of action mandated by that higher power). (Once again these categories may overlap, but should be distinguished for purposes of this definitional presentation.) Belief is thus the foundation for all subsequent actions in the domain of the sacred.

KEY CONCEPTS

Be sure you can define the following terms, and give at least one illustrative example of each:

- assumption
- baraka
- beliefs
- confirming religious experience
- cosmology
- culture hero
- deity
- dharma
- dimensions of belief
- ecstatic religious experience

- fact
- fetish
- ghost
- grateful dead
- mana
- responsive religious experience
- revelatory religious experience
- supernatural
- trickster

RESEARCH EXPLORATIONS

1. Interview a person who is a devout believer in a religious tradition other than your own. Write a paper using concepts introduced in this chapter in which you discuss the basic assumptions and beliefs of this person's belief system. You should then go on to discuss how someone becomes a believer in this tradition. Discuss the five dimensions of belief as they apply to this person and his/her tradition. Describe the kinds of religious experience(s) he/she has had or has observed among fellow believers.

   Make very sure that the person you are interviewing understands that this is a class project and that you are not at this point interested in being converted. If he/she will not discuss these matters with you unless you promise to consider conversion, respect his/her position, but find someone else to interview.

   Be very sure to check with your instructor about your university's norms regarding the signing of "informed consent" forms for projects of this nature.

2. Find a video or DVD copy of one of the following films: *The Apostle* (starring Robert Duvall); *Dead Man Walking* (starring Susan Sarandon and Sean Penn); *Malcolm X* (starring Denzel Washington); *The Believer* (starring Ryan Gosling). Write a paper or prepare a talk for in-class presentation in which you discuss the dimensions of religious belief as presented in this chapter as they apply to the major character(s) in the film.

3. If your local cable provider includes channels featuring religious programming, watch several segments of any preacher or evangelist speaking to a congregation. What does he/she have to say about his/her personal belief? How does he/she try to influence the beliefs of those in the audience? Prepare an in-class talk about your findings; you may want to use taped examples of preaching to illustrate your analysis.

Notes

[1] The *Gita* emphasizes Krishna's divine status; he is a source of cosmic wisdom as he advises Arjuna to uphold the *dharma*. In other Hindu tales, however, Krishna appears as something of a trickster, teasing, tempting, and testing humans. This is a relatively rare example of a trickster who is fully divine rather than semi-divine.

[2] There are, to be sure, alternate explanations. Some scholars claim that in at least some cases of human sacrifice, the bulk of the meat was consumed by people after the choice parts were offered to the higher powers. Sacrifice thus satisfied a need for protein in a diet largely lacking in that nutrient. Even if that were the case, we would still be interested in seeing how the people covered that motive in elaborate, solemn ritual and mythology.

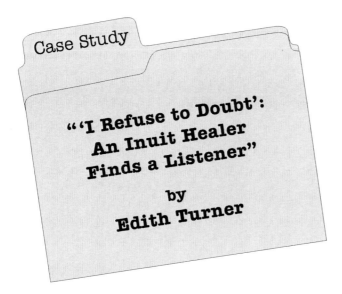

Case Study

" 'I Refuse to Doubt': An Inuit Healer Finds a Listener"

by
Edith Turner

Turner describes her friendship with an Inuit healer and discusses the way her own belief system compared and contrasted with that of the people she had come to study. Turner approaches Claire, the healer, in a way that is not strictly scientifically objective. In fact, she asks for instruction on how to become a healer herself. She approaches learning how to heal with faith in her own ability.

In a small village in the north of Alaska lives a healer whom I will call Claire. Her people may generically be classed as Inuit, tribes possessing a long history of survival in climatic regions that would scare most of us. Their religion, now largely defunct, once recognized various classes of spirits and the power of shamanistic contact with spirit helpers.

Why did I go to the Inuit? Research leads one where it must. I had been studying from a very close-up view the work of ritual doctors in Africa (1986, 1992) and chose to publish my material in a more humanistic style than was the norm in academia, at the same time including much context and analysis. Now came a chance to study a non-Western woman healer in a different culture, a personality who was one of her culture's most richly complex members.

I lived for a year in this Alaskan village, which I am naming Ivakuk, "Hunting," because that is how the inhabitants always lived. I myself was hunting down some of the peculiar details that might possibly be associated with the people's traditional healing and which might be making the healing work. However, in doing the research I found I caught neither subsistence food nor mere fieldnotes, but a living and dear and fascinating friend.

In Ivakuk there were nine healers, seven of whom were women, and there were at least five child apprentices learning the craft. Claire was the principal practitioner in

From Bruce Grindal and Frank Salamone, Editors, *Bridges to Humanity: Narratives on Anthropology and Friendship.* (Prospect Heights, IL: Waveland Press, Inc., 1995).

the village, with a clientele on one side who supported her, and on the other, detractors who preferred another curer. Like the various healers whose work I studied and whose stories I heard, Claire possessed gifts of clairvoyance and direct healing that went beyond the provenance of the medical profession.

Claire told me this story: "A young man came to me about his back. I passed my hand along his back and I prayed. Then I *saw* the original accident. I saw that kid fall off his snowmobile and become twisted by his gun because he couldn't get it off his back." She said to me, "You know what it's like—it's like fantasy. I might write a book."

Claire told me that the young man with the bad back answered her, "Yes, that's exactly what happened, ten years ago." His back was already healed.

This kind of gift appears to resemble the Inuit ability to make spirit journeys, as recounted in former times. Claire had moved back in time and to a different place, and had *seen* what happened.

I remember my first meeting with Claire. This is the story. I was thinking the time had come to visit her—though wouldn't she be secretive and reserved, as Native Americans are said to be? I found my way to her prefabricated house. Now it stood before me, painted dark red, with wooden steps going up from the tundra gravel toward a door on the left. I ascended and knocked. Would she be at home?

A distant voice hollered, "Come in!" I opened the door. It was pitch dark inside. Ah, there was another door beyond: this was just the storm porch. Shutting the first door against the bitter September wind, I opened the further one and found myself in a large living room.

A small woman was busying about and turned to me. She had a fine oval face and straight look, somewhat like an unthreatening version of the dark-haired sibyl in Michelangelo's Sistine frescoes, only carrying in her eyes the more delicate epicanthic structure of the Native American. I introduced myself to this healer person, thinking, "Come on, Edie, your own dad was a doctor. And you're not just an anthropologist. You're fascinated by healing for what it is. You've seen a thing or two." This woman had some gift I did not rightly understand. I was ready and open to hear.

She knew that I was ready as we sat down.

I started out, "I've heard of your work. I've a great respect for Inuit healing."

"What made you interested in it?" she asked.

"I once saw my husband, Vic, heal somebody. This man had a heart attack in our living room, and his heart stopped. Vic put his hand on the man's heart, and it started again. I wondered what was going on—if I might learn what's behind it. I've respect for what you do."

"I'm very glad. I've been getting discouraged, frustrated."

"Are the medical doctors getting you down?"

"Yes."

"Don't let 'em," I said. "It's a good work you're doing."

She explained that she had just come in from the distant village of Bristol. "They flew me there to work on some of the sick."

She and I liked each other. Her adopted children crowded around, Jeanie, seven, and Ann, ten. She also had older adopted children and two grandchildren. We began to talk about our families and grandchildren.

Then she was silent, pondering a minute. "Inuit healing is *different.*" She lingered over the word. "Come into the kitchen and talk while I work."

In a few minutes she was due to attend a teleconference education class in anthropology at 5:00 P.M. and needed to hurry. "Anthropology?" I thought. "She could *teach* them that, couldn't she?"

Did she have to go out right now? She'd just come back from a trip, and now she had to go out again. The kitchen was high with dirty dishes—the family hadn't washed them for days. But she told me how proud she was of her family, proud of her grown-up son of thirty: he had recently obtained his first job and bought a TV and stereo. "I'm *proud,*" she told me.

She suddenly turned to her daughter of [ten], Ann, and spat a command. "What math homework do you have?" Ann showed her the book.

"You can do that quickly. Do the dishwashing, then the homework."

"I'll do the dishwashing," I said, and got to work. It was easy because there was plenty of hot running water.

A message came over Claire's CB radio. She cocked an ear. "Claire. Claire. Come on in," the voice said. "Go at once to Atiq, she's sick, she's throwing up."

The anthropology class would have to be missed because Atiq, an elderly lady, came first. I had learned to respect Atiq too, a healer and a bold personality. Before leaving, Claire opened the refrigerator where she kept three bags of an herb called stinkweed. This was *Artemista tilesii,* wormwood, the best of the Inuit medicines. Claire took out some of the boiled infusion, a dark fluid, and she drank a cupful; she handed me a little to drink. It was bitter. She said it would give her strength to heal. Quickly she grabbed her coat and left for Atiq's house. After finishing the dishes, I thought for a moment and decided to go to Atiq's too.

As I approached Atiq's door, a woman came out. She passed me and jumped on her Honda ATV.

"How is she?"

"Atiq plays too much Bingo," she said sharply. "So of course she doesn't eat properly. That's why she's sick." This was the head of the clinic health aides.

I went into the house. There were many people in old Atiq's living room. I made my way along the passage to the bedroom and found my friend Clem, who was Atiq's adult grandson, at the entrance of the bedroom. His flat features were loosened into solemnity, unseeing. I peeped into the room. The old lady with her familiar face— though now her little pinched eyes were weary—was lying on a mattress on the floor, not on her bed. She was still clothed in her skirt and a fine blouse. Claire was at her side with seven-year-old Jeanie sitting between her knees, acting as her healing apprentice.

Atiq's senile old husband was sitting on the unoccupied bed. He arose and stood near, then went wandering off down the passage. After a time back he came again, and this went on all the while—the old man shuffling to and fro, to and fro. Ardell, another health aide, was sitting on the unoccupied bed, backstage as it were to Claire. Claire told me Atiq's stomach was in the wrong position: it was hard and tight. Claire could feel air pockets that were stopping the stomach from working. There was something wrong that was causing Atiq to vomit blood. Atiq had not been able to eat for three days.

The house was occupied by many people. I went back to the living room and greeted the elders, Kaglik, who was Atiq's brother, and Atiq's son, Clem's father. Both of them were old men. They sat like statues on straight chairs. There was silence. I felt a little frightened. Then I went back to Atiq and tried to massage her feet to relax her. But she vomited, groaning, and lay back; then she vomited again and muttered something in Inuit. Claire was working on Atiq's stomach with both hands, working deep into the folds of the old stomach flesh. Claire had "good hands," as the Inuit often said: those hands could soothe the body and take away pain. At one point Claire spread both arms out with her fingers wide in a gesture of relief. She was tired. In Inuit parlance Atiq's stomach had risen and was jammed against the heart and lungs, stopping the organs from functioning properly.

I went to Ardell, the health aide. "What's wrong, d'you think?"

"We don't know. I'm going to have to phone the hospital and get them to send the medevac plane. The senior health aide gave Atiq some Mylanta. That's all we are allowed to do."

Meanwhile Claire was softening Atiq's stomach to bring it down into the right position. But the air pocket gave trouble. As I stood in the doorway, I saw the old woman's face become contorted; then I saw it blank out to nothing. Claire held Atiq's head hard and held on, drawing Atiq to her. I started to pray. Clem looked fearful, as if death penned; perhaps it did. The old lady reared up again in agony to vomit, then fell back. Her body blanked out, and her head sank back. Her whole personality seemed emptied. I went on massaging her feet while Claire massaged her stomach, bending her head very near to Atiq's. At one time Claire put her hands on Atiq's stomach and lay her head upon her hands, right on Atiq's stomach.

Ardell, the health aide, watched, then took herself off to the clinic to make the phone call to the hospital at Bristol. I left the house to fetch some snacks and brought them back to feed Claire and the others. When I returned, I looked at the scene through the door and thought of the Pieta. There it was, the lax figure and the supporting forms: "Oh, Atiq, I'm sad for your pain, sad." I kept praying that Claire would heal her. Everyone involved has to do what she knows how. Atiq lay there exhausted; was she failing or was she resting? Claire stayed right close to her, head to head, with her hand always on Atiq's stomach, warmly there with the "different" knowledge in it, as Claire put it, an intimate contact. I thought, if only they'd done that for me when I was in hospital in 1983 for agonizing stomach cramps.

Atiq stayed as she was, still vomiting occasionally. Each time she vomited we looked anxiously at the clock, wondering when the plane would come. But she did rest. Claire began to talk cheerfully. I loved Claire's ordinary conversation, again about her grown-up son and his new TV. We laughed, subduing our voices. The others all talked in Inuit. [Atiq] was now drinking 7-Up, talking herself, vividly complaining in Inuit about her stomach. She stretched out her feet, which had been reincased in her tube socks. The old man entered the room in his tortoise crawl and stopped at her outstretched legs. After a pause he just managed to walk across her legs and go to sit on the bed.

Atiq asked for some tea. There was a quiet rush to fetch her a cup. Clem began to smile. Gradually we became aware that the immediate crisis was past. We waited.

The plane was flying over. Everyone heard it. The people in the living room, dressed in grand printed velveteen-and-ruff parkas, passed to and fro to look through the windows, telling each other, "There it is." Clem, being the adult grandson, started worrying about intravenous feeding, IVs—"She must have fluids. The doctor will have to do the IV in the house; the ambulance is too small." Clem's wife fussed over what clothes to send with her. Even so, they forgot her dentures.

As we stood waiting, Clem said to me in his slow voice: "Her spirit went out of her body three times. Three times it went out of her, and Claire brought it back and pulled it down into her stomach. When it leaves for good, it goes up through the hole in the top of the head." I touched my long-closed fontanel (the site of some of my headaches—a place that was aching a little that day).

Clem smiled. "That's right, there."

I surmised that Claire's healing acts of drawing back the fleeing spirit were basically the same ones that used to be carried out by the ancient Inuit shamans. But this occasion had been *now.*

I stood with Clem, still frightened for Atiq's safety, finding I was already dominated by love for the old lady, for Claire, and for this crowd which had become my crowd of "forever" acquaintances. "Forever?" After three weeks? I realized that a leaping tie of love had come from them to me and back again; I was involved.

There was a stir. The ambulance was here in the shape of a new, yellow, low-slung vehicle outside the door. The white pilot came in; then a tall, dark-haired white man, distant of manner, who turned out to be the doctor; another very beardy little fellow, quite fun; then a huge white ambulance man, easy to talk to. The place was full of people milling around in a confused way. I peered into Atiq's room. A blond nurse was already inside the room, putting a blood pressure sleeve on Atiq's arm. The team became occupied in following the stereotypes of "medical practice." They took the blood pressure, pulse, and temperature, asked questions, and then the stretchermen gathered in the bedroom.

Clem told the doctor, "She's been spitting out very dark stuff, black, like blood." The doctor came into the bedroom and looked into the old lady's vomiting can. "A little blood," he said disparagingly. I returned to the living room, and the doctor came and stood by the wall. We grew silent. After a moment the ambulance men emerged from the passageway with their stretcher—Atiq was inside. They carried her out of the door and into the ambulance. We saw her wrinkled face lifted to look out of the ambulance; then the tailgate was shut, and they were off to the airstrip.

The following day Claire had to send in her assignment for the teleconference course in anthropology. She wrote well and knew the facts and traditions for the subject of her essay, which was on subsistence. After all, her husband was a hunter and she was his absolutely indispensable hunter's wife. Who would process the hunting meat but her?

The next time I visited Claire, I found her living room crammed with five large plastic laundry baskets full of dirty laundry, and the sofa was piled high with clean clothes. She was cooking bacon and eggs for her husband, who was back from his construction job. People kept coming in and out to consult Claire about their food stamp forms, for she was also the volunteer food stamp official in town. She said to me, "Have some coffee," then dashed into the utility room where an old style washer-agitator was working, in the process of rinsing a full load of men's jeans. An electric mangle was attached above it. I helped her mangle and turn the clothes inside out; then she made me put them through the mangle again. I helped with much of the laundry, hung up the jeans on the overhead pipes, swept the floor of the living room, and folded the clothes piled on the sofa while she talked and worked alongside me. She was speaking of healing and how healers could feel the pain of the sufferer. (It struck me that this "feeling" would well be covered by a possible concrete glossing of the word "sym-pathy"—"feeling" "with.") Given the power to heal, it would not help much if Claire herself developed the sickness in some mystical way. However, she was able to block the harm of the disease halfway up her arms while she worked on the sufferer's body. She was still able to "feel the pain, feel where it is." This was different from feeling swelling, lumps, heat, and throbbing in the body. It existed as some sense of the misery of the tissues.

She told me how a woman 250 miles away called her on the phone and said, "I'm having a miscarriage." The woman was four months pregnant. When the woman spoke, Claire's second sight told her what was wrong, and then Claire knew what to do, also by virtue of her second sight. She gave the woman the corresponding instructions and the fetus was saved, and later the baby was born full-term.

Claire said yet again in her soft voice, "My healing is *different.*" She went on: "The doctors say to me, 'You're wrong, Claire.' They think I'm trying to predict—I don't predict, I know when someone is pregnant and for how long. Then it turns out I'm right. The health aides say, 'You must go by what the doctors say'—but I *know.* They finished my contract at the clinic; I don't know why. One woman came to me. She put out her hand and said, 'Don't touch me.' She was scared. I didn't touch her. I told her she was two weeks pregnant. I *knew.* Later she had the test, and she was pregnant."

"Why should people be scared of what is so good and useful?" I remarked.

Claire turned back to her cooking. There she was, slaving for her family, waiting on them with food and services.

"I'm glad you came," she went on. "For thirty years no one's helped me in the house." She picked up a glittering peacock blue velvet bathrobe, wet from the wash-tub. "I made this myself, for my husband," she said proudly. Her husband was in the back room watching TV. She went in there later to hang up the nicer things, knitteds and so on. I was thinking how her gifts needed backing up, and how mundane was her husband's construction work in comparison—except when he was hunting.

Claire talked a blue streak. She said to me, "You are different." I told her that I knew other countries where I had witnessed unusual healings—Africa, Brazil. I had even seen a spirit. Then I talked about Atiq.

"If you hadn't been there when Atiq was so sick, she might have died," I told her.

"I saw the spirit leaving her several times," Claire said, just as Clem had told me earlier. "I had to be there. The health aides just up and leave when it's five o'clock. What would Atiq have done? You can't just leave."

She caught me washing the half-moon Inuit knives. "You have to wipe them dry at once," she warned me, drying her own on a towel.

"—Or they'll get rusty," I said. She had ten half-moon knives inserted in the groove behind the sink.

Her living room bore photographs of relatives crowding the walls, just as my own mother used to crowd her own walls. Claire had a large color photograph of her mother-in-law. The face was drawn and severe, yet with a kind of cheerful beauty that burned in the highcheeked Inuit face, well framed by a fur ruff. There were trophy pictures of animals the family had caught. There was a picture of Jesus praying at Gethsemane, beautiful and sad. There was the usual large clock and a sewing machine in its table with an Eddie Bauer down jacket waiting to be repaired, the zipper already tacked into place—her husband's favorite jacket. A milk crate stood against the wall with neat files for the food stamp job, with easily available forms. Claire ran things well.

There were no photos of Claire herself, so I give a pen portrait of her. Claire looked out from herself, all alive, from that oval face with the high brow, with a considering look in her eyes: she was an immediate character, with strength and energy. She moved with an easy walk and big fluid motions. When I came to know her well, she used to take off her jacket in my house and sit down, ready for anything, her eyes a little hooded as became an Inuit (it was rude to look straight into a person's eyes). She was capable; she asked for what was not on the table, such as honey for her tea. We'd talk. Her voice wandered into great variations of tone, from rasping when in a state of uncertainty—still with self-assertion; sometimes slumping in falling tones—in complaint, still with that rasp. Then, when she was musing or reminiscing, her voice became wandering and soft, musically keyed, her eyes inward, her mind seeing pictures that leapt into existence one on top of the other—her voice leapt as the pictures came. And when teaching me language pronunciation, her voice went like this: it carried tones of sorrowful rasping, searching, and persistence, coming near to despair with a frog in the throat and much doubt—then a little hope. She tried again, *"qaaggaq!"* and I repeated, "kargak," wrongly, and her hands flopped uselessly by her side. She laughed, cackling like the grandmother she was—a young grandmother.

I knew a certain thing about her from long ago, and I could not bear to think about it. It was when she stood before her burning house in which lay her first three children, her own children trapped and dead. Her spirit must have been dead and tortured inside her. A screaming impossibility, Claire.

Already with six more children—adopted this time—and two grandchildren, with an easy job she liked, sitting in City Hall, typing on a computer, running the teleconferences as well as taking the courses—this was the life (only they had begun to cut down her hours). And a telephone, and a CB radio.

The radio crackled and said, "Claire, are you on? Come and see little Lee, he's hurt." She went, unhooking her jacket and donning it as she strode down the office stairs out to her Honda ATV and whirled off—with little Jeanie and myself on the back. . . . She entered the house, all gentle, already knowing the trouble, for there existed a preliminary time of clairvoyance for Claire. Inside the house the child was screaming (shades of the burning house). He'd taken a jump off a high shelf and gone crash on both knees. Now he couldn't stand and couldn't walk and was on his mother's lap crying. Claire brought up a chair and sat opposite Lee with Jeanie kneeling close by to watch. Like me, Jeanie was very much interested. Claire took the child's foot gently and turned up the pants leg. Lee's crying got worse. Claire turned her hand over the throbbing knee, almost not touching it.

"I can't hurt you; *I can't hurt you,"* she told him as an obvious truth, in her musical voice. "See, I'm making it better." She was so used to seeing inside. Claire's hand was like an X-ray, so she used to tell me. All inside was as clear as daylight. The mother held Lee, and Claire felt both lower legs, not the knees. Lee's crying began to give way. She felt down the muscles of each lower leg, drawing down the legs neatly and together. She worked each ankle, the flat of the foot, and the toes, bending them gently until they were flexible, showing Lee how good they were. Her hands went back to the knees. The right one bore a bruise and a big swelling below the kneecap. She placed the kneecaps one after the other centrally and pressed them gently into position as if they were jigsaw pieces, completing the action by pressing carefully with her palm. She went to the better knee and worked the dimpled areas while swiveling the leg back and forth. Then she returned to the swelling on the right knee. I noted that she left the trickiest side until last. She pressed the swelling slightly here and there, and I saw it diminish a little. She left that work alone for a time and turned down Lee's pants legs. He slid off his mother's lap and tried a few steps, using his legs like little sticks.

Claire chatted to the mother about financial matters. She turned to Lee. "Auntie Claire's going to make you some mukluk boots. How about that, eh?" Lee was busy making eyes at Jeanie.

"Come on my lap," Claire told him. "Auntie's going to work on you a bit more." She caressed the swelling on the right knee again, showing me how it was going down.

See? It's simple." Before my eyes the swelling went away altogether, leaving the normal muscle curves visible around the kneecap. I was attending carefully, remembering now the occasions when Claire had managed to teach me to heal. Once, under her careful tutelage, she had made me heal an injured rib on her own back. This is what happened. She said, "There." I put my hands on the place. OK, I felt a nasty lump on the rib; but not only this. It was as if it were sending off rays or something; there was a kind of sizzling. What I experienced was an odd message of misery, a call—"I hurt!"—coming out of that bit of sick human tissue. I felt a rush of sympathy for that pain. "Poor Claire." The lump and its mushiness was not just a sign of its physical disruption. My hand knew that and knew it was there to help. I began to work it tenderly in Claire's fashion. To my surprise, the swelling began to go down until it was just a sliver and went away. How? Rationally speaking, I don't know.

And I also experienced being healed myself and noted how the pain seemed to leak away from my body and just not be there anymore.

Now Claire drew down Lee's pants legs and let him go. He walked easily. She went to the sink and washed, getting rid of whatever it was. "The pain goes into my own arm," she would say. "My hand gets hot. *Hot!*"

She went on talking. Lee's mother was hard up, awaiting a welfare check. The place lacked a carpet, with torn vinyl chair seats and only a garish rainbow window shade to cheer the room. Lee was now jumping from the empty stereo shelf to the sofa.

"That's how he did it in the first place," said Claire. "Jumping and falling on his knees. Stop that." We left before more treatment might become necessary.

Claire's healing tantalized me. As the process was indeed deeply physical and focused and particularized, the healing itself was very hard to explain verbally. Claire would say—having seen TV—"It's the power of mind over matter." Was it that? She was working intimately with matter, with her actual hands on actual bodies, searching and taking out pain. "Cancer you can feel—little things—" She drew on paper:

```
        o                      o                    o
                 o                          o
   o                              o
                 o
```

and also drew 1½-inch lumps. "These little things are in the skin or muscle itself, not moving, in it."

"Can you get them out?"

"You can work on some of them and get them to go. Not all, not all at once. You can cure it."

I thought to myself, "Does the mind enter the hands and cure the body?" Other healers said, "My old hands are gone, these are God's hands." I saw in this a theory of healing corresponding to the old Inuit shamans' theory of healing by spirit possession.

Claire told me how she knew when she herself was pregnant, against the opinion of three out of five doctors. She had twice been operated on for cancer; now she was healthy. Once she told me she was very tired; she kept on yawning. She said it was because she had been working on a pneumonia patient—"I took the trouble into myself." The grateful pneumonia patient, now cured, gave her a huge ornate clock decorated with a silver swan, which she put up on her wall.

On another occasion Claire was on a plane trip with her relatives. The weather was tricky. As they started across tundra and ocean for the distant village, she saw a bright, sharp line right across the sky—golden, not cloud-colored. As they rose, higher conditions became bad, with 60-m.p.h. winds and cross gusts. This was extremely dangerous flying weather. "But we flew in the golden line all the way and the plane was perfectly steady. We landed fine." She spoke in a tone of outrightness and wonder, a proposition for my belief, a marvel that does happen. There were old accounts of shamans creating a similar tube of quiet weather in which their dogsleds traveled safely in stormy weather. It was quite obvious to the Inuit that there was such a power.

As for Claire, she constantly ascribed that power to a source outside her: "The good Lord gave me the gift of healing."

We can follow how that gift developed from the way the Claire described her life history. At first I did not know how to go about obtaining her life story, from a cold start as it were; but eventually there occurred a small special event that stimulated us both. One day I was awkwardly trying to ask Claire about her memories of childhood, but the awkwardness only increased, and conversation became impossible. Then in came old Auntie Nora, who had no thumb—it had been eaten off by bees when she was adopted as a baby. Auntie Nora was tiny, well less than five feet tall. She started talking to Claire about an illness of hers, epilepsy, which only bothered her when she was nervous. She said she was conscious during her seizures, feeling bad all the time. And she went on to complain that her nephew used to take her welfare check away from her for food purchases, so that she had no spending money. She was full of complaints.

When she eventually tried to put on her parka to leave, I saw her try to close the zipper. Having no right thumb, it was a difficult matter.

"She needs a tag on that zipper," said Claire.

I happened to have a large tag on the side zipper of my purse—it was a brass triangle with JR on it. Claire and I managed to get it off and put it on Nora's zipper. Nora was very pleased and hugged me, and from then on my awkwardness vanished. Suddenly Claire began to pour out the story of her childhood. She told it as if it were happening now, in a voice that gathered richness as it went along. I listened spellbound. At last all the honey and tea, the language sessions, her awareness that I did in part actually feel with her in what she was doing, her actual seeing of me as a person, came together and formed into her spontaneous tale.

"I was born at the time they had that epidemic, measles. I never did get sick. There were a few of us who didn't. The epidemic was more powerful before I was born, and it was subsiding. I was born in August or September when it was at its worst. So many people got it that they had to use tractors to bury them when they died. They couldn't figure out how it was I lived. I remember my grandfather when I wasn't yet a month old; he died when I was about two months old. I described what he looked like, what he was wearing, how his hair was, and his complexion; and upstairs that little hole in the window—it wasn't really a window—and the bed rolled up, and the floor, I gave descriptions of how they pulled the bed up, the cupboard on this side, the table and on it the white cup with a red rim around it. To the right there was a stove, and it had a little door where they put in the firewood, and there was some driftwood on the floor. And on this side there was an oven, and they were making biscuits that summer, and there was something on top. On this side there was a nurse who had helped me be born, and I described her. I was one of the last ones to be born before she left, which means when you get right down to it that I must have been about a month old at that time. And they were giving shots, and there was a thing on the window—an emblem of the Red Cross, and there was a big sign. I couldn't see the word QUARANTINE; I saw it backward. They said they took those off that summer when I was a month or two old. They had to have those signs on there if somebody was sick in the house.

"And what happened was this. I remember getting up, trying to stand up. I knew my feet were for standing up, I knew what my hands were for, I knew my eyes were to see, but I couldn't stand up, my legs wouldn't hold. They did hold if I went like *that*"—Claire shoved her legs—"and I kept going like that, and then I would roll over and use my hands like this"—Claire shoved with her hands—"and I was going on like this, until I got to that place where there were people talking. My mom said I was about a month old when this happened. I almost fell down from that place, and they could *never* figure out how I rolled from that bed. You know? And I explained it to her later, and she said, '*Claire,* it can't be true, you were only about a month old, just a little baby.'

"I could go all the way back to about a month and a half. All those years I could flash back"—she snapped her fingers, her warm olive face amazed, telling me. "I could go way back and remember every word they said to me. If I just think about it, it comes back to me, picture that house, I could just *feel* it, I'd *be* there—as I described visiting and listening to another old lady. I used to rub her back. I didn't realize she had back trouble and that the only time she felt good was when I was there and had been massaging her. 'Yeah,' she'd say. 'Go like that.' And then I'd get my hands and press. I remembered her house and can describe it. Not long ago an old lady told me, 'That was my mother.' She said, 'What I want to know is what you did when you used to rub her back for her. Describe the house. No, you can't!'

"But I did. I was only two years old.

"I remember that I had long hair and an old lady used to braid it. I was a year or so old when that woman died. I was one year old, and I remember her. I told my mom about the little tiny braids. But when I do that I picture everything. For some reason when I was growing up I could understand everybody; but I couldn't speak, maybe because I was small. When I was growing up, the most I could do was when they let me work on their fingers or their muscles or back muscles or arms. The old people taught me. They said, never use your fingernails, keep your fingers flat and massage the people. You could *press* them, but not use your fingernails at all. But they used to get me all the time for broken bones, fingers, hands, arms, and back, and I didn't do anybody's stomach. Those old people wouldn't let me touch those until later on. My mother, grandmother, and great-grandmother were all healers, and I learned from them. I remember healing someone when I was four, just like my daughter healed my stomach when she was four.

"When I was a teenager I used to work on myself. There was never anything wrong with my body. I was new. I can't really say I learned it. I *feel* it. I get the symptoms from those people. I—they get sick. That's the most important part, the feelings, and I know it, I always felt it. I could *sense* it. The old people would hardly ever let anybody watch them work on a person. I had the authority to do it, authority to watch; I was *given* the authority by the old people. I could, my grandfather did, my grandmother did, my great-grandmother did. It went down from generation to generation. I'm one of the very few people that could work on myself. It's very rare. I have to pray about it a lot of times, though. I don't do the healing myself; I know the good Lord gave it to me, so I'm not going to take all the credit for it. I just never *doubt* it too. I *don't doubt* and I *refuse* to doubt. It's one of the main things.

"Like the other day I was getting bad symptoms in my side, in my stomach. I lay down but I *couldn't* get it away. And the next day a woman came to me with all the symptoms that I had the night before I saw her. I couldn't eat and didn't want to eat; I wasn't really nauseated, but I was uncomfortable. And here she was thinking about me all the time. Every time I work on her, I get her symptoms beforehand. It's more powerful when they think about me. I was affected really easily by that, badly affected. Sometimes I just feel for them to come, and I know they will. You talk about somebody and they'll walk right in. It's happened like that so many times; I always know it. But I could block it off. Another good thing about it—it goes on until they come, and then it'll go away. So any time they come in, after I work on them it goes away. If they don't give me anything I just constantly have it, and I don't like that. Most of the time I ask to work at their house so that I can get a bite to eat or something to drink. They're giving me something.

"When I was growing up I benefited from talking to people. I always had that, with old people. I was never scared to talk to them, although I was supposed not to. Me, I always wanted to find out.

"At one time—I must have been about seven, I was never scared—there was this old lady, she probably had epileptic fits, and everybody used to be scared of her. We were out walking. My cousin told me, 'I bet you can't go in there and talk to her.'

"And I said, 'I bet you there's nothing wrong with that person. All she needs is somebody to talk to, it's just that nobody visits her. How would you feel if nobody visited you? What she needs is somebody to love her or talk to her, and so . . .'

"I was not allowed to go there. But I could! I went in there. When I closed that door, I didn't have the nerve to go on. We knew that her daughter was out; the daughter used to say, 'Don't go in when I'm out.'

"I went in. You had to go through a door. When I looked over in this area out-side—it wasn't too far away—there was a dog on a chain. I was more scared of the dog than anything else. The chain couldn't reach me. In order to get away from the dog I'd have to go inside. It wasn't growling at me. That feeling. It wasn't mean. A low growl.

"When I knocked I heard somebody in there. I braced myself and went in. The first thing I noticed was a skin curtain. Usually doors went up like a curtain. There was a small kitchen, with one bed that had a curtain. This old lady walked out. She was *old! If* her hair had been combed she'd have looked pretty. She was clean. Her clothes were not really dirty; it was as *if* she had slept in them for two days or so. She had a chain on her hand or her leg, I can't remember, her leg. I remember her hands: her nails were really long. She tried talking to me, and I told her the only reason I went in there was because of my cousin; and I asked her, 'Don't tell my mom.'

"She couldn't talk because her tongue was like that, she was tongue-tied. But she *could* have. Anyway I told her she could have, and went back.

"I asked my mom about her. I forgot I wasn't supposed to talk to her. I kept think-ing about it—why didn't they comb her hair? 'Mom, how come you don't comb Kin-naun's hair? How come they keep her on a chain?'

"She said, 'You were there!'

"I said, 'Where?' "—Claire smiled.

"Mom said, 'You were over there, weren't you?' " I never did lie to my mom.

" 'Yes. But I pitied her.'

" 'What did she say to you?'

" 'I was trying to talk to her, I was being nice to her. But I didn't *touch* her.'

"When that old lady was young—about twenty—she got lost. It must have been after her daughter was born—she had twins, you see. After her twins were born she went out—and her mind was boggled, she couldn't think. Instead of going home she got lost. It was a long walk. There was all kinds of water all over the place, she must have forgotten which way she went. At that time it was just a small village anyway. She got lost. I don't know if this is true or not but her track turned from the leg of a human—she had no foot—to a brown bear's legs. Maybe a brown bear was around; I like to think that way. I may say that she later died. She ended up in the insane asylum. They sent her back home and she eventually died. But all she needed at that time was affection."

All this time I was making assenting noises and pouring out more tea and honey. Claire's voice and her speaking style were inseparable from the subject matter, and the story came in a series of vivid pictures. The style itself spoke of great self-confidence such as one encounters in the personal histories of exceptional people. For instance, *"I dared to visit the old lady"*—no one else did. She understood speech practically from birth. The subject matter and style were all one with the flow of knowledge, "I just knew." It was a life that unfolded by its own dynamic: the unitary principle was very strong in her.

She had at least four episodes of what is labeled by psychologists in our culture "fugue" or "psychosis"—but we do not have the right to label them psychosis. They appeared to be the classic irruptions of shamanic experience just as the ancient Inuit knew them, typically lasting for four days, during which something fearful, a spirit of the dead or of an animal, first afflicts the incipient shaman, then changes its nature into a helper.

A friend of Claire's related the first episode. About twenty years previously Claire was in Anchorage alone, for reasons unknown, staying in an expensive hotel for four days. There she had some kind of transformation. (The friend looked disturbed on recounting this.) The friend continued, "Claire told me on the phone—I was at the airport—that she had had some kind of revelation about me. There were certain things that would happen. A person who didn't know Claire's powers would think she'd gone crazy. What she was doing was glossolalia. This was a bad time for Claire. I've no idea what she went through in that hotel for four days all by herself."

Some years later Claire again had a very bad time. At her peripheral vision she would continually see a devil figure. According to a close affine of hers, an educated woman, Claire kept uttering a whole lot of blah-blah-blah nonsense words. It was glossolalia again. This greatly upset the affine. Claire told her, "Don't be like that, you don't think I am anything, do you? I can't help it, it comes to me." But at the end of it Claire could pray to Jesus, and afterward her healing was stronger. The affine, who later also signed up as a student in the anthropology teleconference course, told me that she came to realize that the personality of a shaman or healer could not be expected to be like that of other people.

A further episode occurred during my own fieldwork. One Thursday when I went to see Claire, I found her smoking all alone on her couch, very depressed. She wouldn't say a word. Then she said in a dull voice, "My husband has gone north, he doesn't tell me where, maybe he's drinking. He hasn't come back. Here I am with all the kids and the bills and everything." She shut her eyes, turned to the wall, and wouldn't speak anymore. As for me, I sat there crying and furious with men in that dim place, and frightened because she was angry. Was she angry with me? Claire finished her cigarette and went to sleep. I left, having kissed her. I loved her and it hurt me too. On Sunday when I visited her again she was not around. Her husband was back and told me she was in her bedroom, still feeling bad. I left her some pears and went home. Later still Claire was herself again. She thanked me for the pears, laughing. "I hid them in my room in case the kids got them, and I ate them all myself." What I saw had all the hallmarks of the shaman's episode.

During a later visit yet another episode seems to have occurred. I had just arrived and heard that Claire had returned from hospital, where she had been a patient for four days. I went to her house.

"Where's Claire?"

"Washing dishes," said young Ann.

I entered the kitchen. A small dark figure was at the sink, and she didn't turn around.

"Claire, Claire, look here. I've brought you something." She still didn't turn. Her gray hair was scrawny, her figure thin. I immediately thought, "An episode again? Isn't this fieldwork pitiful! My dear friend caught up in . . . something so mysterious! OK, I have to try to understand."

Claire peeped into the shopping bag I brought and saw peacock blue velveteen for a new parka, and a peacock blue zipper. She turned convulsively and flung herself into my arms. We were crying. I stroked her wild gray hair and haggard face.

"Dear Claire. You've given me everything, my sweet friend." When we recovered she told me the doctor at the hospital had given her the wrong medicine. She was really mad at him. "I'll get an attorney," she said. Now she was off all medicines and was feeling better by the minute. I wondered what the doctor thought he had prescribed the medicine for.

The four-day period puzzled me. An old account has survived about an ancestor of Clem's, the shaman Kehuq. When Kehuq was a young man, he was out on the tundra when he heard the sound of paddles up in the air. He looked up and saw a boat floating in the sky. It landed, and Kehuq saw within it a shaman with one big eye, who danced and gave him pleasure. The vision disappeared, and by the time Kehuq reached home, he had forgotten about it. Late that night Kehuq started up naked and left the tent for no reason. They brought him back, but for four days he was crazy and could not eat.

But when he recovered, Kehuq could dance. When he did so, his spirit left him and he was possessed by the tutelary shaman's spirit. Kehuq taught the people the shaman's songs and also taught them how to carve the shaman's face in wood. He was now gifted with supernatural powers.

This is just one of many accounts featuring a four-day crazy period, typically followed by a supernaturally successful hunting period, also by healing gifts and other benefits.

One of Clem's brothers also had four-day episodes in which he would not talk to anyone. Furthermore Jean Briggs (1970:254–255) mentions that during her fieldwork among the Inuit of Canada, the father of the family with whom she lived appeared to become withdrawn at periods, with the same moodiness and dislike of disturbance as Claire. The so-called "arctic hysteria" (Foulks 1972) may not have been a matter of light deprivation so much as the four-day crazy phenomenon. My own late husband, Vic Turner, suffered black periods from time to time. We both noted that they lasted for four days.

I do not know exactly what happened to Claire during those four-day episodes. I think she was only learning about herself gradually—including what she learned from her readings in the anthropology of her own culture. But she mainly learned because of a shadowy return of faith in her own traditions, battered as those traditions had been, when she was young, by a determined Christianity. And her life's focus was on using her gift. No systematizing was necessary for it to work; what was needed was just its simple activation. The life itself naturally organized the development of the gift, and this is why the depiction of it in this essay needed to be embedded in the events of that life.

A major point is at the center of the account. It can be seen that Claire felt the existence of pain in others, and I had sensed some of it. Pain is supposed to be purely subjective—that is, closed to the individual. I would say it is not so closed.

The ability to approach near enough to this, I believe, stemmed from actual friendship with my difficult opposite number, Claire—from an increasing odd and mutually amused familiarity between us, culminating in that sweet embrace after the fourth episode. Still, what had been going on in Claire in these episodes remained a mystery. If any others in the discipline have had those four-day episodes, they might not be able to put them into words either. My own dark times—I have had them; I have clambered out of them with poetry, then gained at the end a sense of utter glory. It seems clear that the Inuit in the cold regions have latched onto some key that poets have also struggled to use.

It is Claire herself, her experience with her own personality, who is the hero of the piece. Her role and reputation in the village were always up for discussion. She was praised by many because of those gentle hands. "She has The Blessing," said a pillar of the local church. A few of the others said her healing did not work; they preferred her rival, whose hands were "real strong." I felt those strong hands myself. Claire was therefore sometimes on the defensive and wondered if her critics were out to get her. But always she "refused to doubt."

About future research into the four-day episode: we are anthropologists, after all. It is for us to probe, to reexamine the Inuit shamanic roots of Claire's work, to put her care for others in a context of a long line of gifted spirit workers. Anthropologists cannot but be researchers, but the truth is that they are also turning out to be something like midwives of their hosts' developing cultures. So we may hope that our researches may actually help our people. Reconsidering the four-day period, its very existence in Claire throws into doubt the possible next step, which might be psychiatric study. The doubt remains whether psychiatry would cover the shadowy psychic elements involved. I hold out more hope in anthropology, with its richness of data and its growing and flourishing humanism. Humanism itself can dissolve the barriers of the academic conventions and reach in and really embrace the humanity we are studying. For we are inescapably an embracing species. Then we will *feel*—perceive with our senses—those things we have been in the habit of calling *symbol,* representation, and metaphor in the ritual cultures of the peoples whose experience we may not have yet shared. And it is my argument that the proper study of such frontier phenomena as Claire defended will ultimately prove to supply the missing link in the study of ritual and symbol.

So the issues are indeed the actual presence of the anthropologist in the research scene, the possibly profound depths of her subject matter, the liveliness—unsterilized by inappropriate scientific superimpositions—to be found in almost every experience of a fieldworker, and the finding of words truly to convey the complexities to responding readers. Moreover, we are saved by the fact that even those words themselves come not from some all-knowing individual but derive from their nest in our own living culture. The natural social humanism of our bodies will continually bring anthropology back to its old subject matter.

QUESTIONS FOR DISCUSSION

1. What were some of the characteristics that Claire shared with other Inuit healers? What were her special gifts?

2. Discuss the interaction between indigenous religion and Christianity as it affected the belief of Inuit such as Claire.

3. What does Turner mean when she says that Claire always "refused to doubt"?

Suggested Readings or Other Resources

General Works

Klass, Morton. 1995. *Ordered Universes: Approaches to the Anthropology of Religion.* Boulder, CO: Westview Press.

Smart, Ninian. 1996. Doctrine, Philosophy, and Some Dimensions. In *Dimensions of the Sacred: An Anatomy of the World's Beliefs* by Ninian Smart. Berkeley: University of California Press (pp. 27–69).

Illustrative Case Studies

Chagnon, Napoleon A. 1983. My Adventure with *Ebene*: A "Religious Experience." In *Yanomamo: The Fierce People* by Napoleon A. Chagnon. New York: Holt, Rinehart and Winston (pp. 206–212).

Griaule, Marcel and Germaine Dieterlen. 1954. The Dogon. In *African Worlds: Studies in the Cosmological Ideas and Social Values of African Peoples*, ed. Daryll Forde. London: Oxford University Press (pp. 83–89).

Videos

Community of Praise (First Run Icarus Films) is a 60-minute examination of faith working in the lives of a fundamentalist family.

Saints and Spirits (First Run Icarus Films) is a 26-minute exploration of the personal dimensions of Islam during three religious events in Morocco.

4

The Ritual Component of the Sacred

featuring

"Ethnometaphysics of Iroquois Ritual"
by Elizabeth Tooker

A widely used dictionary of religion[1] admits in some despair that "experts do not agree on how to define ritual, nor do they agree about its role in society." Nevertheless, because just about everyone agrees that **ritual** is absolutely vital to religion, some definition seems to be in order. The dictionary offers the following: ritual consists of "repetitive, formalized, stylized acts and forms of speech that are engaged in purposively in order to communicate with or become closer to the supernatural world." In light of our previous discussion, we might want to add that it is acts engaged in by a *group*, not an individual, which is the concern of the anthropological student of religion. Moreover, if we keep in mind that "supernatural" can mean *any* phenomenon not knowable through the five senses—and not necessarily something having to do with spirits or divinity—then this definition will suffice.

We sometimes use the term "ritual" in a pejorative sense in everyday language; it seems to connote an activity that is mindless in its repetition. Indeed, in classical psychoanalytic theory, excessively ritualized behavior was a symptom of extreme neurosis. While it is certainly possible that some people engage in rituals in a "mindless" or mechanical manner, it is highly unlikely that rituals would long survive as cultural institutions if they were nothing more than products of habit. There must be some positive reason for people to participate. One such reason might be a simple comfort factor: we enjoy doing familiar things because we know what to expect (the thrill of the unknown can be fun on occasion, but not, for most people, as a steady diet). Moreover, doing familiar things enriches the experience of the moment with memories, allusions, and resonances. For example, a family might always do the same thing for Thanksgiving (always at the same place, with the same people, with the same foods, and the same ancillary activities—e.g., watching football, looking over photo albums, napping, gossiping) but it is hardly a "mindless" activity. The family Thanksgiving is a way of affirming the identity of this particular small group; the family actively engages in its own traditions. The family knows that other families across the country are engaging in variants of the same process, but it understands that there are certain aspects of the celebration that are particularly theirs. Even if those things seem small or trivial, they mean something to the participants.

Ritual is also a way in which we put our abstract beliefs into formalized action. In fact, we have already seen how participation in ritual reinforces belief and may be part of the process of conversion. It is therefore very important that the ritual have a set form and an expected content; individuals may respond to it in various ways, but always within a standardized, culturally sanctioned framework. Rituals are thus a way to put into practice the ideas generated by the belief system. We said at the end of the last chapter that beliefs are the foundation of any religious system. But if all we have are beliefs, we would hesitate to think in terms of a fully developed domain of the sacred. Those ideas need to come alive in particular settings, involving particular people doing particular things at specified times in order for them to become embedded in the collective memory of the group.

The anthropologist Roy Rappaport contends that ritual is "the social act basic to humanity" because it is a way of organizing (and hence controlling) things that might otherwise be chaotic. He points out that when people participate in a ritual they are publicly communicating their acceptance of the order embodied by that ritual, as opposed to merely paying lip service to an intellectual proposition about the universal order. Indeed, the propositions that stand behind the ritual need not ever be enunciated (unless a visiting anthropologist asks about them) or even understood by all the participants. For Rappaport, the "sacred quality" generated by the ritual act "can then radiate throughout the rest of the social and symbolic system and give it a sense of certainty."[2]

HOW ANTHROPOLOGISTS OBSERVE RITUALS

We can look at what goes on in a ritual in terms of five major factors. First, we will want to observe and document the **material dimension of the ritual**. What are the physical objects that are used (e.g., books, musical instruments, food, candles, bells)? In what sort of physical space does it take place (e.g., indoors or outdoors? large room or small? how is the room furnished and decorated?)? How are participants dressed? What is the physical ambience of the space (brightly lit or dim? smoke-filled or clear? what are the noticeable smells or other sensations?)? In sum, what makes this space "sacred"?

Second, we need to pay attention to the **active dimension of the ritual**. What are the participants doing (e.g., singing, dancing, sitting still, in a trance)? In what sequence do actions take place? What is the mood or attitude of the participants as they engage in specific actions? It should be noted that ritual action does not take place in a vacuum. Every ritual must be prefaced by some sort of preliminary action that prepares participants for their entry into sacred space and time, and it will usually be followed by some actions that allow the participants to re-enter the profane world in a gradual manner.

Third, every ritual has a **human dimension**. Who are the participants (not the specific individual people, but the categories to which they belong, e.g., elders, young people, women, men, people of certain social classes)? Is there a discernible difference between those who seem to be leading the proceedings and those who form the "congregation"?

Fourth, we will want to study the **supernatural dimension of the ritual**. What being/force/idea stands at the heart of the ritual (i.e., what is the nature of the "supernatural world" with which participants want to engage, in the words of the dictionary definition cited earlier?)?

And finally, we need to inquire about the **mythological dimension of the ritual**. What kinds of stories are told to explain why everyone is gathered at this time, in this place, for this purpose? Who tells those stories? Are they explicitly recited, or is it tacitly assumed that everyone already knows them?

When doing anthropological fieldwork, it is usually a good idea to begin by making observations and recording every detail, no matter how seemingly trivial. Even if the ritual space is one that is already familiar, take nothing for granted—treat it as if it were a completely new, never-before-perceived experience—and write up your observations as if you were intending to convey a sense of what is happening to someone who is also completely unfamiliar with the scene. Taking pictures or making sketches (if permitted) is a good way to orient yourself and also to convey a visual impression of the ritual to your audience. If you continue to participate in the ritual, you will gradually come to an appreciation of what is and is not important. You will also have the opportunity to talk to participants to see how they understand and respond to what is going on. Remember that their perspective as insiders may well be different from yours as an anthropologist (because you are able to see what is happening in a cross-cultural, comparative way) so that it is necessary to record and account for both.

TYPES OF RITUAL

There are five general categories of ritual, typically described in terms of their principal function. As is usually the case with typologies, there is considerable overlap in the real world, although it still is useful to separate the categories for purposes of definition.

Technological Rituals

The first type of ritual is the technological, which is concerned with achieving some sort of control over natural forces. If we seek such mastery, it is helpful to know what is causing a certain situation so that we can remedy it if need be. Just as a doctor cannot prescribe a course of medical treatment without first diagnosing the patient's illness, so too must people know what they are up against before they can take steps to solve their problems (or, conversely, to maintain a situation they consider to be beneficial). When the process of diagnosis deals with supernatural causes of some sort, and when that process is carried out in the context of a "repetitive, formalized, stylized act" in which a group is participating, then we have a technological ritual that serves the purpose of **divination**. To "divine" a supernatural cause is analogous to diagnosing a physical condition.

There are many ways in which divination can be carried out. Some of the most common include the analysis of *dreams* (found in modern psychotherapy as well as in many traditional cultures in which dreams were believed to be accurate messages from the spirit world), *presentiments* (i.e., hunches), the *visions* that appear to people in a state of supernatural **possession**, or *body actions* (especially involuntary ones like sneezing, which are believed to be portents of things to come).

Divination rituals may also take the form of *ordeals* in which people are required to undergo painful or dangerous tests in order to prove their guilt or innocence. In the days of the witchcraft trials in Europe and North America, a suspected witch was subjected to the ordeal of "dunking"—the accused was immersed in water on the theory that the guilty would float while innocents sank, small consolation to the poor woman who had been drowned in the course of proving her innocence.

Necromancy is divination accomplished by consulting the spirits of the dead (a séance) or observing a (human) corpse for signs (a supernatural version of the modern autopsy). When the dead body being observed is not human, the process is called *haurispicy*; the entrails of birds seem to be favored in many cultures. Signs might also be found in the actions of live animals, in which case the process is known as *augury*; in ancient Rome the presence of an eagle flying over a funeral pyre was taken as a sign that the deceased had ascended to the realm of the gods.

Some forms of divination involve the observation of naturally occurring phenomena. *Astrology*, for example, is a system for reading the portents in the configurations of heavenly bodies. By contrast, divination might involve the observation of objects or actions deliberately brought into the ritual space. For example, there might be the casting of lots (or tossing dice), or the use of devices such as ouija boards (that spell out messages from the beyond), or divining rods (still used in some rural areas to find water).

Therapeutic Rituals

The second type of ritual is the therapeutic, which is designed to prevent or overcome misfortune or illness. It is usually necessary to preface a therapeutic ritual with a technological one, as it is important to divine (diagnose) the probable cause of misfortune or illness before one can treat it. There are five ways in which cultures may characterize the source of misfortune. Sorcery is the action of a **sorcerer**, who is a person knowledgeable about spells and who is in contact with supernatural forces; such a skilled practitioner can use his or her powers both to cause harm to others and to cure or undo the harmful effects caused by other sorcerers. **Object intrusion** is a process by which some alien physical object has somehow entered a body and is causing disruption and malfunction; our modern notion of germs that cause disease is a variant on the theme of object intrusion.

Spirit intrusion is a process by which some alien spiritual force has somehow entered a body and is causing disruption and malfunction; our modern notion of "unconscious" forces causing psychological or psychiatric illness is a variant on the theme of spirit intrusion. **Soul loss** occurs when a person's vital spiritual essence has somehow escaped or has been stolen, leaving only the physical husk. And finally **breach of taboo**, or the violation of a very strong prohibition that offends some higher power, brings misfortune to the perpetrator and sometimes to his or her whole family.

Ideological Rituals

The third type of ritual is the ideological. Such rituals are designed to reinforce group values. The most widely studied ideological rituals are **rites of passage** which are social occasions marking the transition of members of the group from one important life stage to the next. Birth, puberty, marriage, and death are transition points that are important in many different cultures, although there may also be points that are marked in one but not in other cultures. Even cultures that share transition points do not always give them the same weight. For example, in our own culture weddings are major occasions while puberty, although marked as a significant event in private settings, is not the occasion for any sort of formal public acknowledgement. But among many traditional people, puberty is marked by a major social ritual activity, to which the wedding—which may happen shortly thereafter—is a barely noted appendage. Such people believe that once a person has been officially acknowledged as an adult, then marriage follows more or less automatically. In cross-cultural perspective, there are both male and female initiation rites at the time of puberty, although in any given culture there tends to be an emphasis on one over the other. In general, male puberty rites often involve some sort of physical ordeal carried out in a public way, while the most noteworthy feature of female rites is (temporary) isolation from the group.

One widely studied form of the male puberty initiation ritual is the **vision quest** that was found in many Native American cultures, particularly those of the Great Plains that were organized around hunting and warfare. According to the terms of the vision quest, the pubescent boy was expected, after instruction from elders, to go out into the wilderness on his own. In addition to demonstrating his practical survival skills, he was expected to have a spiritual experience—to have a vision of his guardian spirit. The latter would typically appear in the form of a significant animal (e.g., buffalo, eagle) and would point out to the boy some apparently ordinary physical object (e.g., a rock or a stick) that would thenceforth be his "medicine," a symbol of the guardian spirit's protection. The boy would show this object to the elders upon his return in order to validate his claim to having experienced a vision, and he would keep the medicine in a bag on his person (or affixed to the central pole of his teepee) until he died. So important was the vision quest that no boy could be considered a full adult without undergoing this physical and spiritual exercise. Boys who for whatever reason decided not to undergo the vision quest were not condemned, but neither could they live as adult men; they had to live the rest of their lives as women. Such people were called *berdaches* by early French explorers in the American West. The berdaches were transvestites; there is some speculation that they may also have been castrated, although this does not seem to have been generally the case. Far from being despised, the berdaches were highly prized members of the society; they would, for example, be taken as wives by powerful men, although it is not clear whether sexual relations were involved in such unions. They also often became shamans (ritual specialists).

While rites of passage mark transitions, **rites of intensification** are those that serve to confirm people in their existing social roles. In most Christian denominations there is an explicit ceremony of "confirmation" that serves as a public acknowledgement that a young person, baptized as an infant, is now old enough to make his or her own commitment to his or her church. The confirmation ceremony also brings together those who previously made this transition, thus reinforcing their position. Homecoming rallies, political conventions, and concerts by long-established popular entertainers are other forms of rites of intensification in our society. While some newcomers among those in attendance might experience some sort of conversion through their participation, the more important function of such rituals is to bond together those who are already committed.

One of the earliest studies of religion by a modern social scientist was that of the French sociologist Émile Durkheim. Around the turn of the last century he analyzed the then-new ethnographic reports about the Australian aborigines, believed by scientists of that day to be the most "primitive" people on earth, and hence those whose culture was closest to those at dawn of humanity. Although we no longer are convinced by these arguments about the "primal" religion, Durkheim's other observations are still very much to the point. The Arunta, an aboriginal people of the central Australian desert, live for the most part in small, widely dispersed foraging groups, as the harsh ecology would not support denser or more sedentary settlement. One might expect that these scattered groups would go their own way with little sense of anything beyond their immediate horizons. And yet they retain a sense of being "Arunta," which Durkheim attributed to their participation in regular rituals that drew them together at designated places *(tjurunga)*—spots in the desert believed to be where heaven and earth meet, and hence places of great spiritual significance. While at the *tjurunga* the Arunta gather to share stories of the ancestors and to exchange gifts. They might also engage in some rites of passage (e.g., the initiation of boys who have come of age since the last get-together), although the overall purpose is one of intensification. In effect, says Durkheim, the Arunta define themselves as those people who "do Arunta things," even if for most of their lives they are not in immediate contact with one another. Whatever else may go on at the ritual, it allows the Arunta in effect to celebrate *themselves*.

Rites of ceremonial obligation are another form of ideological ritual. They are rituals in which bonds that link people in ways that go beyond basic kinship are forged. The practice of godparenting (often referred to by its Spanish name *compadrazco*) is perhaps the most familiar ritual of ceremonial obligation. For traditional Christians, the godparent served as a representative of the community into which the baptized infant was being introduced; he or she was also a surrogate parent, vowing to care for the child's spiritual well-being should the parents be unable to do so. For this reason in Latin America (and Mediterranean Catholicism in general) it was usually the wealthiest and most politically powerful people who were chosen as godparents, since they had the most to offer the children of the rest of the community. But the ceremony did not only obligate the godparent to help the child; it also obligated that child, as he or she grew up, to assist the godparent in appropriate ways. For someone to show disregard for or disrespect to a godparent would be almost as shocking in that culture as for someone to treat his or her own parents in an uncaring manner.

The fourth type of ideological ritual is the **rite of reversal**, a culturally sanctioned occasion on which people can step out of their normal social roles. Carnival (or Mardi Gras) was a popular feature of the plantation/slave societies of the New World; the slaves would be given the hand-me-down clothes of the masters, and for a day or two would be allowed to parade around mimicking the manners and mores of their owners. Doing so outside the confines of Mardi Gras would, needless to say, be grounds for the most severe punishment, but it was tolerated— even widely enjoyed by the masters themselves—during Carnival season. In the traditional Swazi kingdom of southern Africa, the king was an absolute (if supposedly benign) monarch, revered and treated with the utmost deference by his subjects, who saw him as the father of their nation. But at one particular festival, the Incwala, the king was made to dress up in a simple grass skirt and undergo a series of ritualized bodily mortifications and public humiliations for the delectation of the jeering crowd. Again, such disrespect would not have been tolerated the rest of the year, but it was encouraged during the Incwala. It is usually suggested that rites of reversal are found in strictly hierarchical, oppressive societies in order to allow the subordinate classes a sanctioned opportunity to let off steam and vent their frustrations in ways that were not threatening in the long run to the rulers.

Salvationary Rituals

The fourth type of ritual is the salvationary, which is designed to help individuals cope with personal issues. Rituals that facilitate a person's entrance into a state of trance or possession are among the most common of the salvationary rituals. Like the rites of reversal discussed above, which function at the level of the group, possession rituals allow *individuals* who feel powerless or otherwise hopeless to achieve a moment in the public spotlight by becoming a conduit of spiritual power. In Western religion, "possession" is a term usually applied to states that are to be dreaded and avoided; the possessed person is usually thought of as being in the grip of some evil power, which must be **exorcised** or driven away by ritual means. But of course that same religious tradition also recognizes saints and mystics who have visions and enter into trance-like states that are believed to be of divine and hence good origin. Mystics in the West are sometimes thought of as people of a neurotic temperament and even those recognized for their sanctity are rarely thought of as role models for the wider society. In non-Western religious traditions, by contrast, possession may be actively sought out as the only way for powerless people (often women or others on the margins of their society) to achieve power and public recognition.

Various religious traditions that evolved among the slave populations of the New World are examples of possession cults. The best known of them is *Vodun* (voudou, or voodoo) from Haiti, although there is also Santeria from Cuba (and other parts of the Spanish-speaking Caribbean), Xango from Trinidad, and Condomblé from Brazil. It is not difficult to fathom why slaves would find in spiritual possession a welcome reprieve from the terrible circumstances of their daily lives. Indeed, these rituals flourished in the nighttime, after the slaves were released from work in the fields. To their white masters, the nighttime was a sinister setting for magical doings (and not simply a matter of convenience), and so the evil reputation of these cults grew. Vodun played a significant role in organizing the slaves in the rebellion that culminated in 1804 in the overthrow of the French and the establishment of the independent black state of Haiti—a political turn of events that further convinced whites that Vodun was "black magic" in all the pejorative senses of that term. Although Vodun magic can certainly be used for harmful purposes, we should keep in mind that in animist philosophy, magic is inherently neither good nor bad; it is only the purposes to which it is put that can be so evaluated.[3] For practitioners of Vodun, the magic involved in the ceremonies is clearly good, because it helps people by putting them in touch with spirits who give them advice and provide them with an alternative source of social power. In all these New World religions, traditions from Africa (specifically of the Yoruba people of the West African coast) were blended with those of either French or Spanish or Portuguese Catholicism. Anthropologists refer to such blended traditions as **syncretisms**. In Vodun and the others, images of Catholic saints are given the personalities and qualities of Yoruba spirits, presumably on the theory that the religion of the enslavers must have some sort of desirable power that could only augment the power inherent in the traditional African system. Not incidentally, it is likely that these syncretisms occurred in the areas where the slaveholders were Catholic, rather than in those dominated by the Protestant powers (England, the Netherlands). Catholicism, with its baroque imagery typical of that era, its bells and incense and chanting, would have seemed to the slave much closer to familiar African ritualism than the more austere, ascetic Protestantism, thus facilitating the syncretic process.

Revitalization Rituals

The fifth type of ritual is that associated with revitalization movements, which do for the society as a whole what the salvationary rituals do for the individual. Revitalization movements are "deliberate, conscious, organized efforts by members of a society to create a new and more satisfying culture"[4] in the words of Anthony Wallace, the anthropologist who popularized the concept in the 1950s. Wallace developed the concept of revitalization through his study of the Handsome Lake religion of the Iroquois, a Native American people. Throughout the colonial period, the Iroquois were a powerful military, political, and economic force in the area that is now New York State and southern Canada, but by the end of the eighteenth century their fortunes were in sharp decline. They might have gone the way of cultural extinction like other native people of the Northeast were it not for the preaching of a prophet named Handsome Lake. He had fallen into alcoholism but attributed his salvation to the intervention of ancestral spirits who spoke to him and compelled him to speak in turn to his people. Handsome Lake's message involved a renewal of respect for certain ancestral ways (mostly having to do with ritual and social organization), combined with an acceptance of certain beneficial ways of the white settlers, such as agricultural techniques. He must have been a very persuasive speaker (a "charismatic leader" to use the familiar quasi-religious terminology), because within a generation the Iroquois were once more a prosperous people peacefully settled on their own land (although they were, of course, certainly circumscribed by the general restrictions placed on Native Americans in the United States and Canada).

The relative success of the Handsome Lake revitalization stands in sharp contrast to another widely studied Native American phenomenon, the Ghost Dance, which swept the western tribes at the end of the nineteenth century. It was, in effect, part of the last wave of resistance to white encroachment on Native lands in that part of the continent. The Ghost Dance is usually described as a "nativistic" revitalization because, unlike Handsome Lake, its prophets (Wodziwob and Wovoka of the Paiute tribe in what is now Nevada) urged the people to shun all the ways of the whites and place their total trust in the protective power of the ancestors ("ghosts"). The spirits of the latter were invoked in elaborate ritual dances, and initiates wore special clothing that had been blessed at those rituals. The shirts were supposed to make them invincible to the bullets of the whites. Given the political and military circumstances of the United States at that time, this resistance-based form of revitalization was eventually overcome.

The colonized people of the Pacific exhibited a reactive form of revitalization beginning in the late nineteenth century. Their revitalization efforts are usually collectively referred to as **cargo cults** because they seemed to be fixated on the supposedly magical properties of the material goods transported by the Europeans to the islands. From a Western point of view, the cargo cultists seemed to be saying that all they wanted were the tools and appliances of Western civilization, but the underlying idea was really more sophisticated. For the colonized islanders, the Europeans must have seemed to have been in possession of some special magical power that allowed them not only to come from far, far away across the sea but also to achieve domination so quickly and easily. Since it was the material goods that most clearly distinguished the Europeans from the islanders, the latter came to the conclusion that the mysterious source of power was in the cargo being brought in by the conquerors. And so they formed groups in the conviction that as long as they had faith, some day the cargo would come *for them*. It wasn't so much the physical articles they wanted, but the magical power that they conveyed. When a revitalization movement looks forward to a period of social and spiritual bliss (as opposed to one that seeks to create an ideal situation in the here-and-now) it is referred to as a *millennial* movement (i.e., the good times will come "in a thousand years"—a shorthand way of saying "some time in the future"—or, perhaps that they will last for a thousand years).

One of the most widespread and highly publicized of contemporary revitalization movements is Rastafarianism, which began in Jamaica in the 1930s and now has followers numbering in the hundreds of thousands in various parts of the world. This movement began (again among an oppressed, exploited colonial people) when Haile Selassie (one of whose titles was Ras Tafari) ascended the throne as Emperor of Ethiopia. At that time he was the only African head of an independent African state, and when Ethiopia was invaded by Italy, the emperor's impressive appearance before the League of Nations made him an international celebrity and symbol of resistance to fascism. These events inspired some Jamaicans to speculate that Haile Selassie was more than simply an earthly king; he was, they claimed, the reincarnation of Jesus Christ, which would prove that God is black and that all the black people transported to the New World were destined to a triumphal return to Africa upon the overthrowing of white rule (which they referred to as "Babylon," a symbolic reference to the place of exile of the Biblical Israelites). There had been secular, political "Back to Africa" movements active among blacks in the United States and the Caribbean since the early years of the twentieth century, but the Rastafarians wedded that political goal to a spiritual one that captured the imagination of increasing numbers of poor people of color. The vast international appeal of Rastafarianism in our own day may have something to do with its association with reggae music (particularly as popularized by the late, legendary Jamaican artist Bob Marley), and nowadays Rastafarians are noted for their vegetarianism, their fondness for marijuana *(ganja)*, which they smoke as a kind of sacramental substance, and other counter-cultural ways. As the movement has spread, its original harshly racialist rhetoric has been softened, and other modifications had to be made following the overthrow of Haile Selassie and his subsequent death in the 1970s. But Rastafarianism is certainly a noteworthy (and relatively rare) example of a revitalization movement that has grown more vigorous over time.

RITUAL PRACTITIONERS

Rituals must be led by members of the group who have some sort of specialized training that has given them knowledge and power not shared by the rest of the group. Ritual leaders in literate religious traditions oriented to some sort of personalized supernatural being or beings are referred to as **priests** or **priestesses**. They often come from designated families or lineages, although whatever skills they possess are not directly inherited but must be learned through intensive study, usually in places apart from the rest of the community. Priests and priestesses lead the people in acts of prayer (asking the divinities for help) and sacrifice (offering gifts to appease or thank the divinities). In such religions, there is a great gap between the powers of the gods and the ways of humans. Communication with supernaturally powerful beings is therefore not a matter to be taken lightly and so the rituals of priestly prayer and sacrifice are highly formalized; it is believed that they must be performed in exactly the right way in order for them to have the desired effect. Hence, priests and priestesses typically do not act on impulse or inspiration. Instead, they are experts in learning the rules and following them carefully, leading the less knowledgeable members of the community and keeping them from error. Literate religions, based as they are on some recognized sacred scripture, are very conservative institutions, since once practices have been codified and written down they are very difficult to change.

By contrast, ritual leaders in animist or other nonliterate traditions operate in an environment in which the supernatural and the natural are closely intertwined. Prayer and sacrifice, which are conducted at a distance by people of vastly inferior power, would be inappropriate in the animist context, which is relatively more apt to use magic—the manipulation of natural objects to achieve supernatural ends. The practitioner of magic, unencumbered by written scripture, is relatively free to improvise and experiment with his or her operations.[5] As noted above, sorcerers are practitioners of magic. While a propensity toward sorcery may run in families, the skills of a sorcerer, like those of a priest, must be learned, usually as an apprentice to a more experienced magical expert rather than in a formal school. Speaking cross-culturally, sorcerers may be either male or female, although in any given culture they tend to be one or the other.

Shamans are makers of magic who are distinguished from ordinary sorcerers primarily by the fact that they enter into a state of trance or possession when they are conducting rituals. Sorcerers are usually part-time specialists who, while not conducting magical rituals, do the ordinary things other adults in their community do. Shamans, on the other hand, are people who exhibit extraordinary qualities that set them very distinctively apart from everyone else. Their extraordinariness is often noted very early in life. For example, a child who has been seriously ill or badly injured and then recovers may be marked as a potential shaman (particularly if an established shaman was involved in the cure, in which case the youngster may become the elder's apprentice). A child who has had some sort of extraordinary experience (e.g., being struck by lightning, being bitten by a poisonous snake) and comes through unscathed is also likely to be seen as someone with latent spiritual powers. Children born with certain physical features (e.g., various kinds of "birth marks" or a caul—a membrane covering the heads of some newborns) may be said to have been marked by spiritual forces. A young person who makes unconventional life choices, like the berdache of Plains Indian cultures, would also be a candidate for shamanhood.

Perhaps the most common "sign" of someone destined to become a shaman is the manifestation of symptoms that we in the West would, by contrast, consider highly unfavorable marks of serious medical problems. For example, the seizures of epilepsy, during which the body seems abandoned by "mind" and "spirit," may be thought to be ways in which a person enters into communication with the spirit world. After all, if it is desirable to seek out a trance state in order to communicate with the beyond, how much more powerful would it be if those states appeared as if unbidden? Even at earlier times in the history of our own culture epilepsy was seen as a sign of supernatural favor rather than as a dreaded medical condition requiring drastic intervention; Julius Caesar's military and political position was supposedly enhanced by his seizures. Along the same lines, we might think of someone in our culture who heard voices, saw visions, spoke in distorted ways, was sometimes catatonic (rigid and unable to move), and so forth as suffering from schizophrenia, which we consider a dreadful, dangerous affliction requiring heavy doses of medication or highly restrictive incarceration. But in a culture that values visions and puts credence in communications with the spirit world, the "schizophrenic" would have an important and highly valued social role to play. If the door of your classroom were suddenly to burst open and you beheld a teenage girl riding a horse, dressed in armor, and loudly proclaiming that the voices of the saints had ordered her to lead an army to save the nation, you would probably call 911 and have her taken away to a secure psychiatric facility. But just a few hundred years ago, an earlier time in the history of our own culture, someone like that—Joan of Arc—was taken quite seriously. Depending on their political perspective, people of her time thought of Joan as either a witch or a saint, but no one thought she was crazy and in need of supervised medical care.

Shamans, like sorcerers, learn their craft, usually through apprenticeship. One of the things they may have to learn, particularly if they are not "naturally" prone to seizures or hallucinations, is how to enter into an **altered state of consciousness**—a trance. Trances can be induced by the use of hallucinogenic drugs or through rhythmic chanting, dancing, or drumming. Recent archaeological and geological evidence suggests that the famous oracle of Delphi in ancient Greece uttered her prophecies while in a state of trance induced by the inhalation of petrochemical fumes seeping from the earth beneath the shrine. Some people can master the technique of controlling their bodily functions in such a way as to slip into a different level of awareness. Needless to say, anyone who is in such an altered state would be very impressive—and perhaps even a little scary—to the rest of the people, hence the source of the shaman's extra power.

One other category of ritual specialist needs to be mentioned: the **witch**. At this point, we must leave aside our ideas of witches and witchcraft as they have developed in the history of U.S. culture (a matter that will be dealt with in a later chapter). We are here discussing makers of magic in traditional cultures; but unlike shamans and sorcerers, witches are people who are believed to have *innate* rather than learned skills. The witch is therefore even more powerful than the shaman. Once again, witches may be either male or female, although in any given society they will likely be one or the other. Perhaps because their innate powers warp them in some way, witches are generally believed to be antisocial individuals, and ordinary people traffic with them only in the most desperate circumstances. The witch's magic is usually thought of as harmful and the witch himself or herself is to be avoided, as that harmful "vibe" emanates from his or her very person. Some anthropologists have made the case that *accusations* of witchcraft are often more socially important than the practice of witchcraft itself. That is, if a community wants to bring an eccentric neighbor into conformity, a rumor may get started that he or she is a witch. Unless the accused is truly a confirmed non-conformist who relishes being feared and mistrusted by others, he or she will probably start behaving more "normally" so as to avoid social condemnation.

FUNCTIONS OF RITUAL

It is to be hoped that these orienting remarks will dispel the notion that ritual is mindless or meaningless. Rituals are ubiquitous features of religious systems; they are the means by which the abstractions of the belief system are translated into sacred space and time and they allow people to put into practice the ideas their belief system has suggested to them. Rituals provide comfort to the confused, affirmation for the converted, social support for the insecure, a sense of power for the hopeless. They provide the forums in which people communicate their ideas to one another and they provide the channels through which humans deal with the supernatural.

KEY CONCEPTS

Be sure you can define the following terms, and give at least one illustrative example of each:

- active dimension of ritual
- altered states of consciousness
- breach of taboo
- cargo cults
- divination
- exorcism
- human dimension of ritual
- ideological ritual
- material dimension of ritual
- mythological dimension of ritual
- object intrusion
- possession
- priests/priestesses
- revitalization rituals
- rites of ceremonial obligation
- rites of intensification
- rites of passage
- rites of reversal
- ritual
- salvationary rituals
- shamans
- sorcerer
- soul loss
- spirit intrusion
- supernatural dimension of ritual
- syncretism
- technological rituals
- therapeutic rituals
- vision quest
- witch

RESEARCH EXPLORATIONS

1. Conduct a series of observations and interviews in a religious setting with which you are not already familiar. Write a detailed analytical paper, using concepts developed in this chapter, in which you discuss the content, structure, and personnel of the main ritual associated with the religious tradition practiced in this setting. A sketch showing the ritual action and (with the permission of the people involved) photos should be part of your report. Make very sure that the people you are dealing with understand that this is a class project and that you are not at this point interested in being converted. If they will not grant you access unless you promise to consider conversion, respect their position but find another setting in which to conduct your research. Be very sure to check with your instructor about your university's norms regarding the signing of "informed consent" forms for projects of this nature.

2. Attend one or more events of a ritualized nature that are not conventionally thought of as "religious." Sporting events (especially those associated with important symbolic occasions, such as a college's "homecoming" festival), the concerts of long-established performers, or political conventions/rallies are some examples. Discuss the ways in which these events are similar to religious rituals discussed in this chapter. In what ways are they different. Present your findings in a brief in-class talk or a homemade video.

Notes

[1] Levinson, David. 1996. *Religion: A Cross-Cultural Dictionary.* New York: Oxford University Press.

[2] Rappaport, Roy A. 1999. *Ritual and Religion in the Making of Humanity.* Cambridge: Cambridge University Press (p. 31).

[3] Readers may remember the film *Marathon Man* in which the hero is tortured by a sinister Nazi dentist. Obviously no one thinks that dentistry is inherently evil, although the skills of a dentist could certainly be used for evil purposes.

[4] Wallace, Anthony F.C. 1956. Revitalization Movements. *American Anthropologist* 58:264-281.

[5] The sorcerer's "magic" may well include the use of natural substances that have healing powers that can be empirically verified. Any number of such items have been collected and synthesized by Western pharmaceutical companies.

Case Study

"Ethnometaphysics of Iroquois Ritual"
by
Elizabeth Tooker

Tooker takes issue with the idea that rituals are meaningless actions; she characterizes them as "ethnometaphysical" in nature, which means that they are expressions of complex, transcendent ideas acted out in terms that are appropriate to the culture. She analyzes Iroquois ritual in terms of how *they are conducted,* when *they must be conducted,* where *they are supposed to be held, and* who *is permitted to participate.*

In *Primitive Culture,* Edward B. Tylor (1958:448–449) wrote, "In the science of religion, the study of ceremony has its strong and weak sides. On the one hand, it is generally easier to obtain accurate accounts of ceremonies by eyewitnesses, than anything like trustworthy and intelligible statements of doctrine . . . On the other hand, the signification of ceremonies is not to be rashly decided on by mere inspection." Since Tylor's pioneering study in the anthropology of religion, ceremonials have continued to be described in the ethnographic literature, and anthropologists have continued to seek the meaning ("signification") of these rituals, if not always in history as Tylor did, in such areas as psychological and social process and function. In the last several decades, an increasing number of studies of symbolism have also appeared, and the disparity noted by Geertz (1966:42) between the number of studies analyzing "the system of meanings embodied in the symbols which make up the religion proper" and those relating "these systems to social-structural and psychological processes" seems to be rapidly closing.

Few recent studies, however, have either described or analyzed ritual form—the cultural patterns that underlie and govern the performance of religious ceremonies, or what might be called the structure of ritual, although the term *structure* has come to have certain other connotations. Yet, as various students of ritualism (for example,

Reprinted by permission of the Southern Anthropological Society from *Symbols and Society: Essays on Belief Systems in Action,* ed. Carol E. Hill (Proceedings #9, 1975), pp. 103–16.

Kluckhohn and Wyman 1940 and Fenton 1936) have observed, the ceremonials that constitute the practice of a religion are not a haphazardly arranged collection of miscellaneous actions. Rather, like other parts of culture including language, religious practice has form and structure. As a language is not composed of an infinite number of words, so also a religion does not employ a limitless number of rites but a relative few, selecting and arranging them in accordance with customary rules to craft a specific ceremony much as words are combined into longer units of discourse in accordance with customary grammatical rules.

Part of the reason for the paucity of studies of ritual form may well be the largely unconscious nature of such patterns. As Sapir (1949b:549) noted,

> It is strange how frequently one has the illusion of free knowledge, in light of which one may manipulate conduct at will, only to discover in the test that one is being impelled by strict loyalty to forms of behavior that one can feet with the utmost nicety but can state only in the vaguest and most approximate fashion. It would seem that we act all the more securely for our unawareness of the patterns that control us.

And so at times the effort required to ascertain these forms may be considerable.

Nevertheless, the reward for such effort may be of equal magnitude—for if "Concealed in the structure of each different language are a whole set of assumptions about the world and life in it" (Kluckhohn 1949:159), so also a comparable set of assumptions may be concealed in the structure of ritual, in the patterns of religious behavior. Although to some the study of ritual form has seemed dry and dehumanizing, it does not necessarily have these consequences. Rather, studies as these may be of help in understanding such matters as belief, and more generally further the study of what Hallowell (1960:20) has termed "ethnometaphysics," and so, as Whorf (1956:218–219) said of the study of linguistic forms, make a significant contribution to the "greater development of our sense of perspective," indicating

> that the few thousand years of history covered by our written records are no more than the thickness of a pencil mark on the scale that measures our past experience on this planet; . . . that the race has taken no sudden spurt, achieved no commanding synthesis during recent millenniums, but has only played a little with a few of the linguistic formulations and views of nature bequeathed from an inexpressibly longer past. Yet . . . this . . . need [not] be discouraging to science but should, rather, foster that humility which accompanies the true scientific spirit, and thus forbid that arrogance of the mind which hinders real scientific curiosity and detachment.

But even if the study of ritual form should prove not to contribute to the discernment of the signification of ceremonies by indicating what the people themselves regard as important and what they feel can be properly ignored, what things they deem to belong together and thus consider different in some manner from things not so classed, it may be of aid in the task of describing ritual practice. Attention to these forms suggests that eyewitness accounts may not be quite as trustworthy or accurate as Tylor implied, but often are distorted in much the same manner as early grammatical studies of non-Indo-European languages, based as they were on the model of Latin grammar. At least it is the intent of the following discussion to suggest how studies of ritual form may contribute to our understanding of religion and, more tentatively, to our understanding of the mode of apprehension, the conception of the world, held by those who practice them. The example to be used is that of Iroquois ritualism, one of the best described in the ethnographic literature (Morgan 1851; Fenton 1936, 1941, 1953; Speck 1949; Shimony 1961; Tooker 1970).

Although a number of Iroquois now living in the state of New York and the provinces of Ontario and Quebec are Christians, not all are, and the traditional Iroquois religious ceremonies continue to be held in the Longhouses[1] (the "churches" of this religion) and in the homes of believers. The religion itself is sometimes called the "Longhouse religion" and those who practice it are sometimes referred to as the "Longhouse gang." And, although the Longhouse religion probably is not identical in every detail to the religion practiced in preColumbian times by the Iroquois, it undoubtedly derives from this practice, and in large part was affirmed by the Seneca prophet, Handsome Lake, who preached from 1799 to his death in 1815.

But if this religion is one of the best described in the ethnographic literature—for as Oswalt (1973:446) observes, "Anthropologists long have exhibited a particular fondness for the Iroquois"—consulting this literature can also be, as he says, "a frustrating experience." Like others, Oswalt (1973:447) suggests that what is needed is a synthesis of the ethnographic and ethnohistorical work on the Iroquois. However, not even such a compendium is likely to dispel completely suspicions similar to those Aberle (1963:1) has noted of anthropological studies of Navajo social organization, either that there is a certain "fuzzy" quality about this culture or that the fieldwork has been "sloppy." Furthermore, the nature of Iroquois ritual is such that certain types of analyses often regarded as being capable of providing more accurate, complete, and clearer descriptions prove difficult to do. For example, the student of Iroquois religious practice is not confronted with a wealth of data on certain matters frequently discussed in the study of religion.

The Longhouse itself, sometimes called a "council house" in Reservation English, is as starkly utilitarian as a Quaker meetinghouse. Typically, it is rectangular in plan, furnished only with benches along the walls and a fireplace or stove at either end. There is no altar, nor are altars built as part of a ceremony. No sacred objects are kept in the Longhouse, and in fact such objects and other visual symbols figure little in the ritual as do formalistic prayers and stylized gestures. Rather the ritual consists of speeches, songs, dances, and games—many of which may also be performed on secular occasions. Only a tenuous connection exists between ritual performance and myth; ceremonies do not enact myths, nor are myths concerned with the justification of the rituals.

Even the seemingly simple task of classifying Iroquois ceremonials is not without its difficulties. At first glance, these ceremonies would seem to be conveniently grouped under several headings, the four most important being the calendric agricultural ceremonies, the curing rituals of the medicine societies, the rites in which the teachings of the prophet Handsome Lake are recited, and the rites of passage.[2] But, although convenient, such a typology has its awkward features. As the following examples illustrate, sometimes a category includes rituals of a kind not indicated by its descriptive label and sometimes the classification omits rituals that have a place in the religion.

Not all the so-called agricultural ceremonies are, in fact, concerned with agriculture. Often listed in the agricultural series (the series is not identical in all Longhouses) is the Midwinter ceremony (held in January or February), the Maple ceremony (March or April), the Planting ceremony (May), the Strawberry ceremony (May or June), the Green Bean ceremony (August), the Green Corn ceremony (August or September), and the Harvest ceremony (October or November). However, some examination of ritual form indicates that the Maple and Strawberry ceremonies are not properly agricultural ones, Maple more obviously and Strawberry less obviously so. In Iroquois practice, the other five of this series (Midwinter, Planting, Green Bean, Green Corn, and Harvest) include as a major ritual a series of dances (the particular dances vary from Longhouse to Longhouse) called "Our Life Supporter" dances, and are dances for the three principal cultivated plants of the old Iroquois agriculture: corn, beans, and squash. The Our Life Supporter dances are not performed as part of the Strawberry ceremony; aboriginally, strawberries were not cultivated. Neither are they performed as part of the Maple ceremony, but the distinction made by the Iroquois is not between wild and cultivated plants; the principal rites of the Maple differ from those of the Strawberry ceremony.

As all these ceremonies involve foods used by the Iroquois, they might be termed "ceremonies addressed to food spirits" (cf. Speck 1949:37). However, this classification ignores such apparently agricultural-calendric rituals as the Sun, Moon, and Thunder ceremonies. Although in some Longhouses the Sun and Moon ceremonies are held only occasionally or not at all, in others they are performed each year as part of the ceremonial calendar. Similarly, in some Longhouses the Thunder ceremony may be performed in order to bring rain, and in some it is given each spring as a standard part of the calendric cycle.

A distinction between calendric and curing ceremonies as well as Titiev's (1960) somewhat comparable distinction between "calendrical" and "critical" rites also poorly fit the Iroquois data. As has been noted, not all seemingly calendric ceremonies are always part of the ceremonial calendar. Conversely, a few ceremonies of the medicine societies are calendric. These include certain rites of the Little Water and the False Face societies, as well as the rites various medicine societies perform during the most important calendric observance, the Midwinter ceremonial. Furthermore, rituals other than those of the medicine societies may be used to cure illness. Virtually any ritual may be performed (if indicated) to cure a sick individual, including those most commonly performed as part of a calendric ceremony.

Such inadequacies as these may seem trivial compared to the impressive accomplishment of these classifications—that of conveying in a limited number of pages the content of a complex religious system. Yet, the seemingly trivial inadequacies of such typologies may also indicate that the principles used in other cultures are different from those in common use in ours. Thus, some study of the structure of culture, those forms which "establish a definite relational feeling or attitude . . . towards all possible contents of experience" (Sapir 1949a:153) may aid in ascertaining these principles and dispel the idea that there is a fuzzy quality about some cultures.

Although it would be rash to claim that, given the present state of knowledge, anything more than a most tentative characterization of the principles governing Iroquois ritual performance can be given, some inspection of the data suggests that the Iroquois pay particular attention to what may be called "appearance," and more specifically to such matters as where things and beings are located, with whom or to whom or with what they appear, and changes in their appearance. Further study may prove that the underlying structure and categories of Iroquois ritual in particular and Iroquois culture in general are much like those of Western civilization. But contrary to some assertions, a basic universal structure (if it does exist) is little understood, and before it is properly known, more extensive analysis of its variant expressions in different cultures than has been made to date may well be necessary. Perhaps, then, the following outline—tentative as it necessarily is—of the principles governing the how, when, where, and who of Iroquois ritualism ultimately may contribute to such an understanding.

PRINCIPLES GOVERNING THE "HOW" OF IROQUOIS CEREMONIAL PRACTICE

The basic framework of an Iroquois ceremony consists of five parts: Thanksgiving Speech, tobacco invocation, rites and/or speeches,[3] brief Thanksgiving Speech, and distribution of food. Each of these parts may or may not be included in a specific ceremony according to the following rules.

Rule 1. Most ceremonies, or more properly most gatherings (little or no distinction is made between the secular and sacred, the natural and supernatural worlds, and religious ceremonies and ordinary meetings generally have the same form) begin with the Thanksgiving Speech. The principle exception to this rule is various ceremonies for the dead; it would be inappropriate to be thankful for death (Chafe 1961:2).

Although the Iroquois word for this address is usually translated "Thanksgiving Speech," more is implied than just the idea of thanking. As Chafe (1961:1) has noted, "The trouble is that the Seneca concept [of thanksgiving] is broader than that expressed by any simple English term, and covers not only the conventionalized amenities of both thanking and greeting, but also a more general feeling of happiness over the existence of something or someone." There is, then, an element of greeting, and more particularly "greeting" as expressing happiness for the existence of a being or thing in the Iroquois notion of thanksgiving. For this reason, in part, the Thanksgiving Speech begins most ceremonies. The speech greets and "returns thanks to"—to use the Reservation English expression—various beings and things.

The burden of the Thanksgiving Speech is the mention of the various items found on the earth and above. In the long versions (different speakers use slightly different versions and the length of the speech may vary), sixteen such items often are mentioned specifically: the people, the earth, the plants (including special mention of the strawberry), the water, the trees (including special mention of the maple), the animals, the birds, the Three Sisters (Our Life Supporters—corn, beans, and squash), the wind, the Thunderers, the sun, the moon, the stars, the Four Beings (messengers from the Creator who appeared to Handsome Lake), Handsome Lake, and the Creator. In the section of the Thanksgiving Speech devoted to each of these items, mention is made first that the Creator decided on, and so ordained the existence of the item. Next the item is described, and mention is made that it is still present and carrying out the responsibility assigned to it. Finally, thanks are returned for it (Chafe 1961:7). Although various speakers mention the items in a slightly different order, all follow the same general order: the items "below" (those on earth) are mentioned first, then the items "above," and within these categories the order is generally from the things nearest the earth upward to the things above.

Rule 2. In some ceremonies there follows after the Thanksgiving Speech a tobacco invocation, a speech during which a speaker throws loose tobacco into a fire. A tobacco invocation is given as part of the Maple ceremony, the Thunder ceremony, the ceremonies of the medicine societies, and certain ceremonies for the dead. It is not included in the Planting, Green Bean, Green Corn, Harvest, and other ceremonies involving the Our Life Supporters, the Strawberry ceremony, or, in some Longhouses, the Sun and Moon ceremonies.

The general rule suggested by these practices is: A tobacco invocation forms part of the ritual of those ceremonies for beings or things usually found at a distance (that is, beyond the village and its nearby fields), but not those for beings or things nearby. For example, the tutelaries of the medicine societies, such as the False Faces, live in the woods beyond the village and its fields, and a tobacco invocation forms part of the ritual of these societies. The maple trees grow in the forest, and a tobacco invocation forms part of the Maple ceremony. The Thunderers are heard beginning in the spring, but not in the winter—they are not always nearby, and a tobacco invocation is given in the Thunder ceremony. However, the Three Sisters (corn, beans, and squash) and strawberries grow nearby, and a tobacco invocation is not included in the ceremonies honoring them. A tobacco invocation is given if the dead are being addressed collectively or if a deceased person is being asked not to bother a sick individual (that is, make him ill), but not during the funeral ceremonies, those ceremonies for the dead held before the ghost has left for the land in the west.

This rule seems to rest on a basic and pervasive distinction made by the Iroquois between the world of the forest and that of the clearing. To the Iroquois, the forest was the domain of men. Men cut the clearing out of the forest for the fields and the village, building the houses and, if necessary, the stockade surrounding them out of materials of the forest. Once this was done the clearing became the domain of the women in particular and of the people generally.[4] Women spent much of their time in the village and the fields, doing almost all of the planting, tending, and harvesting of the crops, while the men were often away, hunting, trading, and warring. As a consequence, women dominated life in the village, men that beyond the clearing.

Rule 3. Speeches and/or rites appropriate to the occasion follow the Thanksgiving Speech and, if given, the tobacco invocation. If the gathering is held primarily for the purpose of reminding people or deciding what they should do, speeches follow. Speeches customarily are important in the following types of gatherings: If the primary intent is to remind people what a person or persons now dead (as the prophet Handsome Lake or the founders of the League of the Iroquois) said and did, the content of the speeches, although varying somewhat according to the knowledge of the speaker, is fixed by tradition. If the gathering is being held for the purpose of telling someone now deceased what he should do (for example, to tell him to stop making another ill), a speech is addressed to him. If it concerns deciding the responsibilities of people now living (such as matters of the kind discussed at ordinary council meetings), speeches also are given.

However, if the gathering is in recognition of one of the items mentioned in the Thanksgiving Speech, there follow rites drawn from the Iroquois repertoire of songs, dances, and games. The repertoire includes such songs as the Personal Chants; dances such as the Feather Dance, Thanksgiving (Skin or Drum) Dance, War Dance, Corn Dance, Stomp Dance, and those of the type known as social dances; and such games as the Bowl (Peach Stone) Game, lacrosse, and tug of war. In a ceremony given for an individual (for example, to restore or maintain health or other good fortune), the song, dance, or game (or some combination of such rites—more than one may be deemed necessary) is indicated in a dream of the individual concerned or suggested as appropriate by another. If the ceremony is for one of the other items mentioned in the Thanksgiving Speech, the choice from the repertoire of songs, dances, and games is fixed by tradition, a choice perhaps first dictated in a dream.

If the gathering involves items not mentioned in the Thanksgiving Speech (such as the tutelaries of the medicine societies), the rites performed are those songs and dances known only to a segment of the community. Individuals with such knowledge include members of the medicine society and often a few who are not members of the society; participation in such a ceremony is not necessarily restricted to those who belong to the society.

Rule 4. If the Thanksgiving Speech has been given at the beginning of the ceremony, there follows next an abbreviated Thanksgiving Speech.

Rule 5. Food is distributed at the conclusion of all gatherings except those that involve neither those beings or things found beyond the clearing nor those individuals living beyond it. For example, food is distributed at the end of (or forms part of) the medicine society rituals. Food is also distributed at the conclusion of such ceremonies as Maple, Planting, Strawberry, Green Bean, and Harvest and at the conclusion of each day's rituals in such ceremonials as Midwinter and Green Corn that last more than one day. It is not distributed at the end of an evening of social dances in the Longhouse (often an evening social dance is held in the Longhouse if the ceremonial is to continue there the next day), but it is served when people from other reservations have been invited to the affair (for example, to a meeting of the singing societies from various reservations).

PRINCIPLES GOVERNING THE "WHEN" OF CEREMONIAL PRACTICE

Consistent with the general idea of greeting expressed in the Thanksgiving Speech, ceremonials and other gatherings are apt to be held when something or some persons "arrive," "appear," or at least change in appearance, or even when it is wished something (such as rain) will appear. In instances involving only people (for example, council meetings), gatherings are held when an individual or individuals request such a meeting, that is, wish to meet with (appear with or before) others.

If the ritual is for one of the items mentioned in the Thanksgiving Speech, the ceremony itself recognizes a change in appearance, and is so timed. For example, the Maple ceremony is held when the sap begins to flow in the maple trees, the Strawberry ceremony "when the berries hang on the bushes," the Thunder ceremony when the Thunderers are first heard in the west in the spring or when it is wished that thunder will be heard and rain fall, the Sun ceremony when the sun begins to feel warm in the spring, the Green Bean ceremony when the green beans are mature, and the Green Corn ceremony when the first corn is ripe. These ceremonies and others of this type are calendric only in the sense that the changes recognized occur at a certain time of the year and not in the sense that they are set in accordance with a fixed division of the year into arbitrary segments. In fact, the date on which a particular ceremony is to be held usually is known only a week or two in advance.[5]

The importance of the dream in determining what should be done to cure a sick person and consequently when curing rituals should be given also seems to be part of the general Iroquois concern with appearance. To the Iroquois, the dream indicates what should be done to maintain or obtain good fortune in general, and so maintain or restore good health. If an ill individual has not had a dream indicating what should be done to effect a cure, another, sometimes termed a "fortuneteller" (Shimony 1961:270), is consulted. Such a person ascertains the cure, employing one or more of a number of techniques including dreaming, looking into a bowl of water, formerly looking at a robe or skin or into a fire, and more recently looking at tea leaves or cards. In general, then, both the type of cure and the necessity for it are indicated by an appearance of something to someone, often but not always in a dream.

PRINCIPLES GOVERNING THE "WHERE" OF CEREMONIAL PRACTICE

Gatherings, including ceremonials, open to all are held in the Longhouse and ceremonies open only to those who have been invited are held in private houses.[6] The major exception to this principle are ceremonies held in the so-called "closed" Longhouses, that is, those Longhouses closed to whites and sometimes also Christian Indians. However, this practice seems to be a relatively recent innovation, instituted in part to keep out the merely curious. In other Longhouses, no such rule presently obtains and the simple but effective device of not widely advertising the date of an upcoming ceremony keeps the merely curious away.

In general, then, the place the ceremonial or other gathering is held is correlated with who may properly attend or come, that is, who may "appear." The medicine societies are not so much "secret" societies as they have sometimes been termed (Parker 1909) as they are groups performing rituals usually open only to those invited. The so-called calendric ceremonies held in the Longhouse are not so much for the community (or for members of a sect—if the Longhouse may be termed such) as they are for the people generally, and consequently whoever wishes may attend.

PRINCIPLES GOVERNING THE "WHO" OF CEREMONIAL PRACTICE

A concern with appearance is also evident in the selection of those items mentioned in the ubiquitous Thanksgiving Speech. Included in this speech are some items we would classify as supernatural beings (for example, the Creator and the Four Beings), and others as belonging to the natural world including animate (people, animals, birds, plants, and trees) and inanimate things (earth, water, sun, moon, and stars) as well as natural phenomena (wind and thunder). But mentioning these diverse items together and treating them similarly in the Thanksgiving Speech (the section of the Thanksgiving Speech devoted to each follows the same form) suggests that to the Iroquois they all belong to the same class, that they all share some common characteristic. This characteristic may involve appearance: all are items whose appearance may change. Some (such as sun, moon, and animals) appear at different places at different times and others (such as plants, trees, and water) change their appearance at different times.

Thus, they may not be so much "spirit forces," as some (Speck 1949 and Fenton 1936) have termed them, as "appearances."

Somewhat similarly the tutelaries of the medicine societies are known from having been seen. For example, the False Faces are known from having been seen in a dream or in the forest. But these tutelaries have not appeared to all, and hence are not mentioned in the Thanksgiving Speech.

Who participates in the rituals and consequently where the ceremony is held also may well rest on the characteristic of appearance. Anyone (with the exceptions noted above) may participate in the ceremonies held in the Longhouse, and generally these ceremonials are for those appearances known to all. Participation in the rituals of a medicine society is largely limited to those who "belong" to the society, that is, to those who have been cured by the society, and each society generally holds its ceremony in a private house.

More generally, group affiliation in Iroquois society seems to rest on the quality of appearance together. Most Iroquois groups, including religious ones, exhibit few if any of the features usually regarded as characteristic of corporate groups. They are not so much closed, property-holding units as they are collections, of individuals who are apt to interact with each other, to be seen together on certain occasions. For example, one cannot join the Longhouse as one might join a Christian church, and the Longhouse does not own ritual or other intangible property. It is the kind of group quite accurately termed a "gang" in the Reservation English expression "Longhouse gang." Somewhat similarly, a medicine society is a group whose members have participated in the important rituals known to that society, that is, have been patients of and have been cured by the society.

In summary, then, I would suggest that the Iroquois are not the innocents portrayed by Alexander Pope in the lines:

> Lo, the poor Indian; whose untutor'd mind
> Sees God in clouds, or hears him in the wind; [7]

but rather, as Frank Cushing (1896:376) said of the Zuni, "theirs is a science of appearances and a philosophy of analogies."

All people, of course, must to a certain extent judge the nature of things on the basis of appearance. What may distinguish the Iroquois and perhaps also some other people is their attention to particular aspects of appearance that are of little consequence in Western society. At least I believe there is evidence for this in Iroquois religious practice. Ceremonials are held to greet the appearance of things or beings or a change in their appearance, and the things and beings so recognized are those that may change in appearance or may appear in different locations. The consideration of who may appear determines where a particular ceremony is held, and the appearance of the item being recognized by the ceremony dictates what rites are included in it. Even social groups are apt to be defined on the basis of appearance: that of being often seen together.

This attention to appearance may well be grounded in the economy once practiced by the Iroquois. Until the last century, the Iroquois practiced a mixed economy based on horticulture, fishing, hunting, and gathering—activities that required little ownership of land resources or means of production. Crucial for success in obtaining a livelihood probably was not control over property but knowledge of appearance. To be a successful hunter, one must pay attention to the appearance of the environment to know where the animals are. To be a successful fisherman, one must know when and where the fish will appear and how they appear in the waters. To be a successful gatherer of wild plants, one must know when they appear and which ones are useful to man—again to recognize appearance. And, as the Iroquois practiced slash-and-burn agriculture, what land might be cultivated may also have been recognized by its location and appearance.

To an extent, the Iroquois still find that attention to appearance is helpful in gaining a livelihood. Economic opportunities on the reservations are few, and the Iroquois who live on them often must "hunt" for jobs elsewhere. In this search, some find the old Iroquois assumptions about the world and life in it still useful, and as long as they do, the religion of the Longhouse may well continue also.

Notes

[1] There are eleven Longhouses located on various Iroquois reservations in New York and Canada. Three were established in this century: the Oneida Longhouse on the Oneida Reserve in Ontario, the Caughnawauga Longhouse on the Caughnawauga Reserve near Montreal, and the St. Regis Longhouse on the St. Regis Reserve situated on both sides of the Canadian–United States border. Three are located in western New York State: the Coldspring Longhouse on the Allegany Reservation, the Newtown Longhouse on the Cattaraugus Reservation, and the Tonawanda Longhouse on the Tonawanda Reservation. A seventh, the Onondaga Longhouse is located on the Onondaga Reservation south of Syracuse in central New York State. The other four are located on the large Six Nations Reserve in Ontario: the Onondaga, Seneca, Lower Cayuga, and Sour Springs (Upper Cayuga) Longhouses.

[2] Although not all published accounts of Iroquois religion have used precisely this classification, something similar to it is evident in many of them, for example, in those by Shimony (1961), Speck (1949:37–38), and Wallace 1966:75–80).

[3] In Iroquois culture, there seems to be a category of actions that includes speeches, songs, dances, and games which has no exact equivalent in ours. In Reservation English, reference to such activities is included in the word *doings*. For example, instead of saying, "I am going to the ceremony," an Iroquois is apt to say, "I am going to the doings." In a sense, the main events at such gatherings include one or more particular "doings" drawn from the total body of speeches, dances, songs, and games. The scope of the discussion here precludes consideration of certain combinations of doings, such as those combining speeches and dances. However, these practices are not inconsistent with the outline given. For example, the Feather Dance that follows each day's recitation of the Code of Handsome Lake during the Six Nations meetings recognizes the role of the Creator in these teachings: that through His messengers, the Creator told Handsome Lake what He wanted the Iroquois to do. Also precluded is discussion of the brief speeches announcing the dance, song, or game that precedes its performance, of dances as the Thanksgiving Dance that are part speech, and other comparable combinations.

[4] In the Iroquoian languages, the feminine gender is used as the generic for "mankind" rather than the masculine as in English. Thus, in Iroquoian pairs comparable to the English "man/woman," "woman" is the unmarked member and refers either to female human beings or to people generally.

5 This practice gives some further evidence that Titiev's —distinction between "calendrical" and "critical" ceremonies poorly fits the Iroquois data. Titiev (1960:293) states that "Because of their very nature calendrical rituals can always be scheduled and announced long in advance of their occurrence." The timing of Iroquois ceremonies suggests that most could equally well be classified as "critical" ones, ceremonies of the type Titiev (1960:294) regards as being "designed to meet the pressing needs of a given moment" and so "never . . . announced, scheduled, or prepared for far in advance" although they "may be designed to benefit . . . a whole society, a relatively small group, or even a single individual." Calendrical ceremonies (that is, ceremonies based on a true calendar) may be more common among those peoples having a division of labor that organizes society into functional groups, and so have what Durkheim (1933) called "organic solidarity." In Iroquois society, social solidarity seems to rest largely on similarities between individuals, not differences, and so on what Durkheim termed "mechanical" rather than organic solidarity. It may be that in societies with little organic solidarity, ceremonies usually are held in response to a situation known to all, rather than on an arbitrary date, set without regard to the wants and needs of individuals—a feature Titiev (1960:294) suggests means that calendrical ceremonies "can be interpreted only as having value for an entire society."

6 I became aware of this principle when a Seneca told me of a couple who wished to be married in the Longhouse (a relatively infrequently performed ritual that seems to have developed relatively recently in response to white emphasis on their own forms of legal marriage) and to have only invited guests there (in obvious emulation of common practice among whites). They were told that if they wished to have the ceremony in the Longhouse, they could not limit attendance to those receiving invitations because the Longhouse was open to all.

7 *An Essay on Man* (1733), Epistle I, 11. 99–100.

References

Aberle, David F., 1963. Some Sources of Flexibility in Navaho Social Organization. *Southwestern Journal of Anthropology* 19:1–8.

Chafe, Wallace L., 1961. *Seneca Thanksgiving Rituals,* Bureau of American Ethnology Bulletin 183 (Washington, DC: Government Printing Office).

Cushing, Frank Hamilton, 1896. *Outlines of Zuni Creation Myths.* In *Thirteenth Annual Report of the Bureau of American Ethnology* (Washington, DC: Government Printing Office), pp. 321–447.

Durkheim, Émile, 1933. *The Division of Labor in Society,* trans. George Simpson (Glencoe: Free Press).

Fenton, William N., 1936. *An Outline of Seneca Ceremonies at Coldspring Longhouse,* Yale University Publications in Anthropology 9 (New Haven: Yale University Press).

———, 1941. *Tonawanda Longhouse Ceremonies: Ninety Years after Lewis Henry Morgan,* Bureau of American Ethnology Bulletin 128 (Washington, DC: Government Printing Office).

———, 1953. *The Iroquois Eagle Dance: An Offshoot of the Calumet Dance,* Bureau of American Ethnology Bulletin 156 (Washington, DC: Government Printing Office).

Geertz, Clifford, 1966. Religion as a Cultural System. In *Anthropological Approaches to the Study of Religion,* Michael Banton, ed., Association of Social Anthropologists Monographs No. 3 (London: Tavistock Publications), pp. 1–46.

Hallowell, A. Irving, 1960. Ojibwa Ontology, Behavior, and World View. In *Culture in History: Essays in Honor of Paul Radin,* Stanley Diamond, ed. (New York: Columbia University Press), pp. 19–52.

Kluckhohn, Clyde, 1949. *Mirror for Man* (New York: McGraw-Hill).

———, and Leland C. Wyman, 1940. *An Introduction to Navaho Chant Practice,* American Anthropological Association Memoir 53 (Menasha, WI: George Banta).

Morgan, Lewis H., 1851. *League of the Ho-de-no-sau-nee, or Iroquois* (Rochester: Sage and Brother).

Oswalt, Wendell H., 1973. *This Land Was Theirs,* 2nd ed. (New York: John Wiley and Sons).

Parker, Arthur C., 1909. Secret Medicine Societies of the Seneca. *American Anthropologist* 11:161–185.

Sapir, Edward, 1949a. The Grammarian and His Language. In *Selected Writings of Edward Sapir,* David G. Mandelbaum, ed. (Berkeley: University of California Press), pp. 150–159.

———, 1949b. The Unconscious Patterning of Behavior in Society. In *Selected Writings of Edward Sapir,* David G. Mandelbaum, ed. (Berkeley: University of California Press), pp. 544–559.

Shimony, Annemarie Anrod, 1961. *Conservatism among the Iroquois at the Six Nations Reserve,* Yale University Publications in Anthropology 65 (New Haven: Department of Anthropology, Yale University).

Speck, Frank G., 1949. *Midwinter Rites of the Cayuga Long House* (Philadelphia: University of Pennsylvania Press).

Titiev, Mischa, 1960. A Fresh Approach to the Problem of Magic and Religion. *Southwestern Journal of Anthropology* 16:292–298.

Tooker, Elisabeth, 1970. *The Iroquois Ceremonial of Midwinter* (Syracuse: University of Syracuse Press).

Tylor, Edward B., 1958. *Religion in Primitive Culture* (New York: Harper and Brothers). (Originally published in 1873 as chs. 11–19 of *Primitive Culture.)* Wallace, Anthony F. C., 1966. *Religion: An Anthropological View* (New York: Random House).

Whorf, Benjamin Lee, 1956. Science and Linguistics. In *Language, Thought, and Reality: Selected Writings of Benjamin Lee Whorf,* John B. Carroll, ed. (New York: Wiley), pp. 207–219.

QUESTIONS FOR DISCUSSION

1. What does "metaphysical" mean? What does "ethnometaphysical" mean?

2. What are the main aspects of Iroquois ritual as Tooker describes them? Can you distinguish between those elements in the description that reflect Tooker's comparative knowledge as a professional anthropologist and those that are expressions of the Iroquois' own ideas about what they are doing?

3. What does Iroquois ritual have to do with appearances?

4. How would the Iroquois explain the purpose of their rituals?

SUGGESTED READINGS OR OTHER RESOURCES

General Works

Bourguignon, Erika. 1973. *Religion, Altered States of Consciousness, and Social Change.* Columbus: Ohio State University Press.

Crapo, Richley H. 2003. Religious Ritual. In *Anthropology of Religion: The Unity and Diversity of Religions* by Richley H. Crapo. Boston: McGraw Hill (pp. 179-207).

Smart, Ninian. 1996. The Ritual Dimension. In *Dimensions of the Sacred: An Anatomy of the World's Beliefs* by Ninian Smart. Berkeley: University of California Press (pp. 70-129).

Selected Case Studies

Canizares, Raul. 1993. *Walking with the Night: The Afro-Cuban World of Santeria*. Rochester, VT: Destiny Books.

Dugan, Kathleen. 1985. *The Vision Quest of the Plains Indians: Its Spiritual Significance*. New York: Mellen Press.

Fleurant, Gerdes. 1996. *Dancing Spirits: Rhythms and Rites of Haitian Vodun*. Westport, CT: Greenwood Press.

Lewis, William F. 1993. *Soul Rebels: The Rastafari*. Prospect Heights, IL: Waveland Press.

Mooney, James. 1965 [1896]. *The Ghost Dance Religion and the Sioux Outbreak of 1890*. Chicago: University of Chicago Press.

Wallace, Anthony F.C. 1969. *The Death and Rebirth of the Seneca*. New York: Vintage.

Williams, Francis E. 1977 [1923]. *"The Vailala Madness" and Other Essays*. Honolulu: University Press of Hawaii.

Videos

For Those Who Sail to Heaven (First Run Icarus Films) is a 48-minute presentation of the ritual of the Opet Festival (Sufi Rites) in Egypt.

The Night of San Lazaro (First Run Icarus Films) is a 35-minute look at "Cuba's most important parade," one that celebrates a figure some say is a Christian healer/saint and others say is an African deity.

5

The **Mythological Component** of the **Sacred**

featuring

**"Gilgamesh and Christ: Two Contradictory Models
of Man in Search of a Better World"
by Miles Richardson**

In the previous chapter we noted that the everyday use of the word "ritual" is at odds with the connotations of that term as used by students of religion. The ordinary meaning has pejorative implications that we need to set aside when studying religious ritual in an anthropologically sound manner. The same situation holds true in the case of the next element in the system of religion; indeed, in the case of mythology the pejorative connotations are even stronger and so we must work even harder to overcome them.

For most people, a **myth** is any erroneous belief (e.g., "It's a myth that it's always sunny in Florida"), and a "mythology" is any collection of tales associated with an outmoded belief system or exotic culture. It is perfectly acceptable to talk about the myths of ancient Greece and Rome, and to enjoy those stories simply as literature. But if we refer to the mythic elements in the Bible or the Qur'an we are apt to give deep offense to a great many people in our own society, since in this context the word "myth" seems to imply that those scriptures are based on untruths.

In our discussion, however, we will see that mythology is a component of *every* religion, even those that, in accordance with Geertz's definition, seem to be secular in origin. Even "science" might be considered a religion (because it is a system of symbols, etc.) and it has its own mythology. Saying so does not in any way suggest that science is false or outdated, just that it operates in much the same way as any other pervasive, powerful system or belief and action, which means that it does indeed include myth in its framework.

So what is a myth? Perhaps the best way to express it is to say that a myth is a *story*. It is not an isolated belief, but a complete and often complex narrative. More specifically, it is a story that serves several purposes within the framework of a religious system. We will discuss those purposes in greater detail below, but for the moment we can say that any story is meant to be shared; the act of sharing conveys specific bits of information, of course, but it also serves to link the storyteller and his or her audience in a special way. Storytelling, particularly when it

123

involves stories that deal with the origins and identity of a people, is a way to ground abstract ideas in readily digestible form and to make people feel part of something larger than themselves. So mythology is as much a social process as it is a body of completed tales that sit on a bookshelf. As such, we are not concerned with whether a mythology is "right" or "wrong"; as anthropologists our job is simply to document the kinds of stories members of a religious tradition share with one another and to determine the consequences of their decision to believe and to share their belief.

WHY PEOPLE SHARE MYTHS

In the chapter on belief we saw that participating in ritual and myth was one way that people become believers and sustain their beliefs. Ritual reinforces their commitment by allowing them to participate in activities that are common to the group and that differentiate their group from all others (the Durkheim view of the essence of all religious life). In the chapter on ritual, we saw that every ritual has a mythological component—stories that explain why the ritual is conducted and how it should be maintained. In the absence of such explanation, ritual would indeed be as mindless as the popular stereotype would have it. So mythology is intrinsic to the ways in which beliefs are propagated and the ways in which rituals are carried out.

In that sense we might say that myth is a kind of "charter" for religion, much like a constitution for a nation or a set of bylaws for an organization. The capacity of mythology to serve as a charter is based on its explanation of origins. Remember that to be truly religious, any set of ideas must ultimately be expressed in terms of "concepts of a general order of existence"; they must help believers see how everything fits together (since the alternative—chaos—is not an attractive one for most people). But those abstract concepts are sometimes difficult for ordinary people to grasp. The charismatic mystic has had experiences that are almost literally unspeakable. How, then, can that mystic convince others that he or she has come up with a compelling explanation for everyone's perceived problems? Perhaps the most important way is for the leader to convey the essence of his or her revelation in the form of a story, with recognizable characters and a plot that mirrors the actions with which real people can identify.

A story with truly mythic qualities explains not only *how* things are, but *why* they must be that way. For that reason, the characters in mythic stories are usually referred to as **archetypes**—great, transcendent role models for what people are supposed to be and do (or, in some cases, for what they are *not* supposed to be or do). We sometimes refer to westerns as "mythic" stories about American culture, not because there was no Old West or because people like cowboys never existed, but because the western explains how the supposed virtues of American culture (independence, honesty, a concern for justice) were forged out a particular set of experiences; the cowboys, whatever their real qualities may have been, are seen in retrospect to have embodied those virtues in a particularly powerful way. So the mythic cowboy is an archetype of American culture in that he is a recognizable character—a working man doing easily understandable tasks—who goes about his activities in ways that can be taken as exemplary. He is presented to us as having the kind of *character* that supposedly typifies our national identity, and he is the standard to which we are expected to aspire. In exactly the same way, the ancient warrior heroes of the Greek epics may or may not in real life have been as noble as Homer depicted them; but it is Homer's vision that has survived, and for many centuries both the *Iliad* and the *Odyssey* were the gold standards in Western culture for judging human behavior. Both those epics explain quite clearly—in the form of dramatically arresting narratives—the origin of conflict. They spell out the often conflicting ways of gods and humans and present heroes who show us how we are expected to deal with the lot handed out to us in life.

THE ANALYSIS OF MYTH

Just as we learned to look for five categories that define any ritual we might observe, we can now discuss five elements that we will want to pay particular attention to when we study any myth from any religious system.

First, we will want to find out something about the **provenience** of the story. In other words, from what culture does the story come? Sometimes the culture in question is large, of "national" scope (e.g., ancient Greek, Mayan, twentieth century American), but it can also be something relatively specialized (e.g., an Internet-based *Star Wars* fan group). This matter can get complex when we deal with stories that have been translated across one or more cultural lines. For example, there is a story of a great, primeval flood in the mythologies of most of the people of ancient Mesopotamia. Some scholars have suggested that it reflects a dim memory of some long-ago catastrophe, but from our point of view, this speculation, while fascinating, is also irrelevant. Whether or not there was a great flood in actual history, the fact remains that people of many cultures continued to tell the tale. The story apparently had its origin in Sumeria, the first of the great civilizations of the Fertile Crescent. The form in which it is most familiar to us, the story of Noah and his ark, was probably picked up by the ancient Hebrews through their contact with the Babylonians. A complete scholarly disquisition on the flood story would trace its provenience through all these cross-cultural transmissions, but for most purposes (including those in the research explorations on p. 130) we can be satisfied with identifying the culture in which the specific form we are analyzing is told.

Next, we will want to summarize the **content** of the story. What are the main plot points? Who are the major characters? In discussing the content of a myth, we want to stick to the objective facts, almost as if we were journalists concerned with the standard questions: who? what? when? where? We would only be concerned with the question "why?" in terms presented by the story itself. For example, why did Noah build the ark? The story tells us it was because God commanded him to do so. God even gave him very explicit instructions about size, dimensions, building materials, and so forth. Any speculation as to Noah's other possible motives would be left to another part of the analysis.

Every story has, in addition to plot and character, a certain **form** that brings those elements of content together. Stories can, after all, be told in many ways. The same plot and characters can be conveyed via different literary **genres** (e.g., prose narrative, poetry, spoken drama, sung drama), each with its own conventions. For example, the epic poetry of Homer relies on traditional word usage and turns of phrase; the rhyme and meter impose a certain rhythm on the story (particularly when it is recited aloud). The *content* of the *Iliad* could certainly be conveyed as a prose story, a play, or an opera; but its impact on its audience in those forms would be different from the way the epic poem would be received. Whatever the genre, the myth is a story that uses the standard devices of literary language, including symbolism and metaphor. After all, when trying to convey transcendent reality, it is usually most effective to fall back on an "it is like this . . ." strategy rather than to try to describe something directly.

The matter of form also requires us to pay attention to the way in which the story unfolds, regardless of genre. For example, in standard Western narrative, there is an introduction to the setting and the characters, followed by some complicating action that poses a problem that the characters must solve; finally there is a resolution or outcome (happy or otherwise) in which the complications of the plot are unraveled. In general, then, there is an expectation of linear progress. But even in our own culture, we know that this standard form is subject to considerable variation. Many stories are told, for example, in flashback—characters at the "end" of the story relive events that happened previously. The Greeks referred to beginning a story *in media res* (literally, in the middle of things). Some literary artists use the technique of the "flashforward"—the action takes place in the future, even though the characters remain in the here and now. The recent popular movie *Memento* was told "backward," beginning at the end and working its way step-by-step back to the beginning. Different cultures will obviously have their own preferences for the ways in which they like their stories presented, and individual artists within those traditions may be free (up to a point) in playing with those traditions to make their storytelling all the more striking and memorable.

Another matter we will want to discuss is the **context** of the myth. Under what circumstances will the story be told? Who tells it? Who forms the audience? How often will it be told? Are there special accessories (music? furniture? costumes?) that are part of the story-telling process?

And finally, there is the question of *function*. We have already discussed the general functions of any myth in any culture, but in looking at a particular story we have to engage in some informed speculation about what might account for both formal and contextual elements in that story. For example, why are certain characters depicted in a certain way, performing certain actions? Why does the storyteller choose to use poetry rather than prose? Why is the story told only at night? And so forth.

There are, as might be expected, almost as many different ways to discuss the function of myth as there are analysts of myth. But most such discussions fit into one of three general categories. First, there is the **social function**, which seeks to link the elements of the story to particular features of the social organization of the people who share that story. This tradition is often associated with British social anthropologists like Bronislaw Malinowski (although it has been applied by scholars beyond that circle). Malinowski was one of the first scholars to understand the "charter" function of myth, and he believed that myth was a force that in effect maintained the entirety of the social order. Malinowski argued against the tendency to interpret myths in terms of their symbolism; myth is better seen, he believed, as "a narrative resurrection of a primeval reality."[1] In other words, the symbolism of a mythic narrative exists not for its own literary sake, but simply as a way of speaking about everyday things, although the myth invests those things with some sense of higher significance.

Malinowski recounts a myth told by the people of the Trobriand Islands in the western Pacific; he conducted extensive fieldwork in that region in the second decade of the twentieth century. The myth speaks of various conflicts among several animals (iguana, dog, pig, crocodile, snake, opossum) which are resolved when the dog, who originally had high prestige, was observed eating a kind of fruit scorned as dirty. The pig, who disdained such a meal, loftily concluded, "Thou eatest . . . dirt; thou art a low-bred, a commoner; the chief . . . shall be I."[2] According to Malinowski's interpretation, the clan whose totem (symbolic representative ancestor) is the pig now claims the highest social rank of chief. The myth is thus often cited in order to adjudicate disputes over land and fishing rights. Moreover, when visitors unfamiliar with the local system of rank were puzzled as to why the pig clan was preeminent, they would be told the story to explain the situation. It is not unlikely that the pig clan rose to prominence because it somehow managed to amass extra economic and/or military resources, but saying so flat out could be considered offensive. So the myth, which reverts back to a primeval time when the order of things was established (presumably forever), says in effect, "Well, that's the way things are supposed to be—why argue?"

One of the "symbolic" interpretations that Malinowski particularly disliked was that of the Freudian psychoanalysts, one type of **psychological function** of myth (the second of the three major categories). Freud's great insight was to state the equation: as the dream is to the individual, so the myth is to the society. Dreams, in Freudian analysis, symbolically express unconscious wishes; despite the often distorted imagery of dreams, they are very real once we plumb the depths of unconscious motivation. Freud also believed that all unconscious wishes are fundamentally sexual, for "humanity as a whole is oppressed by its sexual needs."[3] Sexual urges are represented in dreams (and myths) as fantasies of incest, castration, physical destruction, masturbation, penis envy, or homosexuality. A famous Freudian explanation of "Little Red Riding Hood" tells of a young woman who has become sexually mature (the color red symbolizes menstruation) but is still a virgin (she carries an unbroken bottle of wine to her grandmother). She meets a wolf (symbolizing predatory men) in the forest (giant phallic symbols). He eats her (a rape fantasy) but is later slain by a woodsman (fantasy of true love) who slices open the wolf (castration fantasy) to release the imprisoned (sexually repressed) girl.[4]

Freud's follower Carl Jung carried on the tradition of the psychoanalysis of myth, although he eventually departed in some significant ways from the master's teachings. For one thing, he came to believe that not all symbolism was necessarily sexual, although it did arise out of basic biological nature, which explains why there are so many similarities in myths from one culture to another. Jung believed that these similarities represented a "collective unconscious" that linked all humankind. The symbols might differ (depending on the physical surroundings of the particular culture), but the underlying mechanisms are universal. One of the recurring themes that particularly fascinated Jung is the *anima*, the Latin word for soul; usually represented as an old woman, she is said to stand in for man's unconscious self. She appears as a woman because she is also "the psychic representation of the minority of female genes in a male body."[5] For Jung, basic biological factors somehow enter the "preconscious psyche" of humans, and are released in the form of (individuals') dreams and (cultures') myths.

The psychoanalytic perspective is no longer in fashion among anthropologists because it seems to downplay the varieties of cultural experience by assuming a universal unconscious dimension to human experience. And yet non-Freudian and non-Jungian psychological interpretations of myth continue to be useful to anthropologists. For example, Clyde Kluckhohn conducted intensive ethnographic research among the Navaho[6] in the 1940s and 1950s. The Navaho, the largest Native tribe in the United States, live in the desert Southwest. In analyzing Navaho myths, Kluckhohn found a surprisingly high number of references to health and illness. Indeed, rather than the sexual anxieties typical of Freudian analysis, the Navaho seemed to be expressing their deep-set medical anxieties in their myths. While the Navaho certainly had a higher rate of illness than their Anglo neighbors, their medical problems were not more numerous or severe than those of their Native American neighbors (the various Pueblo people) whose mythology was not similarly focused on health imagery. Kluckhohn concluded that the Navaho anxiety about health reflected the circumstances of their economic life. The Pueblo people were agriculturalists, and their anxieties centered on natural phenomena (e.g., the weather). But the Navaho, who had traditionally been hunters and gatherers, seemed to be concerned that if they succumbed to ill health they would be unable to be efficient food collectors—the men could not go out to hunt and the women would be unable to join the gatherers. So, in Kluckhohn's view, people's worries do indeed get translated into the imagery of (personal) dreams and (collective) myths; those worries are not universally about sex, but reflect the particular circumstances to which members of a culture have to adjust.

Myth has also been analyzed in terms of its **structural function**, associated with the school of theory influenced by the French anthropologist Claude Lévi-Strauss,[7] who pointed out that while mythic narratives are neither obviously logical nor coherent there is still a striking degree of similarity among the myths of many different cultures. Strongly influenced by scholarship in the field of structural linguistics, Lévi-Strauss came to believe that just as all languages are made up of the same basic sounds rearranged in various combinations, so too myths could be reduced to their basic constituent units. The most fundamental structure of human thought (the one that generates all languages and hence all cultural products that rely on language, as myth certainly does) is the "binary opposition." Just as in language a sound (or combination of sounds) is meaningful only to the extent that it contrasts with another sound (or combination of sounds), so in myth, a story theme is meaningful only to the extent that it contrasts with another story theme. Myths are full of obvious binary oppositions (death vs. life, light vs. dark, culture vs. nature, youth vs. age, male vs. female, and so forth) plus many that are revealed only through the very detailed structural analysis method developed by Lévi-Strauss. Those details, which rely on massive amounts of textual source material in order to be operative, will not concern us here. But we can summarize the structuralist position by saying that the fundamental purpose of myth is to provide a logical model capable of overcoming the apparent contradictions between presumably opposing themes. One frequently cited structural analysis of the Book of Genesis holds that the narrative is built around an opposition of singularity and plurality; "unitary categories such as man alone, life alone, one river, occur only in ideal Paradise; in the real world things are multiple and divided; man needs a partner, woman; life has a partner, death."[8]

MYTHS AS SOCIAL ACTIONS

Myth is a highly formalized, complex type of communication. It involves people on the social level (tellers of stories and their audiences) and on the historical level (the stories are passed down from generation to generation and become part of the identifying markers of a culture). It also implicitly links people with the supernatural forces or beings who are involved in the stories or who stand behind the conflicts that engage the human characters in the stories. As a type of communication, therefore, myth cannot be seen simply as a collection of stories; it must be seen as part of an active process that expresses the most profound beliefs and explains the most important ritual activations of those beliefs. Although a particular mythic story may achieve some sort of "finished" form (as when the myths of the ancient Greeks were synthesized by Homer and then written down by the great playwrights and poets of classical Greece), the process of transmission is an ongoing cultural activity. In effect, when we stop telling stories about a social institution or belief or value, that thing no longer has any cultural relevance.

KEY CONCEPTS

Be sure you can define the following terms, and give at least one illustrative example of each:

- archetype
- content
- context
- form
- genre

- myth
- provenience
- psychological function of myth
- social function of myth
- structural function of myth

RESEARCH EXPLORATIONS

1. Interview a knowledgeable person from a religious tradition other than your own and ask him/her to share with you stories or other narratives of special importance in his/her tradition. Be careful about describing these stories as "myths" to the person you are interviewing (who may well think that referring to his or her sacred stories as "myths" is a kind of put-down), but ask that person to explain why the stories are of particular importance. Analyze one or more of these narratives, describing the provenience, content, context, and form. Discuss the function of the story; compare and contrast a psychological, social, and/or structural explanation of function. Share your results (and the stories) with the class.

2. The Book of Genesis in the Judeo-Christian Bible contains two narratives of creation (Genesis, chapter 1 and Genesis, chapter 2). Compare and contrast these two stories with regard to the elements of mythological analysis developed in this chapter. Prepare an in-class presentation of your findings.

3. Select either of the Genesis creation narratives and compare/contrast it with the "Hymn of Creation" included in the Hindu sacred text, the Rg Veda. Your comparison should include consideration of the five components of mythic analysis. Make sure to place both narratives in their appropriate cultural contexts. Prepare an in-class presentation of your findings.

4. Some apparently secular narratives in pop culture are often described as "mythic" (e.g., the classic western, as in the novels of Zane Grey or the movies of John Ford). In what ways do these narratives conform to the elements of myth discussed in this chapter? In what ways are they different? Prepare an in-class presentation, using dramatic readings or video clips to illustrate your findings.

Notes

[1] Malinowski, Bronislaw. 1992 [1925]. *Magic, Science and Religion and Other Essays*. Prospect Heights, IL: Waveland Press (p. 101).

[2] Malinowski, p. 112.

[3] Freud, Sigmund. 1938 [1900]. *The Interpretation of Dreams*, ed. A. A. Brill. New York: Random House Modern Library (p. 970).

[4] Fromm, Erich. 1951. *The Forgotten Language*. New York: Grove Press (pp. 240–241). Note that some scholars insist on a distinction between myths (which are said to have a high, serious purpose dealing with matters of transcendent importance) and folktales such as "Little Red Riding Hood." But the latter, although sometimes more lighthearted in tone, often deal with highly serious matters (they are, after all, one way in which moral values can be imparted even to young children) and may thus be analyzed in the same way as myths. The Freudians did not adhere to the distinction between myths and folktales, and without endorsing their analytic conclusions, we will follow their lead in that regard.

[5] Jung, Carl. 1938. *Psychology and Religion*. New Haven, CT: Yale University Press (p. 33).

[6] The people now prefer to spell their name "Navajo," but in Kluckhohn's time the spelling "Navaho" was in regular use.

[7] Lévi-Strauss, Claude. 1963. The Structural Study of Myth. In *Structural Anthropology*, tr. C. Jacobson and B. Schoepf. New York: Basic Books (pp. 186–205).

[8] Leach, Edmund. 1961. Lévi-Strauss in the Garden of Eden: An Examination of Some Recent Developments in the Analysis of Myth. *Transactions of the New York Academy of Sciences* 23:386–396.

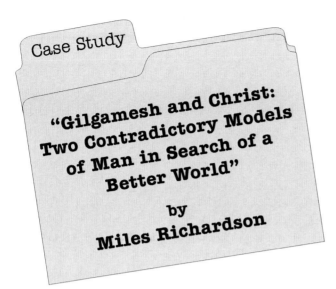

Gilgamesh was the central figure in various epic tales of Mesopotamia; stories in this tradition can be dated to at least 2000 B.C.E. Richardson compares and contrasts Gilgamesh and Jesus Christ as mythic heroes—archetypal characters in grand narratives of origin and moral purpose. He also offers some interesting observations on anthropologists as mythic figures in their own right and suggests that we might be better served with Gilgamesh (only partly divine, and intent on seeking knowledge) rather than with Christ (perfect, immortal) as our archetype.

Into the Temple where his mother dwelt Gilgamish[1] went, and when she saw by the look upon his face that he was bent upon going on some strange journey or upon doing some terrifying deed, his mother cried out to Shamash, The Sun God, asking him why he had given her son a heart that could never keep still. And Gilgamish, hearing her cry, said to her, "Peace O woman! I am Gilgamish, and it must be that I shall see everything, learn everything, understand everything." Then his mother said to him, "These longings are yours, O Gilgamish, because not all of you is mortal. Two thirds of your flesh is as the flesh of Gods and only one third is as the flesh of men. And because of the Gods' flesh that is on you, you must be always daring, always restless. But yet, O my son, you have not immortal life. You must die because part of you is man. Yea, Gilgamish, even you must die, and go down into the House of Dust."

And Gilgamish, hearing his mother say this, groaned loudly, terribly; and tears flowed down his cheeks; no word that was said to him might content him. He groaned, he wept, even although in the court of the Temple he heard the women sing:

Reprinted by permission of the Southern Anthropological Society from *Aspects of Cultural Change,* ed. Joseph B. Aceves (Proceedings #6, 1972), pp. 7–19.

"Who is splendid among men,
Who is glorious among heroes?"

And answer back, one to the other:

"Gilgamish is splendid among men
Gilgamish is glorious among heroes."

In a while he rose up and said, "O Ninsunna, O my mother, what is it to die?"

Then Ninsunna, his mother, made answer, and said, "It is to go into the abode out of which none ever returns; it is to go into the dark abyss of the dread Goddess, Irkalla. They who dwell there are without light; the beings that are there eat of the dust and feed on the mud."

So his mother said, and Gilgamish, the great king, groaned aloud, and tears flowed down his face. (Colum 1930: 19–20)

[Time moves; the scene changes.]

And when they had crucified him, they divided his garments among them by casting lots; then they sat down and kept watch over him there. And over his head they put the charge against him, which read, "This is Jesus the King of the Jews." Then two robbers were crucified with him, one on the right and one on the left. And those who passed by derided him, wagging their heads and saying, "You who would destroy the temple and build it in three days, save yourself! If you are the Son of God, come down from the cross." So also the chief priests, with the scribes and elders, mocked him, saying, "He saved others; he cannot save himself. He is the King of Israel; let him come down now from the cross, and we will believe in him. He trusts in God; let God deliver him now, if he desires him; for he said, I am the Son of God." And the robbers who were crucified with him also reviled him in the same way.

Now from the sixth hour there was darkness over all the land until the ninth hour. And about the ninth hour Jesus cried with a loud voice . . . "My God, my God, why hast thou forsaken me?" (Matthew 27:35–46)

Perhaps since the time of the australopithecines—those tiny brained, large jawed creatures who walked bipedally across Africa at the beginning of Pleistocene—change in the human species has been a series of adaptations to being human. For instance, the increase in brain size from the australopithecines to Neanderthal man reflects an adaptation to the human mode of exploiting the environment (Brace and Montagu 1965). The development of a self, which emerged through man's ability to treat himself as an object, is still another example (Hallowell 1959, 1968). In large measure, adaptation to being human is adjustment to the ability to symbolize, the ability to envisage a future, immediate or distant, and to organize one's energies, experiences, and desires in terms of that future. It is the ability to create a future and then to act as if that future were real and achievable.

Nowhere is this human ability so marked as in the case of death. Apparently man is the only life form that can terrify itself with visions of its own extinction. Once man has terrified himself with his visions, he struggles to overcome them, and the ultimate criterion of any utopia worthy of the name is a world without death.

The figures of Gilgamesh and Christ offer two contradictory models of man confronting his own knowledge. Both figures try to solve the problem of death; they both seek eternal life. Gilgamesh fails; Christ succeeds. Yet it is in Gilgamesh's failure rather than in Christ's success that we get a glimpse of the human condition and an example of our task as anthropologists.

Gilgamesh is the central figure in an epic that dates back to approximately 2,000 B.C.[2] In the epic Gilgamesh is king over the city state of Uruk. Even for those days, Gilgamesh is an extraordinary king. He is restless, strong, and full of lust, "leaving no virgin to her lover, neither the warrior's daughter nor the wife of the noble." He is two-thirds God and one-third man, and none can withstand him.

The people of Uruk begin to mutter among themselves about Gilgamesh and turn to the gods for relief from his restlessness. In answer the gods make Gilgamesh's equal, Enkidu, and send him to live in the wilderness with the animals. Enkidu loses his innocence to a temple harlot and from her hears about Gilgamesh. He brags to the harlot that he will go to Uruk and challenge Gilgamesh.

When he enters the city, he will cry out, "I am the strongest here, I have come to change the old order, I am he who was born in the hills, I am he who is the strongest of all."

Enkidu leaves for Uruk. As he approaches, people compare him with Gilgamesh: "He is the spit of Gilgamesh. He is shorter. He is bigger of bone. Now Gilgamesh has met his match." Gilgamesh walks out in the street. Enkidu blocks his way. "They grappled, holding each other like bulls. They broke the doorposts and the wall shook, they snorted like bulls locked together." Gilgamesh throws Enkidu, and Enkidu immediately recognizes Gilgamesh's superiority. They embrace and become fast friends.

Gilgamesh and Enkidu set out for the Land of the Cedars, for Gilgamesh wants to write his name in that place where no man has been. Enkidu warns him of the monster, Humbaba, who watches over the land. Gilgamesh with scorn replies, "Where is the man who can clamber to heaven? Only the gods live forever with glorious Shamash, but as for us men, our days are numbered, our occupations are a breath of wind. How is this, already you are afraid! I will go first although I am your lord, and you may safely call out, 'Forward, there is nothing to fear.'" With Enkidu shamed into following him, Gilgamesh enters the Land of Cedars. They encounter Humbaba, and after a furious struggle the two friends succeed in killing him. When they return, the goddess Ishtar sees them and is overwhelmed by Gilgamesh's beauty. She offers him her love, but Gilgamesh reminds her of how she has treated her former lovers: how she lured the lion into a trap; how she tricked the stallion into being captured and broken to the bit; and how she turned the shepherd into a wolf, so that "now his own herd-boys chase him away, his own hounds worry his flank." Gilgamesh suggests that the same thing may happen to him.

Ishtar is furious. She rushes off to her father and complains, "My father, Gilgamesh has heaped insults on me; he has told over all my abominable behaviour, all my tainted acts." Her father says that she has brought it upon herself and that he will not listen to her. But she threatens to break open the door of hell and let all the dead

out. So her father changes his mind and makes for her a bull of heaven. She turns the
bull loose on earth, and

> with his first snort he slew a hundred men, and again he slew two hundred, he
> slew three hundred; with his second snort hundreds more fell dead. With his
> third snort he charged Enkidu, but he dodged aside and leapt upon the Bull and
> seized it by the horns. The Bull of Heaven foamed in his face, it brushed him with
> the thick of his tail. Enkidu cried to Gilgamesh, "My friend, we boasted that we
> would leave enduring names behind us. Now thrust in your sword between the
> nape and the horns." So Gilgamesh followed the Bull, he seized the thick of its
> tail, he thrust the sword between the nape and the horns and slew the Bull.

Ishtar looked down at them and uttered a curse: "Woe to Gilgamesh, for he has
scorned me in killing the Bull of Heaven." When Enkidu heard these words he tore
out the Bull's right thigh and tossed it in her face saying, "If I could lay my hands on
you, it is this I should do to you, and lash the entrails on your side."

Shortly afterwards, Enkidu has a number of dreams, each about his own death.
He tells Gilgamesh,

> Last night I dreamed again, my friend. The heavens moaned and the earth
> replied; I stood alone before an awful being; his face was sombre like the black
> bird of the storm. He fell upon me with the talons of an eagle and he held me
> fast, pinioned with his claws, till I smothered; then he transformed me so that
> my arms became wings covered with feathers. He turned his stare towards me,
> and led me away to the palace of Irkalla, the Queen of Darkness, to the house
> from which none who enters ever returns, down the road from which there is
> no coming back. There is the house whose people sit in darkness; dust is their
> food and clay their meat. They are clothed like birds with wings for covering,
> they see no light, they sit in darkness.

Enkidu becomes very ill and after twelve days of suffering he dies on the
twelfth night. At the first light of dawn, Gilgamesh calls together the counse-
lors of Uruk and cries out:

Hear me, great ones of Uruk,
I weep for Enkidu, my friend,
Bitterly moaning like a woman mourning
I weep for my brother.
O Enkidu, the wild ass and the gazelle
That were father and mother,
All four-footed creatures who fed with you
Weep for you,
. . .
The mountain we climbed where we slew the watchman
Weeps for you,
Ula of Elam and dear Euphrates
Where once we drew water for the waterskins,
The warriors of strong-walled Uruk
Where the Bull of Heaven was killed,
Weep for you.
. . .

The tillers and harvesters
Who brought grain for you once
Mourn for you now.
The servants who anointed your body
Mourn for you now;
The harlot who anointed you with fragrant oil
Laments for you now.
The women of the palace, who brought you a wife
With the ring of your choice,
Lament for you now.
O my young brother Enkidu, my dearest friend,
What is this sleep which holds you now?
You are lost in the dark and cannot hear me.

The death of Enkidu awakens the fear in Gilgamesh that he too may well die. "Bitterly Gilgamesh wept for his friend Enkidu; he wandered over the wilderness as a hunter, he roamed over the plains; in bitterness he cried, 'How can I rest, how can I be at peace? Despair is in my heart.'"

Driven by his fear, Gilgamesh travels to find the one human who does have immortal life, Utnapishtim, the Faraway. In his journey, Gilgamesh encounters one difficulty after another. Some of these wear away at his great strength; others, such as the woman of the vine, try to confuse his purpose. She asks, "Gilgamesh, where are you hurrying to? You will never find that life for which you are looking. So fill your belly with good things; day and night, night and day, dance and be merry, feast and rejoice. Let your clothes be fresh, bathe yourself in water, cherish the little child that holds your hand, and make your wife happy in your embrace; for this too is the lot of man." But Gilgamesh's fear, fear of a man who is two-thirds god, will not let him rest nor rejoice.

Gilgamesh crosses the waters of death, and as he nears the shore, Utnapishtim sees him and wonders who is this poor traveler who staggers toward him. Aloud, he asks, "What is your name, you who come here wearing the skins of beasts, with your cheeks starved and your face drawn? Where are you hurrying to now?"

Gilgamesh explains that he is looking for life without death. Utnapishtim snorts, "There is no permanence. Do we build a house to stand for ever, do we seal a contract to hold for all time?" Gilgamesh replies, "How was it that you came to enter the company of the gods and to possess everlasting life?" Utnapishtim then tells him the story of the flood.

Once there was no death. Men did not die. Because they did not die, they became numerous. As men increased in numbers, they began making more and more noise. The noise that they made became so great that the gods complained that they could no longer sleep properly. So the gods decided to wash the world clean of men, and they let loose a deluge. However, one god had a human friend, Utnapishtim, and he told his friend to build a boat because the world was to be flooded. Utnapishtim listened to his god and built a boat big enough to contain all of his gold, his family and kin, the beasts of the field, and his craftsmen. The rains covered the earth, and only those in the boat did not drown. When the waters subsided, Utnapishtim prepared a sacrifice. When the gods smelled it, "they gathered like flies over the sacrifice." Satiated with the sacrifice and feeling remorseful over flooding the world, the gods granted Utnapishtim immortal life.

When Utnapishtim is finished with the story, he says to Gilgamesh, "As for you, Gilgamesh, who will assemble the gods for your sake, so that you may find that life for which you are searching?"

But Utnapishtim relents and puts Gilgamesh to a test. If Gilgamesh can stay awake for six days and seven nights, Utnapishtim will help him. No sooner than the test begins, Gilgamesh falls asleep. Utnapishtim remarks with scorn, "Look at him now, the strong man who would have everlasting life, even now the mists of sleep are drifting over him."

Utnapishtim lets Gilgamesh sleep for seven nights and then awakens him. When Gilgamesh realizes what he has done, he asks in despair, "What shall I do, O Utnapishtim, where shall I go? Already the thief in the night has hold of my limbs, death inhabits my room; wherever my foot rests, there I find death."

Wearily, Gilgamesh turns to go, but Utnapishtim tells him of one more chance to gain eternal life. At the bottom of the waters of death is a plant which restores lost youth to man. Gilgamesh goes to the bottom of the ocean and succeeds in getting the plant. In the company of Urshanabi, the ferryman, he crosses the waters of death and makes for Uruk. The two stop to rest beside a well of cool water. While Gilgamesh is preoccupied, a snake comes from the bottom of the well and eats the plant. Gilgamesh sits down and weeps, "O Urshanabi, was it for this that I toiled with my hands, is it for this I have wrung out my heart's blood? For myself I have gained nothing; not I, but the beast of the earth has joy of it now. I found a sign and now I have lost it. Let us leave the boat on the bank and go."

On the outskirts of Uruk, Gilgamesh looks at his city and says to Urshanabi, "Climb up on the wall of Uruk, inspect its foundation terrace, and examine well the brickwork; see if it is not of burnt bricks; and did not the seven wise men lay these foundations? One third of the whole is city, one third is garden, and one third is field, with the precinct of the goddess Ishtar. These parts and the precinct are all Uruk."

This too was the work of Gilgamesh, the king, who knew the countries of the world. "He was wise, he saw mysteries and knew secret things, he brought us a tale of the days before the flood. He went on a long journey, was weary, worn out with labour, and returning engraved on a stone the whole story."

The epic of Gilgamesh is the account of a man who wants to see everything, learn everything, and understand everything. He has these desires to an extraordinary degree because he is two-thirds God. He feels the approach of death more than the ordinary man, and he strives to conquer it. Yet he fails. He fails because he is one-third man. As his godly part drives Gilgamesh to risk great achievements, so his human part insures that he will fail. He is a tragic hero, a person magnificent in strength, splendid in appearance, courageous in heart, but with one fatal fault: he is one-third man. His epic is an account of what constitutes man's lot. Man's lot is that he question, but it is equally man's lot that he receive no answer.

The figure of Christ provides a very different model of man in search of a better world. There are, of course, several Christs. There is the Christ of Spanish America who teaches man how to suffer (Richardson, Bode, and Pardo 1971); there is King Jesus who rides his white horse ahead of the black congregations of the South; and then there is the swingingest figure of them all—Jesus Christ: Superstar.

The figure that I am referring to is the Protestant Christ, especially the traditional, orthodox one. This is the Christ who is somehow both an effeminate figure who bids you in a sweet voice to turn the other cheek and a merciless individual who will watch you burn in Hell—and not bat an eyelash. In any attribute, he is perfection, unalterable perfection. If there are any of his movements, desires, or expressions that you do not understand, it is because of your inability to comprehend, because of your limitations as a mere human. Thus, when Jesus said on the cross, "My God, my God, why hast thou forsaken me?" he may have been posing a puzzle for mankind, but he most certainly was not expressing doubt about his own godhood.

This traditional Christ has the same task as Gilgamesh: to conquer death. Yet in every other respect he is in complete contrast to Gilgamesh. Unlike Gilgamesh, Christ is fully God. To be sure, he has a human exterior, and he has to suffer the pain and indignities that this human exterior brings him. But within, he is pure God—and he knows it. In contrast to Gilgamesh's aristocracy, Christ on earth belongs to the lower class. While Gilgamesh performs great feats of physical prowess, Jesus works miracles of healing and raising the dead. Only when he chases the moneychangers out of the temple does Jesus exhibit a physical strength. He is almost sexless and is free of lust; Gilgamesh, on the other hand, leaves "no virgin to her lover."

Gilgamesh responds with great feeling only to his close friend, Enkidu. He has no message for other men; what he seeks, he seeks for himself. He seeks what only the gods have: eternal life. Driven by the hope that he will not fail, Gilgamesh risks all in the effort. With success literally in his hand, he is careless for a brief moment and fails. Jesus, on the other hand, is sensitive to the conditions and feelings of all people, even strangers. He is a teacher with a message. He teaches that if people will follow him and believe in him, they will have eternal life. To demonstrate that he is God, he does the one thing that only God can do: he conquers death. Knowing that he cannot fail, Jesus allows himself to be crucified. He is reborn after three days, and in doing so, he shows all that he is God. All those who believe in him will likewise be reborn.

The model that the image of Christ provides is a model of progress, success, utopia. It is the picture of man as God. If man has sufficient faith in God, he can conquer any obstacle, even death. If man will but submit himself to the right authority, if he will but follow the right creed, then he will succeed. He can remake the world. Man can achieve perfection—if not now, then in the next five minutes; if not then, a year from now, a century, two centuries, a thousand years from now. The millennium will come. The perfect world, a world without sin, without oppression, without racial hatred, without atomic fallout, without pollution, without all those actions and emotions that make man less than God, is attainable. Man can aspire to be God.

Such an aspiration, of course, is not limited to Christians. As Peacock and Kirsch (1970:202–217) have pointed out, the Christ model has become secularized into a basic tenet of American culture. Working with a model which calls for man to remake his evil world into the shape of God's saintly one, secular American culture has produced a model of two contrasting types. One type is a constellation of all the undesirable characteristics; the second type is the epitome of all that is good, true, and useful. Despite occasional minor reverses, movement is from the first, the bad, to the second, the good.

Such polar contrasts appear frequently in the scholarly discussions about modernization-developmental processes into a type of evolutionism that is as ethnocentric as the brashest Victorian theoretical scheme (Hoetink 1965). The scholar proceeds by contrasting type one, traditional society, with type two, modern society. Societies become modernized and developed to the extent that they leave type one and approach type two. So far so good. But the traditional type is often a patchwork construct pieced together with features of the most backward societies. The traditional type is Papa Doc's Haiti in Hell. The modern type is a glittering edifice elegantly devised from the best features of the most advanced societies. The modern type is General Ike's America in Heaven.

In a recent seminar on Latin American agricultural development, the speaker was contrasting the agricultural practices of type one, the Nicaraguan peasant, with type two, the American agro-businessman. To make his point, the speaker showed a slide of the peasant striding alongside his oxen as they pulled a solid wooden-wheeled cart across the Nicaraguan landscape. The speaker asked us to compare the cart with automated mechanical creatures that waddle their way through the California lettuce fields. In his accompanying remarks the speaker showed no appreciation of the antiquity of the cart or of its effectiveness in uneven terrain. He ignored the ingenuity of the peasant in utilizing scarce resources, nor did he mention the asymmetrical power relations between Nicaragua and the United States, relations that may have helped create the limited, scarce environment in which the Nicaraguan works.

The employment of the model of contrasting types is not restricted to agricultural studies. The management field utilizes the model when it compares the practices of management in traditional society with those of modern society. One student of management contrasts the Mexican and North American organization men in this fashion: "Fear" characterizes the relationship between the typical Mexican manager and his superiors. He attempts to "avoid" or "outmaneuver" his organizational equals. He sees subordinates as "unreliable and untrustworthy tools." In contrast, the typical United States type "respects" his superiors, "cooperates" with his equals, and sees his subordinates as "helpers" (Fayerweather 1959:31–41; Richardson 1966).

In political science the employment of the model of two contrasting types makes the Latin American system of elite replacement equal to political instability and immaturity, unrepresentative government, and apathetic masses. It makes the system that the United States uses to replace its elite equal to political stability and maturity, democratic government, and a participating, involved citizenry. These equations justly earn Leeds's contempt as being "pernicious in their ethnocentricism [and in] their evangelical assurance of righteousness" (1968:85).

Evangelical arrogance is by no means restricted to political science. One can detect it, now and again, among the voices raised in the not so deliberate meetings of the American Anthropological Association. In that nervous body, it passes as very radical chic, expounded by bourgeois adventurers and adventuresses, their minds bedazzled by the image of themselves as Christ—Che Guevara incarnate leading the admiring masses to victory against the capitalistic, imperialistic, warmongers of Wall Street.

The Christ model of man in search of a better world is at its best when it is used as a model for action. Any model which guarantees that whosoever follows it will live forever (and succeed always) is going to be popular. However forceful the model may be in stimulating action, as a model for comprehension it produces farcical results. For it is a model that lacks tolerance, humor, and skepticism, that lacks an appreciation of alternatives, that lacks all those attributes that characterize the anthropological perspective.

Instead of depicting man as God, the Gilgamesh model pictures man as hero. Instead of being a model of utopia, it is a model of effort, of drive, of risk, and of failure. Gilgamesh strives to be perfect, but he is man and he fails. In these two acts of effort and of collapse, we find ourselves.

We utilize the magic of symbols, of culture, to construct an image of the future. With our magic, we reify that image and convince ourselves and others that the image is not an image but reality itself. With the pure commitment of the insane, we proceed toward that tantalizing image, full of confidence that we will succeed.

The future that we seek may be immediate or distant; it may evoke the behavior of a few or stimulate action on the part of many. It may be the modest image of two anthropologists at the bar discussing Lévi-Strauss over bourbon and branch, or it may be the hopeful vision of a nation meeting its obligation to its poor. But the future in the image is imaginary; it is our fantasy of what we expect to encounter, and not what we will actually meet. Even our best images, our most scientific models, our most elegant ethnosemantic charts have this flaw. Because we as men live within a world that is symbolic and not real, we err, inevitably so. Sooner or later our symbols depart too far from reality and we crash against the unexpected. Instead of discussing Lévi-Strauss, the two anthropologists get drunk (which may be an improvement); instead of offering dignity to its poor, the nation casts them out. The very thing that leads us on insures that we will fail. It is because of the ability to utilize symbols that we strive; it is because of the same ability that we fail.

Although we fail, we cannot rest with failure. That which makes us human picks us up from the floor and we are off, as Utnapishtim might say, on another fool's errand. Only when we cease being human will we cease failing, and only when we cease failing will we cease striving to accomplish what cannot be accomplished. Yes, we may be fools, but we are heroic fools. We will end the world not with a whimper, but with a big, loud bang.

If this is the way man is, then cannot he, like Gilgamesh, take satisfaction in what he can accomplish and in what he is? If he cannot achieve perfection, he can nonetheless build what no other animal can build, and if he cannot be God, he can be what he is. What man is, is what he is now—and what he was at the beginning of the Pleistocene. He is a two-legged primate, struggling. He is "always daring, always restless, with a heart that can never keep still"; he is "bent upon going on some strange journey or upon doing some terrifying deed."

To recite the epic of man is the task of the anthropologist. He has the unique charge of celebrating man's acts. He is man's poet. As man's poet, the anthropologist tells of how man plays his part in a drama that is simultaneously one of horror and one of hope. He has to tell of Auschwitz where man bathed his own kind in poison gas. He has to tell of My Lai and to recite to the rhythm of his own guilt the words of our time: "Waste them." The anthropologist must speak of man's failures, for these are the things that men do. But when he is weary of man's defeats, he can sing of other occasions when man somehow reaches out to other men and expresses with a few words the hopes of all. Such an occasion took place when a Southern black man stood in Washington, D.C., and shook the world with "I have a dream." Still another occasion took place when after a long, bitter war Chief Joseph of the Nez Perce Indians spoke for us:

I am tired of fighting. Our chiefs are killed. Looking Glass is dead. Toohulhul-sote is dead. The old men are all dead. It is the young men who say no and yes. He who led the young men is dead. It is cold and we have no blankets. The little children are freezing to death. My people, some of them, have run away to the hills and have no blankets, no food. No one knows where they are—perhaps they are freezing to death.

I want to have time to look for my children and see how many of them I can find. Maybe I shall find them among the dead. Hear me my chiefs, I am tired. My heart is sad and sick. From where the sun now stands, I will fight no more forever.

Anthropology has the unique charge of celebrating the whole of mankind, but it has a special obligation to those groups who have little power, who live at minimal subsistence levels; whom the currents of history have bypassed, whom the superpowers ignore or manipulate to their own advantage. Paul Radin wrote in 1933 that it is to these people that the anthropologist owes his first loyalty (1933:x). Surely by now we are aware of this obligation. Likewise we are by now aware of the delicate nature of this relationship. The fine strands of the relationship between the anthropologist and these groups cannot support the heavy sentiment of the romantic anthropologist leading "his people" on to victory, just as they cannot withstand the scientific arrogance of those who look for subjects and not for informants.

Yet anthropology is anthropology. It is not the study of men, but of man. To contemplate man we cannot use a model based on the smooth flow of action produced by the uneventful life of a god, but rather we need a model based on the outrageous contradiction of an imperfect man seeking perfection. The god model of Christ leads us away from the study of man because it bedazzles us with the promise that someday we will cease to be human and become God. The man model of Gilgamesh holds out no such hope. With it we can come closer to understanding what it is to be human. With it we can tell the story of man. In the future, in the distant future, perhaps some will find the epic that we have written and read there that man knew the countries of the world. "He was wise, he saw mysteries and knew secret things, he brought us a tale of the days before the flood. He went on a long journey, was weary, worn out with labour, and returning engraved on a stone the whole story."

NOTES

[1] The English spelling of Gilgamesh varies, with Gilgamesh being most common. Colum spells the name Gilgamish.

[2] This summary and the quotations contained within it are from Sandars (1960). Sandars has done an excellent job of combining scholarship with a highly readable text, and the reader is referred to this source for additional background material on Gilgamesh and his times.

REFERENCES

Brace, C. Loring, and M. F. Ashley Montagu, 1965. *Man's Evolution* (New York: Macmillan).

Colum, Padraic, 1930. *Orpheus: Myths of the World* (New York: Macmillan).

Fayerweather, J., 1959. *The Executive Overseas* (Syracuse, N.Y.: Syracuse University Press).

Hallowell, A. Irving, 1959. Behavioral Evolution and the Emergence of the Self. In *Evolution and Anthropology: A Centennial Appraisal,* Betty J. Meggers, ed. (Washington, DC: Anthropological Society of Washington).

————, 1968. Self, Society and Culture in Phylogenetic Perspective. In *Culture: Man's Adaptive Dimension,* M. F. Ashley Montagu, ed. (London: Oxford University Press).

Hoetink, H. 1965. El nuevo evolucionismo. *América Latina* 8:26–42.

Leeds, Anthony, 1968. Comment on Political Instability in Latin America: The Cross-Cultural Test of a Causal Model. *Latin American Research Review* 3:79–86.

Peacock, James L., and A. Thomas Kirsch, 1970. *The Human Direction* (New York: Appleton-Century-Crofts).

Radin, Paul, 1933. *Method and Theory in Ethnology* (New York: McGraw-Hill).

Richardson, Miles, 1966. The Possibility of an Anthropology-Management Symbiosis. *South Eastern Latin Americanist* 10:1–3.

————, Barbara Bode, and Marta Eugenia Pardo, 1971. The Image of Christ in Spanish America as a Model for Suffering: An Exploratory Note. *Journal of Inter-American Studies* 13:246–57.

Sandars, N. K., 1960. *The Epic of Gilgamesh* (London: Penguin Books).

QUESTIONS FOR DISCUSSION

1. What are the main differences between Gilgamesh and Christ? What were their respective goals in life?

2. Why, according to Richardson, is Christ an enduring hero in our culture?

3. What implications does the Christ narrative have for the way Christians live their lives? What implications does it have for non-Christians who nonetheless live in Christian-influenced societies?

SUGGESTED READINGS OR OTHER RESOURCES

General Works

de Waal Malefijt, Annemarie. 1989 [1968]. Myth and Ritual,. In *Religion and Culture: An Introduction to the Anthropology of Religion* by A. de Waal Malefijt. Prospect Heights, IL: Waveland (pp. 172–195).

Eliade, Mircea. 1960. *Myths, Dreams, and Mysteries,* tr. Philip Mairet. New York: Harper.

Smart, Ninian. 1996. The Mythic or Narrative Dimension. In *Dimensions of the Sacred: An Anatomy of the World's Beliefs* by Ninian Smart. Berkeley: University of California Press (pp. 130–165).

Selected Case Studies

Boretz, Avron A. 1995. Martial Gods and Magic Swords: Identity, Myth, and Violence in Chinese Popular Religion. *Journal of Popular Culture* 29:93–109.

Doniger, Wendy. 2000. The Mythology of the Face-Lift. *Social Research* 67:99–125.

Dundes, Alan. 1962. Earth-Diver: Creation of the Mythopoeic Male. *American Anthropologist* 64:1032–1051.

Middleton, John. 1954. Some Social Aspects of Lugbara Myth. *Africa* 24:189–199.

Videos

Eyanopapi: The Heart of the Sioux (Insight Media) is a 30-minute retelling of creation stories of the Sioux, a native people of South Dakota.

The Mahabharata (Insight Media) is a 166-minute film adaptation of the great ancient Hindu saga of war and the epic battles of feuding clans.

6

The Ethical and Moral Components of the Sacred

featuring

"The Navaho View of Life"
by Clyde Kluckhohn and Dorothea Leighton

Religion is a way for people to orient themselves to the supernatural—a way of understanding realities that transcend those that can be perceived through the five ordinary senses. But it is also a way for people to orient themselves to one another. Beliefs about even the loftiest supernatural and transcendent things are ultimately translated into everyday behavior because people always want to know, "What is the right thing to do?" "How am I supposed to act?" "What constitutes the good life?"

Every society therefore has a *moral* code, accepted notions of right and wrong. **Morality** is usually enshrined in the traditional **value system** of a society; it is part of the customary lore of a people and is handed down from one generation to another either by formal instruction or (more likely) through informal processes of transmission (e.g., the sharing of exemplary stories). The moral code of any given society provides guidelines for the making of decisions about how to behave. **Ethics** is a term used to describe the rational discussion of that process of moral decision making. Ethics is also the social dimension of morality: we can think "immoral" thoughts in private, but there is only a question of ethics that must be discussed and solved when we act on our thoughts and our actions impinge on others.

When moral principles and ethical guidelines are backed up by **sanctions**, they become **laws**. Sanctions are means by which actions are either rewarded (positive sanctions) or punished (negative sanctions); the punishments and/or rewards may be administered by authorized members of society (civil sanctions) or dealt with by deities or other nonhuman agents (supernatural sanctions); the punishments/rewards may be written into a consistent legal system (formal law) or they may be carried out arbitrarily or capriciously (informal sanctions). Sanctions or laws thus express a society's judgment about those elements of the general moral code that are most worthy of attention. In Western culture, for example, the taking of a human life is (with just a few exceptions) against the law; stepping on an ant is not a punishable offense. But a Jain (an adherent of a religion of South Asia derived from Hinduism) might disagree, because in that religious tradition, the taking of *any* life is morally objectionable.

Anthropologists recognize that certain values might be universal, but while principles may be general, the applications are not. Take, for example, the prohibition against murder. Some cultures define human life in the broadest possible terms, such that the taking of any life, for any reason, is wrong. But many traditional cultures had more narrow boundaries. The tribal names of many traditional groups can be translated as "the people," as if to imply that everyone else is somehow less than human. Outsiders might thus treated with suspicion, perhaps even hostility and aggression; killing an outsider would be a considerably lesser offense than killing a member of "the people." In a similar fashion, it is certainly true that the incest taboo is universal. But the application varies widely. In our society, kinship organization is focused on the nuclear family, and while we might be unhappy over sexual relations involving cousins, they would not evoke the same horror as mating between parents and children, or between siblings. But in societies with extended kinship systems (lineages, clans, etc.), all members of that large group would be covered by the incest taboo. In unilineal descent systems, one traces one's blood kin only on one "side" of the family—that is, one is descended either from the mother *or* the father, not both, as in our system. The incest taboo in cultures featuring unilineal descent would apply only to the "blood" side of the family, the other side being relatives only by marriage, and hence appropriate mating partners.

SOURCES OF MORALITY

Where do customary notions of right and wrong come from? In some traditions, it is believed that humans are intrinsically good—they know instinctively what is just and fair. But it seems to be more common to assume that moral ideas come from outside. The outside source might be a divine personage, such as the creator God of Judaism, Christianity, and Islam who is understood as the source of all goodness. In those religious traditions, one acts in a righteous way because God has commanded us to do so, and He has provided us with guidelines for acting in accordance with His will. On the other hand, some religious traditions feature divine figures who are super-powerful, but not necessarily super-good (e.g., the gods and goddesses of the ancient Indo-European people, including the ancestors of the Greeks, Romans, and Hindus). In that case, the source of good is said to be some sort of impersonal cosmic force, such as the Hindu *dharma*, the principle of universal order that was discussed in the chapter on belief systems. In the Confucian belief system, by contrast, the principle of order does not reside in some cosmically transcendent force, but in the bonds of society. In that system, therefore, goodness comes from our tendency to act in accordance with the social order, for to do otherwise would be to live in chaos. It is thus apparent why in traditional China people were inclined to set aside personal preferences in favor of working toward the collective good, particularly as it was embodied in the family, the basic organizational unit of Chinese society. This system valued **filial piety**—the respect and honor due to one's family as a whole, embodied in its elders. The individualist would be a source of disruption and disorder, and even if he or she engaged in actions that might be considered moral in other societies, his or her dissent from the social norm would be viewed as inherently bad according to the terms of the Confucian system.

Whatever the source of morality is believed to be, every culture adheres to its moral code because it is a source of both stability and identity. Some religious systems (such as Islam or Mormonism) explicitly aim to be a total way of life, pervading every aspect of believers' day-to-day experience. In such systems, therefore, the moral code governs not only "religious" behavior in the narrow sense, but behavior that might, in other societies, be thought of as economic or political. The forms of Christianity that dominate the contemporary U.S. society are much less totalizing; indeed people often express resentment when "religious values" are introduced into the political discourse. In a social system like that of the contemporary United States, where there are so many groups living side-by-side, there might be a tendency for traditional moral codes to slide together. But some minority groups, mindful of their separateness, uphold special ideas of right and wrong precisely to distinguish themselves from the assimilated mainstream population. Jewish laws of *kosher* dietary practices are one way in which contemporary Jews, otherwise fully assimilated into American culture, can maintain a sense of their distinctive identity, since non-Jews do not abide by the rules of *kosher*.

VIRTUE

The person who does "the good" as his or her culture's moral code defines that term may be said to be a *virtuous* person. The word "virtue" has been weakened in meaning in English over the years; it is nowadays usually restricted to matters of sexual morality ("Virtuous people delay sexual relations until they are married.") But the word originally had a broader, more forceful connotation. It comes, in fact, from a Latin root indicating strength. So to be virtuous is not merely to be some sort of goody-goody, but to be an upholder of all that maintains a society's identity and cohesion. Virtuous people are in harmony with each other and with the larger cosmic forces.

Every society, as should be obvious, promotes virtue. Once again the principle is general, but the applications vary widely. Let us consider some moral systems and see what constitutes virtue in each of them.

Buddhism, for example, promotes four great virtues that make for a truly good person. The Buddhist should strive for: benevolence *(metta)*, a willingness to help those in need; compassion *(karuna)*, literally the ability to "suffer along with" another, to "feel their pain" in modern psychological terms; joy in others' joy *(mudita)*, somewhat more difficult for most people than reaching out to others who are suffering or in pain; and equanimity *(upekkha).* The latter virtue is the one most readily misunderstood by non-Buddhists, especially those in the West. There is a tendency to stereotype Buddhists as "fatalistic," even "passive" because they strive to accept whatever happens without feeling unduly attached to one outcome over any other. Buddhists believe that the world as we know it is illusory rather than real (despite the "evidence" of our senses). And yet we cling to it and attach value to it, all the while increasing our suffering. After all, what but suffering could come from persistent attachment to the unreal? The Buddhist's goal is not "eternal life" in the Christian sense, but *nirvana*—not a place like Paradise, but a state of being, or, more accurately, of non-being. To achieve *nirvana* is to be beyond sensual pain or pleasure; it literally means the extinction of the consciousness. So the individual must die and be reborn as many times as it takes for him or her to achieve that final freedom. That being the case, the virtue of equanimity makes good sense; one must cultivate the practice of detaching oneself. As the presence of the other virtues on the list makes clear, the Buddhist does not disallow friendship or fellowship or charity. The Buddhist, mindful of the need to achieve "extinction" of the individual consciousness, is involved with others but is not attached to them. He or she is active in the world, but should not be desirous of any of the apparent fruits of that action. (For example, one gives alms to a poor person because it is an intrinsically virtuous thing to do, not because one will then receive thanks or public recognition of one's generosity.)

Jainism derives from Hinduism, as does Buddhism, and it shares some of the same values. But its ethical system is quite distinctive. Its five basic principles are supposed to be carried out strictly by monks and nuns (ascetic holy men and women), although laypeople may adjust some of them to fit their particular life situations. The overriding Jain virtue is nonviolence *(ahimsa);* this virtue is shared by Hindus and Buddhists, but Jains are the most scrupulous in its interpretation. The great Jain sage Mahavira is said to have swept the ground in front of him as he walked and before he sat down, lest he inadvertently harm an insect. And so Jains have come to believe that no life form, even the tiniest and most apparently insignificant, should be destroyed. Jains in India have established hospitals for sick animals, and have been known to buy caged animals in order to set them free. They are also strict vegetarians. Because of the principle of *ahimsa,* Jains avoid occupations that would be harmful to life (like hunting or fishing or the making of leather goods); some of them go so far as to avoid farming, as plowing a field might inadvertently hurt small animals or insects living in the soil. Jains have thus gravitated to jobs in the helping professions (medicine, law, education) and as a result they make up a powerful middle class in India, where their reputation for virtue earns them the trust of others.

Other Jain virtues include truth-telling, honesty (avoidance of anything that could be construed as theft), and chastity. Like the Buddhists, they also advocate nonattachment. Jains assert that all attachments lead to bondage of some sort, and that some kinds of attachment (especially to money and material possessions) can take complete control of a person. Mahavira is said to have taken this principle so seriously that he even abandoned his clothes, and went around preaching while totally naked. One aspect of nonattachment that is particular to Jainism is the support of suicide. But is not suicide the taking of a life, and would doing so not run counter to Jain principles? As the Jains see it, all life is a preparation for the liberation of the spirit from the body, and when a person is sufficiently evolved spiritually, that person can make the final choice to shuck off bodily existence. Someone who commits suicide out of despair would not be approved by the Jains; only those who could demonstrate that they had reached the highest levels of spiritual awareness could be said to be making a righteous decision to die. The most highly esteemed form of that decision, the one taken by Mahavira himself, is self-starvation (*sallekhana*, literally the "holy death"). Jains prepare for *sallekhana* over the years by rigorous fasting. The "final fast" involves giving up food but continuing to drink liquids; death comes in about a month, depending on the physical condition of the person. Death by self-starvation is seen as the ultimate, most noble expression of nonattachment and freedom.

Buddhism is a religion without a supreme deity (the Buddha himself was simply a seeker who found enlightenment, not a divine being) and hence the practice of the four virtues is a kind of inward exercise, a way of cleansing the personal mind, heart, and soul. By contrast, Christianity is a religion focused on an omnipresent, omnipotent creator who is the source of all that is good and loving. Christian virtues are therefore focused outward; the aim of the Christian is to be with God in heaven for all eternity. To that end, Christians have focused on three "theological" virtues, so called because they derive from God, are defined in relation to God, and are believed to lead to God. These virtues are faith, hope, and charity. Faith is a firm belief in something for which there is no proof (in the ordinary, scientific sense of that term). Hope is desire with some expectation of fulfillment. (For example, "I *hope* I can pass this course, and I have *faith* that I will.") Charity in Christian theology does not mean simply giving to the poor (although that act can certainly be an example of the larger virtue); it means "love" in the fullest sense. For the Christian, the most complete model of love is Jesus Christ's self-sacrifice—he died on the cross to save humanity from its sins. So people are called to be "Christ-like" in their charity, which means not writing checks to worthy institutions and then calculating the tax write-off, but the willingness to give everything for others if need be, without counting the cost. In eternity, according to St. Paul, there will no longer be need of either faith or hope (since the souls of the saved will already be in God's presence); only charity (love) endures, because being in God's presence is the very definition of complete love.

The Buddhist and the Jain stand outside time, and their goal is to transcend physical categories such as time and space. The Christian is deeply involved in time, dedicated as he or she is to a god who intervened in human history and who calls everyone, in a kind of linear process, to a defined end-time. Although there is some overlap between Buddhist/Jain and Christian virtues, these systems have very different goals, and they shape their approved virtues to help adherents achieve those goals.

Confucianism presents us with yet another option when it comes to the definition of virtue. Although not a religion as some definitions would have it, it is certainly an ethical system that fits well within the Geertz definition; moreover as a philosophy that has served as the underlying organizing and stabilizing force of Chinese civilization for more than two millennia, it certainly commands our attention. Confucius was a sage primarily concerned with matters of governance, and he wrote extensively about the kind of person needed to make government work for the good of all. His system of virtue is thus addressed to a kind of idealized civil servant or bureaucrat who is responsible ultimately for the righteous order of society, on which the happiness of all individuals is ultimately dependent. And so Confucius urged his followers to exhibit proper behavior *(li)*, which is defined by the virtue of *jen*, a term without a precise English translation, encompassing as it does several attitudes, including sincerity, generosity, and earnestness. The Confucian goal is not the achievement of the non-being of *nirvana*, nor eternal life with God, but the orderly society in the here-and-now. And it is up to the "superior person" *(chun-tzu)* to bring about that social order and to maintain it thereafter. The superior person understands the mandate of heaven (which is to achieve stable order on earth), loves the people (which means that he is their leader and instructor), is courageous and wise, is eager to follow what is morally right, and who always studies deeply.

THOU SHALT NOT . . .

The moral codes of some religious traditions are based on an enumeration of "sins" rather than of virtues. They emphasize the kinds of behaviors and attitudes that are to be avoided, rather than the ones that should be practiced.

The Jivaro, an indigenous people of the South American rainforest, specify seven major categories of "sin." *Pegkkegchau* refers to any interaction with things that are ugly, deformed, dirty, bad-tasting, damaged, or worthless. *Tudau* describes anyone engaged in one or more specifically condemned activities, including incest, bestiality, wife-beating, adultery, sexual exhibitionism, and theft; it also includes, perhaps to the wonderment of outsiders, complaining about the food one's wife or mother has prepared. To be *yajau* is to be cruel, brutish, malicious, without scruples. Examples of *yajau* behavior include killing a neighbor's animals, offering one's sister to a stranger, molesting women at night, drawing or carving images of female genitals on the earth or on a tree; gender-specific *yajau* behaviors include women killing their own infants in anger or actively pursuing extra-marital sexual affairs. *Katsek* sins are those that bring about ruination, harm, damage, or destruction; the term literally refers to the act of burning down a house, but it is also used metaphorically to describe acts that "burn down" the social order. Examples include adultery, theft, lies, homicide. *Detse* is the failure to conform to the ideal norm of behavior (which is gender-specific). *Tsuwat* (literally "something filthy") refers to the act of slander. And finally *antuchu* (which literally means "doesn't listen") describes anyone who is disobedient or refuses moral instruction or correction.

The Jivaro do not make much reference to "higher powers" that stand behind these principles, and there is little apparent sense of spiritual beings that stand ready to punish transgressions. Rather, these are primarily *social* sins—acts or attitudes that harm the fabric of society—and they are likely to be punishable within the context of recognized social authority.

KNOWING WHAT IS "RIGHT"

No society could long survive if it did not have an active sense of right and wrong or if it did not have the means to achieve some consensus among its members as to how people are supposed to act. Indeed, certain moral principles may well be universal, although the ways in which they are defined and applied will vary depending on the cultural and physical contexts in which people live. While ethnocentrism often leads us to conclude that people who have values different from our own must be somehow bad or immoral, we must be willing to look at the larger social context of different groups in order to better understand their value systems.

KEY CONCEPTS

Be sure you can define the following terms, and give at least one illustrative example of each:

- ethics
- morality
- value system
- filial piety
- sanctions
- virtue
- laws

RESEARCH EXPLORATIONS

1. Several political issues confronting our own society have a strong moral component (e.g., abortion, the death penalty, affirmative action, welfare reform, minority rights). Select any one of them and find out how members of different religious traditions in your community deal with that issue. Interview representatives of those religious traditions, and, if time permits, do some library or Internet research to find out more about the moral codes of the religious traditions you have dealt with.

2. Attend a court trial in which the defendant is accused of a violent crime (e.g., murder, rape, arson, child or spousal abuse, armed robbery). Then attend a trial in which the defendant is accused of a "victimless" crime (e.g., prostitution, possession of marijuana). Finally, attend a trial in which the defendant is accused of a "white collar crime" (e.g., embezzlement, credit card fraud). Compare and contrast the ways in which prosecutors and defense attorneys present their cases in these three trials. What elements of law (sanction), ethics, and morality are brought to bear on these arguments? What inferences can you make about the wider culture from an analysis of law, ethics, and morality? Present your findings as an in-class talk.

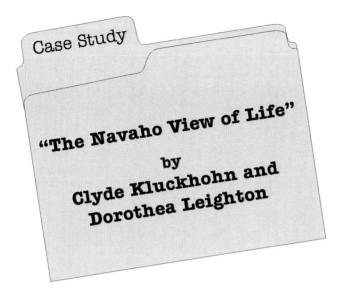

Case Study

"The Navaho View of Life"
by
Clyde Kluckhohn and
Dorothea Leighton

This classic ethnographic study of the largest Native American tribe in the United States is famous for its psychological insights into the beliefs and behaviors of the people. In this chapter, Kluckhohn and Leighton describe and analyze the Navaho perspective on matters of law, ethics, and morality. For the Navaho, life goals must make sense to the individual, but a sense of individual fulfillment is always filtered through an understanding of group-sanctioned morals and unconscious habits. Navaho ethics do not appeal to an abstract morality, nor do they depend on a higher power; rather, the Navaho are concerned with group cohesion and loyalty to tradition. We therefore cannot fully appreciate Navaho ethics unless we understand the full cultural context in which ethical decisions must be made.

In our survey of The People's way of life, the least tangible but by no means the least important subject has been reserved for the last. The problems the Navahos face and the techniques they have developed for coping with them—their material technology and their ways of handling human relations and of dealing with superhuman forces—have been considered. Through the survey of their language in the last chapter, the view of life that lies behind the special character of the Navaho adaptation was partially revealed. This subject must now be further amplified in more direct and explicit terms.

Adjustments and adaptations are always selective. Almost always more than one solution is objectively possible. The choices that a people make and the emphasis they give to one problem at the expense of others bear a relationship to the things they have come to regard as especially important. All people have to eat to survive, but whether they eat to live or live to eat or live *and* eat is not fixed by uncontrollable forces. Even if they live to eat, there will be choices as to what they eat. No society utilizes all the foods present in the environment that can be handled by the available technology. For example, neither Navahos nor white people commonly eat snake flesh although it is perfectly nutritious. The external facts—important though these always are—are not the only determinants of what people do.

The way of life which is handed down as the social heritage of every people does more than supply a set of skills for making a living and a set of blueprints for human relations. Each different way of life makes assumptions (and usually somewhat different assumptions) about the ends and purposes of human existence, about what human beings have a right to expect from one another and from the gods, about what constitutes fulfillment or frustration. Some of these assumptions are made explicit in so many words in the lore of the folk; others are tacit premises that the observer must infer by finding consistent trends in deed and word.

All of the specific things that The People approve or disapprove cannot be mentioned. Many of these have already been stated or implied. But the central directions of Navaho goals and values need to be indicated. It must, however, always be remembered that in this respect also The People are in a transitional stage. They are torn between their own ancient standards and those that are urged upon them by teachers, missionaries, and other whites. An appreciable number of Navahos are so confused by the conflicting precepts of their elders and their white models that they tend, in effect, to reject the whole problem of morality (in the widest sense) as meaningless or insoluble. For longer or shorter periods in their lives their only guide is the expediency of the immediate situation. One cannot play a game according to rule if there are sharp disagreements as to what the rules are. The incipient breakdown of any culture brings a loss of predictability and hence of dependability in personal relations. The absence of generally accepted standards of behavior among individuals constitutes, in fact, a definition of social disorganization.

A stable social structure prevails only so long as the majority of individuals in the society find enough satisfaction both in the goals socially approved and in the institutionalized means of attainment to compensate them for the constraints that ordered social life inevitably imposes upon uninhibited response to impulse. In any way of life there is much that to an outside observer appears haphazard, disorderly, more or less chaotic. But unless most participants feel that the ends and means of their culture make sense, disorientation and amorality become rampant. Synthesis is achieved partly through the overt statement of the dominant conceptions and aspirations of the group in its religion and ethical code, partly through unconscious apperceptive habits, habitual ways of looking at the stream of events.

In this chapter an attempt will be made to describe not only Navaho ethics and values but also some of those highest common factors that are implicit in a variety of the doings and sayings of The People. In the not distant past these recurrent themes, these unstated premises, gave a felt coherence to life in spite of social change, in spite of the diversity of institutions, in spite of differences in the needs and experiences of individuals. These distinctly Navaho values and premises still do much to regulate group life and to reconcile conflicts and discrepancies. But the basic assumptions of The People are now under attack from a competing set of assumptions. The majority of Navahos no longer feel completely at home and at ease in their world of values and significances, and an appreciable minority are thoroughly disoriented. This [case study] will portray the Navaho view of life in its integrated form as still held by most older people and many younger ones, for probably no Navaho alive today is completely uninfluenced by this set of conceptions of the good life, of characteristic ways of thinking, feeling, and reacting, although it should be remembered that many younger people partly repudiate some of these notions and find themselves in an uneasy state between two worlds.

NAVAHO "ETHICS"

In no human group is indiscriminate lying, cheating, or stealing approved. Cooperation is of course impossible unless individuals can depend upon each other in defined circumstances. Societies differ in how they define the conditions under which lying or stealing is forgivable or tolerable or even perhaps demanded. In their general discussions The People make virtues of truth and honesty, much as white people do. In the advice fathers give their children, in the harangues of headmen at large gatherings, these two ideals never fail to be extolled.

The difference in the presentation of these ideals by whites and Navahos lies in the reasons advanced. The Navaho never appeals to abstract morality or to adherence to divine principles. He stresses mainly the practical considerations: "If you don't tell the truth, your fellows won't trust you and you'll shame your relatives. You'll never get along in the world that way." Truth is never praised merely on the ground that it is "good" in a purely abstract sense, nor do exhortations ever take the form that the Holy People have forbidden cheating or stealing. Certain other acts are commanded or prohibited on the basis that one or more of the Holy People did or did not behave in similar fashion, but never in the modes which would seem "natural" to Christians: "Do this to please the Holy People because they love you," or "Don't do this because the Holy People punish wrong-doing." The Navahos do most definitely believe that acts have consequences, but the nature of the consequence is not wrapped up in any intrinsic "rightness" or "wrongness" of the act itself. In the matters of truth and honesty, the only appeal to the sentiments (other than those of practicality and getting along with relatives and neighbors) which Navaho "moralists" permit themselves is that of loyalty to tradition. The old Navaho way was not to lie, to cheat, or to steal. The prevalence of such vices today, they say, is due to white corruption. So much for theory.

When it comes to practice, it is harder to put the finger on the differences between Navaho and white patterns. One gets the impression that Navahos lie to strangers with fewer qualms than the average well-socialized white adult would feel. (However, the white adult's easy acceptance of "white lies" must not be overlooked.) There are also occasions on which stealing seems to be condoned "if you can get away with it." Again, though, a qualification must be entered; in many parts of the Navaho country, one can leave an automobile containing valuable articles unlocked for days and return to find not a single item missing. Thefts occur chiefly in the areas under strongest white influence, especially at "squaw dances" frequented by ne'er-do-well young men who are souls lost between the two cultures. There is undoubted evidence that white contact brings about—at least in the transitional generations—some breakdown in the moralities. This much, however, seems to be a distinctive part of the native attitude: a Navaho does not spend much time worrying over a lie or a theft when he is not found out; he seems to have almost no "guilt" feelings; but if he is caught he does experience a good deal of shame.

Offenses more strongly condemned are those that threaten the peaceful working together of The People. Incest and witchcraft are the worst of crimes. Murder, rape, physical injury, and any sort of violence are disapproved and punished, but some of the penalties seem relatively light to white people. By Navaho custom, murder, for instance, could be compounded for by a payment of slaves or livestock to the kin of the victim. To this day the Navaho way of dealing with violent crimes against the person is not ordinarily that of retaliation or even of imprisonment of the offender but of levying a fine which is turned over, not to "the state," but to the sufferer and his family to compensate for the economic loss by injury or death—a custom bearing marked resemblance to the old Teutonic wergild, or "blood money."

The positive behaviors that are advocated center on affectionate duty to relatives, pleasant manners to all, generosity, self-control. It has already been pointed out that the widest ideal of human conduct for The People is "to act to everybody as if they were your own relatives." A courteous, nonaggressive approach to others is the essence of decency. Polite phrases to visitors and strangers are highly valued. If an English-speaking Navaho wishes to speak approvingly of another Navaho with whom he has had a chance encounter, he is likely to say, "He talks pretty nice." Generosity is uniformly praised and stinginess despised. One of the most disparaging things that can be said of anyone is, "He gets mad like a dog." Women will be blamed for "talking rough" to their children. The Navaho word which is most often translated into English as "mean" is sometimes rendered "he gets mad pretty easy." In short, one must keep one's temper; one must warmly and cheerfully do one's part in the system of reciprocal rights and obligations, notably those that prevail between kinfolk.

Navaho "Values"

Health and strength are perhaps the best of the good things of life for The People. If you aren't healthy, you can't work; if you don't work, you'll starve. Industry is enormously valued. A family must arise and be about their tasks early, for if someone goes by and sees no smoke drifting out of the smokehole it will be thought that "there is something wrong there; somebody must be sick." In enumerating the virtues of a respected man or woman the faithful performance of duties is always given a prominent place. "If you are poor or a beggar, people will make fun of you. If you are lazy people will make fun of you."

By Navaho standards one is industrious in order to accumulate possessions—within certain limits—and to care for the possessions he obtains. Uncontrolled gambling or drinking are disapproved primarily because they are wasteful. The "good" man is one who has "hard goods" (turquoise and jewelry mainly), "soft goods" (clothing, etc.), "flexible goods" (textiles, etc.), and songs, stories, and other intangible property, of which ceremonial knowledge is the most important. An old Navaho said to W. W. Hill, "I have always been a poor man. I do not know a single song." The final disrespect is to say of a man, "Why, he hasn't even a dog."

A good appearance is valued; while this is partly a matter of physique, figure, and facial appearance, it means even more the ability to dress well and to appear with a handsome horse and substantial trappings.

However, as Adair[1] says:

> This display of wealth is not a personal matter as much as it is a family matter. It is not "see how much money I have," but "see how much money we have in our family."

Thus possessions are valued both as providing security and as affording opportunities for mild ostentation. But to take the attainment of riches as the chief aim of life is universally condemned. This is a typical pronouncement by a Navaho leader:

> The Navaho way is just to want enough to have enough to eat for your family and nice things to wear sometimes. We don't like it when nowadays some of these young men marry rich girls for their money and waste it all right away. The old people say this is wrong. You can't get rich if you look after your relatives right. You can't get rich without cheating some people. Cheating people is the wrong way. That way gets you into trouble. Men should be honest to get along.

Many skills carry prestige. We have spoken of the ability to dance, to sing, to tell stories. Skill at speaking is important and is expected of all leaders. "He talks easy" is high praise. Conversely, "He doesn't talk easy. He just sits there," is a belittling remark. Training in certain occupations is emphasized: a man will spend all the time he can spare from subsistence activities in order to learn a ceremonial; grandmothers and mothers are expected to teach young girls to weave. Knowledge is power to Navahos as to other peoples, but the kinds of knowledge which are significant to the Navaho are naturally limited by his technology and his social organization. The skillful farmer or stockman is admired. So also is he who excels at cowboy sports, but the runner comes in for his meed of praise too, even though this skill is today of minimal social utility.

Personal excellence is thus a value, but personal "success" in the white American sense is not. The Navaho lack of stress upon the success goal has its basis in childhood training but is reinforced by various patterns of adult life. A white man may start out to make a fortune and continue piling it up until he is a millionaire, where a Navaho, though also interested in accumulating possessions, will stop when he is comfortably off, or even sooner, partly for fear of being called a witch if he is too successful. This statement represents tendency rather than literal fact, for a few Navahos have in this century built up fortunes that are sizable even by white standards. The attitudes of the Navaho population generally toward these *ricos* are very mixed. Envy, fear, and distrust of them are undoubtedly mingled with some admiration. But there is almost no disposition for parents to hold these individuals up as models to their children. No elder says, "If you work hard and intelligently you might get to be as rich as Chee Dodge."

Navaho ideas of accumulation are different from those of whites. Riches are not identified so much with a single individual as with the whole extended family and "outfit." Indeed the social pressure to support and share with relatives has a strong leveling effect. The members of a well-off family must also spend freely, as in the white pattern of "conspicuous consumption." But all wealth is desired for this purpose and for security rather than as a means of enhancing the power and glory of specific individuals. The habit of whites in the Navaho country of attributing full control of the incomes of *rico* families to the male head of the family is a falsification, a projection of white ways. As a practical matter, he does not have the same freedom as a white millionaire to dispose of his fortune.

That individual success is not a Navaho value is reflected also in the avoidance of the types of leadership that are familiar in white society. To The People it is fundamentally indecent for a single individual to presume to make decisions for a group. Leadership, to them, does not mean "outstandingness" or anything like untrammeled power over the actions of others. Each individual is controlled not by sanctions from the top of a hierarchy of persons but by lateral sanctions. It will be remembered that decisions at meetings must be unanimous. To white persons this is an unbelievably tiresome and time-wasting process. But it is interesting to note that experiments with "group decision" in war industry have shown that the greatest increases in production have been attained when all workers in a unit concurred. Majority decisions often brought about disastrous results. (In passing it may be remarked that these experiments offer perhaps another lesson for the government in its dealings with The People: when the groups of workers were allowed to set their own goals, far more was achieved than when they were asked to strive for goals set by management.)

Some personal values that bulk large among whites have a place among The People, which is measured largely by the degree of white influence. Cleanliness, for instance, is an easy virtue where there is running water, but where every drop must be hauled five miles washing is an expensive luxury. Navaho social and economic life is not geared to fine points of time scheduling. If a Singer says he will arrive "about noon," no one takes it amiss if he appears at sundown, though an arrival a day or more late would call for explanation. Work is not, as it is in our Puritan tradition, a good thing in itself. The Navaho believes in working only as much as he needs to.

In sum, the Navaho concept of "goodness" stresses productiveness, ability to get along with people, dependability and helpfulness, generosity in giving and spending. "Badness" means stinginess, laziness, being cruel to others, being destructive. The concept of value stresses possessions and their care, health, skills that are practically useful. Concerning all of these topics The People are fully articulate. Such sentiments are enunciated again and again in the oral literature, in formal addresses, and in ordinary conversation.

SOME PREMISES OF NAVAHO LIFE AND THOUGHT

To understand fully the Navaho "philosophy of life" one must dig deeper. The very fact that The People find it necessary to talk about their "ethical principles" and their values suggests that not everybody lives up to them (any more than is the case in white society). But many characteristically Navaho doings and sayings make sense only if they are related to certain basic convictions about the nature of human life and experience, convictions so deepgoing that no Navaho bothers to talk about them in so many words. These unstated assumptions are so completely taken for granted that The People take their views of life as an ineradicable part of human nature and find it hard to understand that normal persons could possibly conceive life in other terms.

Premise 1. Life Is Very, Very Dangerous

This premise is of course distinctive only in its intensity and its phrasing. All sensible human beings realize that there are many hazards in living; but to many whites, Navahos seem morbid in the variety of threats from this world and from the world of the supernatural which they fear and name. Of course this is largely a point of view. To some detached observers it might seem more healthy to worry about witches than about what you will live on when you are old or about the dreadful consequences of picking up some germ. Whites also tend to personify evil forces. They found relief in "discovering" that World War I was all due to J. P. Morgan. All human beings doubtless have the tendency to simplify complex matters because this gives the gratifying illusion of understanding them and of the possibility of doing something about them.

However, while this is clearly not a matter of black or white, The People do have a more overwhelming preoccupation than whites with the uncertainty of life and the many threats to personal security. The great emphasis laid upon "taking care of things," upon the industry and skills necessary for survival, and upon the ceremonial techniques bear witness to this. There are five main formulas for safety.

Formula 1: Maintain orderliness in those sectors of life that are little subject to human control. By seeming to bring the areas of actual ignorance, error, and accident under the control of minutely prescribed ritual formulas, The People create a compensatory mechanism. These prescriptions are partially negative and partially positive. The Navaho conceives safety either as restoration of the individual to the harmonies of the natural, human, and supernatural world or, secondarily, as restoration of an equilibrium among nonhuman forces.

This is achieved by the compulsive force of order and reiteration in ritual words and acts. The essence of even ceremonial drama is not sharp climax (as whites have it) so much as fixed rhythms. The keynote of all ritual poetry is compulsion through orderly repetition. Take this song that the Singer of a Night Way uses to "waken" the mask of each supernatural supposed to participate in the rite.

> He stirs, he stirs, he stirs, he stirs.
> Among the lands of dawning, he stirs, he stirs;
> The pollen of the dawning, he stirs, he stirs;
> Now in old age wandering, he stirs, he stirs;
> Now on the trail of beauty, he stirs, he stirs.
> He stirs, he stirs, he stirs, he stirs.
>
> He stirs, he stirs, he stirs, he stirs.
> Among the lands of evening, he stirs, he stirs;
> The pollen of the evening, he stirs, he stirs;
> Now in old age wandering, he stirs, he stirs;
> Now on the trail of beauty, he stirs, he stirs.
> He stirs, he stirs, he stirs, he stirs.

He stirs, he stirs, he stirs, he stirs.
Now Talking God, he stirs, he stirs;
Now his white robe of buckskin, he stirs, he stirs;
Now in old age wandering, he stirs, he stirs;
Now on the trail of beauty, he stirs, he stirs.
He stirs, he stirs, he stirs, he stirs[2]

The song goes on like this for many verses. To white people it has a monotonous quality, but infinite repetitions in an expected sequence seem to lull the Navaho into a sense of security.

Formula 2: Be wary of non-relatives. This is, to some extent, the obverse of the centering of trust and affection upon relatives. If one feels thoroughly at home and at ease when surrounded by one's kin, it is natural that one should distrust strangers. In white society (and probably in all others) there is a distrust of strangers, members of the "out-group." But the Navaho fears also the other members of his own people who are not related to him. Hence antiwitchcraft protection must always be carried to a "squaw dance" or any other large gathering. This tendency to be ill at ease when beyond the circle of one's relatives is a truly "primitive" quality and is characteristic, to varying degrees, of most nonliterate folk societies.

This formula is closely related to the preceding one; if one wins security by reducing the uncharted areas of the nonhuman universe to familiar patterns, it is natural that unfamiliar human beings should be regarded as threats.

Formula 3: Avoid excesses. Very few activities are wrong in and of themselves, but excess in the practice of any is dangerous. This is in marked contrast to the puritanical concept of immorality. To Navahos such things as sex and gambling are not "wrong" at all but will bring trouble if indulged in "too much." Even such everyday tasks as weaving must be done only in moderation. Many women will not weave more than about two hours at a stretch; in the old days unmarried girls were not allowed to weave for fear they would overdo, and there is a folk rite for curing the results of excess in this activity. Closely related is the fear of completely finishing anything: as a "spirit outlet," the basketmaker leaves an opening in the design; the weaver leaves a small slit between the threads; the Navaho who copies a sandpainting for a white man always leaves out something, however trivial; the Singer never tells his pupil quite all the details of the ceremony lest he "go dry." Singers also systematically leave out transitions in relating myths.

This fear of excess is reflected also in various characteristic attitudes toward individuals. There is, for example, a folk saying: "If a child gets too smart, it will die young." The distrust of the very wealthy and very powerful and the sanctions and economic practices that tend to keep men at the level of their fellows have already been mentioned.

Formula 4: When in a new and dangerous situation, do nothing. If a threat is not to be dealt with by ritual canons, it is safest to remain inactive. If a Navaho finds himself in a secular situation where custom does not tell him how to behave, he is usually ill at ease and worried. The white American under these circumstances will most often overcompensate by putting on a self-confidence he does not in fact have. The American tradition says, "When danger threatens, do something." The Navaho tradition says, "Sit tight and perhaps in that way you may escape evil."

Formula 5: Escape. This is an alternative response to Formula 4, which The People select with increasing frequency when pressure becomes too intense. Doing nothing is not enough: safety lies in flight. This flight may take the form of leaving the field in the sheer physical sense. Navahos have discovered that they don't get very far by trying to resist the white man actively; so they scatter. The white man then cannot deal with them as a group—he can't even locate and exhort or admonish or punish them as individuals. Escape may be this sort of passive resistance or it may be simple evasion, as when a Navaho woman, who was otherwise fairly happy in a government hospital, left it rather than ask for one kind of food that she desperately missed. Had she asked, it would have been given her, but she found it simpler to leave. Flight also takes the even more unrealistic form of addiction to alcohol or of indiscriminate sexuality. In effect, the Navaho says, "My only security is in escape from my difficulties."

These types of behavior in the face of danger are documented by the following episode related by a fifth-grader in one of the boarding schools.

> We look down to the river, we saw a lot of cows at the river. My brother said, "I am not scared of those cows that are at the river." Soon the cows were going back up the hill. We just climb up on a big tall tree and sit there. The cows come in closer and closer. We stay on the tree. Soon they come under the tree. My brother and I were so scared that we just sit there and not move. Soon my brother start crying. When the cows go away we laugh and laugh. My brother said, "The cows were scared of me." I said, "They are not scared of you." We say that over and over. Soon my brother got angry, then we fight in the sand. After we fight we go home.

Premise 2. Nature Is More Powerful Than Man

Navahos accept nature and adapt themselves to her demands as best they can, but they are not utterly passive, not completely the pawns of nature. They do a great many things that are designed to control nature physically and to repair damage caused by the elements. But they do not even hope to master nature. For the most part The People try to influence her with various songs and rituals, but they feel that the forces of nature, rather than anything that man does, determine success or failure of crops, plagues of grasshoppers, increase of arroyos, and decrease of grass. If a flood comes and washes out a formerly fertile valley, one does not try to dam the stream and replace the soil; instead one moves to a floodless spot. One may try to utilize what nature furnishes, such as by leading water from a spring or stream to his fields, but no man can master the wind and the weather. This is similar to the attitude toward sex, which is viewed as part of nature, something to reckon with, but not a thing to be denied.

Many white people have the opposite view; namely, that nature is a malignant force with useful aspects that must be harnessed, and useless, harmful ones that must be shorn of their power. They spend their energies adapting nature to their purposes, instead of themselves to her demands. They destroy pests of crops and men, they build dykes and great dams to avert floods, and they level hills in one spot and pile them up in another. Their premise is that nature will destroy them unless they prevent it; the Navahos' is that nature will take care of them if they behave as they should and do as she directs.

In addition to all the other forces that make the acceptance of the current program of soil erosion control and limitation of livestock slow and painful, this premise plays an important and fundamental part. To most Navahos it seems silly or presumptuous to interfere with the workings of nature to the extent that they are being told to do. Besides, they believe it won't bring the benefits the white people promise. If anything is wrong these days, it is that The People are forgetting their ways and their stories, so of course anyone would know that there would be hard times. It has nothing to do with too many sheep.

Premise 3. The Personality Is a Whole

This assumption also must be made explicit because white people so generally think of "mind" and "body" as separable units. The whole Navaho system of curing clearly takes it for granted that you cannot treat a man's "body" without treating his "mind," and vice versa. In this respect Navahos are many generations ahead of white Americans, who are only now beginning to realize that it is the patient, not the disease, which must be treated. Successful physicians who understood "human nature" have acted on this premise always, but it has found verbal expression and acceptance only recently; at present it is receiving the most publicity in the specialty known as "psychosomatic medicine."

Premise 4. Respect the Integrity of the Individual

While the individual is always seen as a member of a larger group, still he is never completely submerged in that group. There is an area of rigidity where what any given person may and may not do is inexorably fixed, but there is likewise a large periphery of freedom. This is not the "romantic individualism" of white tradition, but in many respects the Navaho has more autonomy, more opportunity for genuine spontaneity than is the case in white society. Rights of individuals, including children, over their immediately personal property, are respected to the fullest degree, even when their wishes run counter to the obvious interests of the family or extended family. White people seeking to purchase a bow and arrow that they see in a hogan are surprised to have the adults refer the question to the five-year-old who owns the toy and whose decision is final. If a youngster unequivocally says he does not want to go to school or to the hospital, that is, in most families, the end of it. Husbands and wives make no attempt to control every aspect of the behavior of the spouse. Although individuals are not regarded as equal in capacity or in all features of the treatment that should be accorded them, still the integrity of every individual is protected from violation at the hands of more powerful people.

Where survival is held to depend on cooperation, the subordination of the individual to the group is rigorously demanded. Such interdependence is felt to exist in all sorts of ways that are not, from the white point of view, realistic. Success in hunting is thought to depend as much upon the faithful observance of taboos by the wife at home as upon the husband's skill or luck in stalking game. The individualism that expresses itself in social innovation is disapproved as strongly as is that which expresses itself in too obtrusive leadership. The following quotation (which, incidentally, is also a nice illustration of Navaho logic) brings out the Navaho feeling exactly.

> You must be careful about introducing things into ceremonies. One chanter
> thought that he could do this. He held a Night Chant. He wanted more old

people so he had the dancers cough and dance as old people. He also wanted an abundance of potatoes so he painted potatoes on the dancers' bodies. He desired that there should be a great deal of food so he had the dancers break wind and vomit through their masks to make believe that they had eaten a great deal. They surely got their reward. Through the coughing act a great many of the people got whooping cough and died. In the second change many of the people got spots on their bodies like potatoes only they were measles, sores, and smallpox. In the part, where they asked for all kinds of food, a lot died of diarrhea, vomiting and stomach aches. This chanter thought that he had the power to change things but everyone found out that he was wrong. It was the wrong thing to do and today no one will try to start any new ceremonies. Today we do not add anything. [3]

On the other hand, where autonomy does not seem to threaten the security of established practices or the needful cooperative undertakings, individuality is not only permitted but also encouraged. Men and women feel free to vary their costumes to suit their temperaments, to experiment with variations in house style and other technological products, to break the day's routine with trips and other diversions spontaneously decided upon, while displays of jewelry, saddles, and horses bring admiration more than disapproval. He who makes up a new secular song or coins a new pun or quip wins many plaudits. Unity in diversity is the Navaho motto.

Premise 5. Everything Exists in Two Parts, the Male and the Female, Which Belong Together and Complete Each Other

With the Navaho this premise applies to much more than biology. The clear, deep, robins-egg-blue turquoise they call male, and the stone of a greenish hue they call female. The turbulent San Juan River is "male water," the placid Rio Grande "female water." The mountains of the north where harsh, cold winds blow are "male country," the warm open lands of the south "female country." There are male rains and female rains, the one hard and sudden, the other gentle; there are male and female chants; male and female plants are distinguished on the basis of appearance, the male always being the larger. The supernaturals, as seen in the sandpaintings or mentioned in the songs and prayers, are nearly always paired, so that if Corn Boy appears, one can be sure that Corn Girl will soon follow.

Premise 6. Human Nature Is Neither Good Nor Evil— Both Qualities Are Blended in All from Birth On

The notion of "original sin" still lurks in white thinking. But the premise that children are "born bad" and have to be beaten into shape seems completely absent from the Navaho view. On the other hand, white "liberals" act upon the assumption that human beings can be educated into almost complete perfection, that if ignorance is removed people will act in full enlightenment. Similarly, at least some Christian groups hold that "grace" can permanently transform the wayward into paragons of virtue. The Navaho assumption is that no amount of knowledge and no amount of "religious" zeal can do more than alter somewhat the relative proportions of "bad" and "good" in any given individual.

Premise 7. Like Produces Like and the Part Stands for the Whole

These are two "laws of thought" almost as basic to Navaho thinking as the so-called Aristotelian "laws of thought" have been in European intellectual history since the Middle Ages. Of course, *similia similibus curantur* has been important in the thinking of most human groups since the Old Stone Age or earlier; but among whites this principle is now largely relegated to the realm of folk belief, whereas among The People it still dominates the thought of the most sophisticated members of the society.

Let a few examples do for many. Because the juice of the milkweed resembles milk it is held to be useful in treating a mother who cannot nurse her infant. Since the eagle can see long distances, the diviner who does stargazing must rub a preparation that includes water from an eagle's eye under his own eyelids. Witchcraft performed over a few hairs from an individual is as effective against the owner of the hairs as if done upon his whole person. In chants small mounds of earth stand for whole mountains.

Premise 8. What Is Said Is To Be Taken Literally

[T]he easy ambiguities, the fluidities of English speech are foreign to the Navaho. There is little "reading between the lines," little exercise of the imagination in interpreting utterances. A student was asking about a girl who was said by a white person to be feeble-minded. He asked, "Can so-and-so's daughter speak?" The Navaho replied very positively, "Yes." Observation showed that the girl uttered only unintelligible sounds. When this was later thrown back at the original informant he countered, "Well, she *does* speak—but no one can understand her." And this was said without a smile or even a twinkle in the eye.

Similarly, a Navaho will seldom take it upon himself to attribute thoughts or sentiments to others in the absence of very explicit statements on their part. White workers among The People find it irritating when they ask, "What does your wife (or brother, etc.) think about this?" and get the reply, "I don't know. I didn't ask her." Their supposition is that spouses or close relatives or intimate friends have enough general knowledge of each other's opinions to answer such questions with reasonable accuracy even if there has been no discussion of this precise point. But the Navahos do not see it this way.

Premise 9. This Life Is What Counts

Because the Christian tradition is so prevalent in white society, it is necessary to bring this premise out explicitly. The People have no sense whatsoever that this life is a "preparation" for another existence. Indeed, except for the (by no means universally accepted) view that witches and suicides live apart in the afterworld, there is no belief that the way one lives on this earth has anything to do with his fate after death. This is one reason why morality is practical rather than categorical. While the Navaho feels very keenly that life is *hard*, his outlook is quite foreign to that of "life is real, life is earnest, and the grave is not the goal." White life is so permeated with the tradition of Puritanism, of "the Protestant ethic," that much Navaho behavior looks amoral or shiftless.

Another reason would seem to be that Navahos do not need to orient themselves in terms of principles of abstract morality. They get their orientations from face-to-face contacts with the same small group of people with whom they deal from birth to death. In a large, complex society like modern America where people come and go and where people who never see each other must carry on business and other dealings, it is functionally necessary to have abstract standards that transcend an immediate concrete situation in which two or more persons are interacting.

SEEING THINGS THE NAVAHO WAY

To most people most of the time, the habitual ways of speaking, acting, feeling, and reacting to which they have been accustomed from childhood become as much a part of the inevitables of life as the air they breathe, and they tend unconsciously to feel that all "normal" human beings ought to feel and behave only within the range of variation permitted by their own way of life. Then, however, when they have to deal with other groups who have been brought up with a somewhat different set of unquestioned and habitual assumptions about the nature of things, they all too often label the other group as "ignorant" or "superstitious," "stupid" or "stubborn." Many teachers and administrators of the Navajo Agency have very unrealistic expectations as to the capacities of Navahos to think and respond in white terms, forgetting that the median schooling of the Navaho adult is nine months!

Difficulties arise largely because, on both sides, the premises from which thought or action proceeds are unconscious—in the simple sense of unverbalized. Teachers, for example, urge Navaho children to strive for what the teachers want most in life without stopping to think that perhaps The People want quite different things. If a teacher who has had great success in teaching white children does not get comparably good results with Navaho children, she thinks this is because the Indian children are less bright. As a matter of fact, the trouble is often that the incentives which have worked beautifully to make white children bestir themselves leave Navaho children cold, or even actively trouble and confuse them.

For instance, the teacher holds out the hope of a college education with all that this implies for "getting on" in the white world; to at least the younger Navaho child, this means mainly a threat of being taken even further from home and country. The teacher reads or posts a complete set of grades for her class. To her, this is a way of rewarding the students who have done well and of inciting those who have not done so well to more strenuous efforts. Her students, however, may feel quite differently about the matter. Those at the top of the list may find it embarrassing to be placed publicly ahead of their contemporaries, and the list may seem cruel ridicule to those who have lagged behind. The whole conception that individuals can be rated on a scale from 0 to 100 is foreign to The People.

Or suppose a primary teacher sets both boys and girls to making pottery. From her point of view this is an interesting and worthwhile class activity, for white people do not make a sharp distinction between what six-year-old boys and girls should do. Yet this is as grievous a humiliation to a Navaho boy as a ten-year-old white boy would feel if he were made to appear at school in lace petticoats. A high-school teacher tries to induce a boy and a girl to fox trot together; when they refuse, she says:

"They acted like dumb animals." But they are from the same clan, and the thought of clan relatives having the type of physical contact involved in white social dancing gives Navahos the same uncomfortableness the teacher would feel if the manager of a crowded hotel demanded that she and her adult brother share the same bed. There is nothing "reasonable"—or "unreasonable"—about either attitude. They are just different. Both represent "culturally standardized unreason."

The People have only "object taboos" as regards sex, none of the "aim taboos" which are so marked a development of western culture. That is, Navahos do feel that sexual activity is improper or dangerous under particular circumstances or with certain persons. But they never regard sexual desires in themselves as "nasty" or evil. In school and elsewhere, whites have tended to operate upon the premise that "any decent Navaho" will feel guilty about a sexual act that takes place outside of marriage. This attitude simply bewilders Navahos and predisposes them to withdrawal of cooperation in all spheres. To them sex is natural, necessary, and no more or no less concerned with morals than is eating.

The Navaho and the white administrator may see the same objective facts, and communication may be sufficiently well established so that each is sure the other sees them. Naturally, then, there is mutual irritation when the same conclusions are not reached. What neither realizes is that all discourse proceeds from premises and that premises (being unfortunately taken for granted by both) are likely, in fact, to be very divergent. Especially in the case of less sophisticated and self-conscious societies where there has not been much opportunity to learn that other peoples' ways of behaving and of looking at things differ from their own, the unconscious assumptions characteristically made by most individuals of the group will bulk large.

Let us put this in the concrete. A wealthy man dies and leaves considerable property. He has a widow but no children by her. There are, however, two sons by another woman to whom the deceased was never married in either white or Navaho fashion. He left, of course, no written will, and it is agreed that he gave no oral instructions on his deathbed. These are the facts, and there is no dispute about them between the Navaho and the white administrator.

Nevertheless the prediction may safely be made that before the estate is settled the white man will be irritated more than once and some Navahos will be confused and indignant at what seems to them ignorance, indifference, or downright immorality. The white man will unconsciously make his judgments and decisions in terms of white customs. Navahos will take Navaho customs as the standard except in so far as some may deliberately try to get a share, or more than their rightful share, by insisting upon the application of the white man's law. But the main difficulties will arise from the fact that the premises are never brought out into the open and discussed as such.

The Indian Service administrator is likely to take white customs and legal system for granted as "part of human nature" and to act upon the unstated assumptions in the following left-hand column. Navahos, unless they happen to be familiar with and to want to take advantage of white patterns, view the situation in the light of the very different principles in the right-hand column.

The white administrator would be likely to say that the *only* heirs to *any* of the property were the wife, children, and perhaps the illegitimate children. Such a decision would be perplexing or infuriating to the Navaho. To say in the abstract what disposal would be proper at the present complicated point in Navaho history is hardly possible. But it is clear that a verdict, which seemed so "right" and "natural" to a white person as to require no explanation or justification, would probably appear equally "unjust" and "unreasonable" to the Navaho involved.

The pressure of such double standards is highly disruptive. Just as rats that have been trained to associate a circle with food and a rectangle with an electric shock become neurotic when the circle is changed by almost imperceptible gradations into

White	Navaho
1. Marriage is an arrangement, economic and otherwise, between two individuals. The two spouses and the children, if any, are the ones primarily involved in any question of inheritance.	1. Marriage is an arrangement between two families much more than it is between two individuals.
2. A man's recognized children, legitimate or illegitimate, have a claim upon his property.	2. Sexual rights are property rights; therefore, if a man has children from a woman without undertaking during his lifetime the economic responsibilities which are normally a part of Navaho marriage, the children—however much he admitted to biological fatherhood—were not really his: "He just stole them."
3. Inheritance is normally from the father or from both sides of the family.	3. Inheritance is normally from the mother, the mother's brother, or other relatives of the mother; from the father's side of the family little or nothing has traditionally been expected.
4. As long as a wife or children survive, no other relatives are concerned in the inheritance unless there was a will to that effect.	4. While children today, in most areas, expect to inherit something from their father, they do not expect to receive his whole estate or to divide it with their mother only; sons and daughters have different expectations.
5. All types of property are inherited in roughly the same way.	5. Different rules apply to different types of property: range land is hardly heritable property at all; farm land normally stays with the family which has been cultivating it; livestock usually goes back (for the most part) to the father's sisters and maternal nephews; jewelry and other personal property tend to be divided among the children *and* other relatives; ceremonial equipment may go to a son who is a practitioner or to a clansman of the deceased.

an ellipse, so human beings faced with a conflicting set of rewards and punishments tend to cut loose from all moorings, to float adrift and become irresponsible. The younger generation of The People is more and more coming to laugh at the old or pay them only lip service. The young escape the control of their elders, not to accept white controls but to revel in newly found patterns of unrestraint.

The introduction of the white type of individualism without the checks and balances that accompany it leads to the failure of collective or cooperative action of every sort. The substitution of paid labor for reciprocal services is not in and of itself a bad thing. But there is not a commensurate growth of the white sort of individual responsibility. There tends to be a distortion of the whole cultural structure that makes it difficult to preserve harmonious personal relationships and satisfying emotional adjustments. Widespread exercise of escape mechanisms, especially alcohol, is the principal symptom of the resultant friction and decay. Human groups that have different cultures and social structures have moral systems that differ in important respects. The linkage is so great that when a social organization goes to pieces morality also disintegrates.

Instead of a patterned mosaic, Navaho culture is becoming an ugly patchwork of meaningless and totally unrelated pieces. Personal and social chaos are the byproducts. The lack of selective blending and constructive fusion between white and Navaho cultures is not due to low intelligence among The People. They are perfectly capable of learning white ways. But when the traits of another culture are learned externally and one by one without the underlying values and premises of that culture, the learners feel uncomfortable. They sense the absence of the fitness of things, of a support that is nonetheless real [but] difficult to verbalize.

For every way of life is a structure—not a haphazard collection of all the different physically possible and functionally effective patterns of belief and action but an interdependent system with all its patterns segregated and arranged in a manner which is *felt,* not *thought,* to be appropriate. If we wish to understand The People in the world today, we must remember that, like ourselves, they meet their problems not only with the techniques and the reason at their disposal but also in terms of their sentiments, of their standards, of their own hierarchy of values, of their implicit premises about their world.

Let us not hastily dismiss as "illogical" their views. If we do, we are probably just reacting defensively to the fact that their views and ours often fail to coincide. If "romantic love" plays a very small part in their lives, if women find plural marriage tolerable and sometimes even invite their husbands to marry a younger sister, it is not that The People are "unnatural." As a matter of fact, so far at least as "romantic love" is concerned they are acting the "normal" way, in the statistical sense that this sort of love is the accepted tradition among only a few groups of human beings.

Nor must we say: "Yes, the Navahos are different. I grant that. But they are so different that I can't see how any effective communication is possible." No, The People are also human beings. Like us, they must eat and have shelter and satisfy sexual urges. And they must do this with the same biological equipment and in a physical world where heat and cold, summer and winter, gravity and other natural laws set limits as they do for us. In a certain ultimate sense the "logic" of all peoples is inescapably the same. It is only the premises that are different. When we discover the premises we realize that the phrase "a common humanity" is full of meaning.

Notes

[1] John Adair, *The Navajo and Pueblo Silversmiths* (Norman: University of Oklahoma Press, 1944), p. 98. By permission of the author.

[2] Washington Matthews. *The Night Chant, a Navaho Ceremony,* Memoirs of the American Museum of Natural History, 6 (1902), 110–111.

[3] Willard W. Hill, "Stability in Culture and Pattern," *American Anthropologist,* 41 (1939), 260.

BIBLIOGRAPHY

Adair, John, *The Navajo and Pueblo Silversmiths* (Norman: University of Oklahoma Press, 1944).

Dyk, Walter, recorder, *Son of Old Man Hat; A Navaho Autobiography* (New York: Harcourt, Brace and Company, 1938).

Hill, Willard W., "Stability in Culture and Pattern," *American Anthropologist,* 41 (1939), 258–260.

Kluckhohn, Clyde, "Covert Culture and Administrative Problems," *American Anthropologist,* 45 (1943), 213–227.

———, "A Navaho Personal Document," *Southwestern Journal of Anthropology,* 1 (1945), 260–283.

Matthews, Washington, *The Night Chant, A Navaho Ceremony,* Memoirs of the American Museum of Natural History, 6 (1902).

Reichard, Gladys A., "Human Nature as Conceived by the Navajo Indians," *Review of Religion,* 7 (1943), 353–360.

———, *Prayer: the Compulsive Word* (New York: J. J. Augustin, 1944).

QUESTIONS FOR DISCUSSION

1. What do the authors claim to be the central directions of Navaho goals and values? How do the authors distinguish between ethics and values in the Navaho context?

2. In what ways do Navaho goals and values correspond to those of European Americans? In what ways do they differ?

3. The authors state that the "logic" of all cultures is "inescapably the same." What do you think they mean by this statement? How do they illustrate it with regard to the situation of the Navaho and the white people they have to deal with? Do you agree with their position? If so, why? If not, why not?

SUGGESTED READINGS OR OTHER RESOURCES

General Works

Klass, Morton. 1995. *Ordered Universes.* Boulder, CO: Westview.

Salamone, Frank A., and Walter Randolph Adams, eds. 1997. *Explorations in Anthropology and Theology.* Lanham, MD: University Press of America.

Selected Case Studies

Harner, Michael. 1962. Jivaro Souls. *American Anthropologist* 64:258-272.

Vallely, Anne. 2002. Moral Landscapes: Ethical Discourses among Orthodox and Diaspora Jains. In *A Reader in the Anthropology of Religion*, ed. Michael Lambek. Malden, MA: Blackwell (pp. 555–569).

Videos

China Institutionalizes Itself (Insight Media) is a 26-minute explanation of the basics of the Confucian code that examines how this philosophical and religious system has remained the primary social and ethical foundation of Chinese civilization despite changes in political organization.

The Jains (Insight Media) is a 25-minute observation of life in a Jain community in India; it outlines the main tenets of the Jain faith and ethical system.

Karma and Care (Insight Media) is a 26-minute discussion of modern virtue theory based on an ethic of care; it examines Buddhist and Christian values related to the practice of care.

A Life Apart: Hasidism in America (Insight Media) is a 95-minute film that examines the Hasidim, a sect of ultra-orthodox Jews who have re-created an Eastern European culture in America, maintaining their separate identity through adherence to the moral codes of Judaism, leading them to reject most aspects of American popular culture.

7

The Environment of the Sacred

featuring

"Religion and Place in Southern Appalachia"
by Richard Humphrey

We have seen that in creating a domain of the sacred, religion alters perceptions of time. Sacred activities take place during special times, and religion in general calls on believers to think about matters of eternity and infinity. But the domain of the sacred also alters conventional notions of space, inasmuch as religious activities take place in special environments. Those environments may be natural ones that are reinterpreted by believers in light of their presumed sacred connotations; or they may be environments that are specifically designed and built for sacred purposes. In this chapter we will therefore consider the ways in which people engaged in religious activities both influence and are influenced by the natural and the cultural environments that they have defined as sacred.

MAKING THE SUPERNATURAL SEEM REAL

Traditional religions deal in one way or another with the "supernatural," which we have defined in its most basic sense: that which is perceived through means beyond the ordinary five senses. Even belief systems that may seem secular in orientation (we have mentioned political movements, economic ideologies, science, and even aspects of popular culture in this regard, and will say more about them in the next chapter) invite participants to think about matters of abstract and transcendent consequence. The problem thus always arises: how can matters that are by definition beyond ordinary categories be depicted in such a way that they seem real—indeed "uniquely realistic"—to potential believers?

In general, there are two ways in which this problem has been addressed. One is the way of **representation**. That is, the supernatural is evoked *by* an image, which may be physical (e.g., a picture, a sculpture), verbal (i.e., a spoken or written metaphor such as "God is our father"), or even musical (e.g., in Vodun each of the spirits is summoned by a particular pattern of rhythmic drumming). The other is

175

the way of the **sacrament**, which means that the supernatural *is* its image. In other words, the supernatural power is somehow believed to be inherent in the picture, sculpture, word, or music that believers can perceive. In some versions of Christianity, Christ is believed to be "remembered" in the communion service, and the communion bread itself is seen as a symbol of Christ's divinity and his bond with the people (a representational image). But in other forms of Christianity, such as Roman Catholicism, the communion bread is believed to *become* the body and blood of Christ through the spoken words of the priest (a sacramental presence).

The Greek god of the sea, Poseidon, is manifested in the sea itself. The sea *is* his body (a sacramental presence) and also accounts for his personality; just as the sea is changeable, so Poseidon is fickle and must be influenced through sacrifice. A temple to Poseidon might have a statue of the god, but that image was purely representational; the true presence of the god was in the sea itself, which is why most temples to Poseidon were built near the seashore.[1]

Some religious traditions are explicitly **aniconic**, which means that they do not permit the making of any physical representation of whatever supernatural being or force is at the center of their faith. Islam and Judaism are two world religions that are zealously aniconic, believing any form of physical representation of God to be blasphemy or idolatry. (By contrast, Christianity and Hinduism have no problem at all with visual, verbal, and/or musical representations of divinity.) But it is also possible to see that the decision to *avoid* physical imagery is itself a very powerful metaphorical statement about the nature of God: God is so vast, powerful, transcendent that He can only be represented by a blank, the better to underscore the vast distance between God and humans. In any case, even aniconic religions find ways to make the supernatural real through the use of physical objects. For example, both Jews and Muslims pay great reverence to the book of scriptures; the unfurling of scrolls of scripture is an important part of Jewish ritual, and Muslims may keep a specially bound copy of the Qur'an in a shrine-like niche above the doorway to a home.

NATURAL SPACE AS SACRED ENVIRONMENT

Religious traditions the world over have looked to certain natural features as essential elements in their perception of the sacred. Mountains are very likely to be identified as the abode of gods or as places that emanate supernatural power. Volcanic mountains are especially good candidates for sacred status since they are so obviously the products of forces way beyond ordinary human power to either replicate or even understand. Rivers are also frequently understood as sacred things, possibly because they bring life (water for drinking, irrigating, bathing) but also the possibility of death (through catastrophic flooding); for people living before the age of scientific exploration, rivers came from unknown sources and went who-knew-where. They were mysterious, powerful, beneficent yet potentially danger-ous forces in and of themselves. Like water, fire could be seen as sacred because it both brought life (warmth, cooked food) and threatened death. Uncontrollable forces such as thunder and lightning were also sources of fear and awe.

Much has been made of the fact that three of the world's great religious traditions—Judaism, Christianity, and Islam—all arose out of a desert environment. In all three of those traditions, the desert represents solitude and quiet; the desert is a place where God can be contemplated most directly, where people are free of the complications and distractions of life in crowded farming villages, commercial cities, or other centers of political or economic power. Some commentators have suggested that all three of these religions developed a monotheistic philosophy (the idea that there is only one God) in that desert environment of vast emptiness, where a single power could be perceived as stretching to the farthest horizons. By contrast, the religious traditions associated with forested areas were more likely to be expressed in terms of multiple, overarching spiritual powers. Like any generalization, this one must be taken with a grain of salt, but at the very least it demonstrates that natural space is not a neutral element in even the most abstract aspects of a belief system.

Ancient people tended to be **henotheistic**; that is, they believed that their gods or spirits were only potent in their own territory. In the Second Book of Kings in the Judeo-Christian Bible, we read of a Syrian general, Naaman, who is cured of leprosy by the Hebrew prophet Elisha. In gratitude, he decides to become a devotee of the Hebrew God; but he takes the precaution of transporting two muleloads of Israelite earth back to Syria on the assumption that the Hebrew God could only exercise his power on his own soil. As monotheism took hold, believers came to the conclusion that God was powerful everywhere and in every circumstance. And yet, there is still a dramatic and fateful connection between a people and their soil. Modern political Zionism was, after all, founded on the assumption that the natural homeland of the dispersed Jews was to be centered around Mount Zion in Jerusalem. And the subsequent political conflict in that region was a result of another people—who also claimed descent from the patriarch Abraham—believing themselves to have an equal claim to a modern state in the land hallowed by their ancestors.

CREATING SACRED SPACE

In addition to perceiving the sacred in elements in the natural environment, people in most cultures try to create sacred space of their own. We can often see much of the belief system and traditions of ritual mirrored in the physical forms of the built elements of the sacred environment. For example, the typical Egyptian temple was conceived as a dwelling place for the gods, and it was suitably monumental in size. It was constructed so that one rose from a ground-level entrance to a much higher inner sanctuary. The god dwelt in those uppermost reaches of the temple and was tended to by a specially designated priesthood. The god was treated as if he were a human being, and the temple was set up to tend to his daily needs (including the provision of food). On the walls were depictions of these ministrations. During public rituals, an image of the god would be carried down from the inner sanctuary and presented in an outer courtyard. By contrast, the Greco-Roman temple was usually relatively small, more like a shrine where people could deposit valuable offerings or make private pledges than a huge space for public worship.

Buddhist temples are typically built around relics of past worthies. These artifacts are enshrined in *stupas*, structures built in the shape of the cosmic egg (mentioned in chapter 3 in connection with Hindu cosmological ideas). Buddhism seems to have been an aniconic religion at the beginning—the Buddha was registered by his *absence* rather than his presence. But after the peoples of South Asia were contacted by the Greeks during the campaigns of Alexander the Great, a tradition of statue building (some of it on a monumental scale) became prominent. Modern Buddhist temples are often multipurpose campuses, with attached monastic dormitories and schools. Large temples also include pavilions where laypeople can gather for public instruction.

The Hindu temple *(mandir)* is conceived as a palace for the gods. Often many different gods have shrines within a common temple area, which is constructed along the lines of a military fortress, the better to preserve the order of the cosmos. The shrine containing the image of a deity is recessed (and may be metaphorically described as a "womb"); above it is a tower representing a cosmic mountain. (Sacred architecture often deliberately echoes sacred features of the natural landscape.) A prominent feature of the Hindu temple is a water tank, as devotees are expected to engage in ritual purification before entering the temple proper. The Hindu temple is usually not constructed for congregational worship. Instead, it is a space designed for multiple private devotions, although a *mandir* in the United States nowadays may look more like the spaces designed as Christian churches.

Confucian temples are symmetrical in design, reflecting that system's concern for earthly order. Their most prominent feature is a set of tablets enshrining words of wisdom. Statues of past officials or locally revered sages may also be on display.

Synagogues, churches, and mosques are usually places of congregational worship as opposed to private devotion. Within Christianity there are several historically important differences in architectural design; the Catholic church is oriented around the altar, while the Protestant church is oriented to the pulpit (reflecting Protestantism's emphasis on preaching the word from scripture). In the Orthodox churches, the main altar is hidden behind an elaborate screen decorated with holy icons, reflecting that tradition's great emphasis on the transcendent mystery of Christ's communion with his faithful. An important feature of the mosque is its attached minaret, a tower from which the call to prayer is issued. In general, Christian and Jewish places of worship are open to all who enter in a respectful way; mosques of particular historic or architectural importance may be open to nonbelievers under supervision, but are usually reserved for the faithful during services. Mosques in particular and Islamic architecture in general strive to evoke the desert; they feature open spaces and light.

Even apparently secular traditions have their designated sacred spaces, such as the great public monuments, which include a specially designed cemetery for national heroes, in Washington, D.C. Sometimes, though, places not deliberately designated as sacred can become so by association. "Ground Zero" in New York, for example, was simply a piece of commercial real estate before 9/11; afterward it became a place hallowed by the deaths of so many people.

The religions of tribal people are no less involved in the creation of the sacred than are those of the literate civilizations. The French anthropologist Claude Lévi-Strauss (discussed in chapter 5 in connection with his important contributions to the study of mythology) has described two indigenous cultures of Brazil that, in their very different ways, illustrate these principles.[2] The Bororo lived in circular villages, a fairly common architectural style in that part of the world; the circle was pragmatic (it made it easier to defend the village against outsiders), but it was also an expression of a philosophical idea (the circle represents completeness or closure). But the Bororo village had some features that distinguished it architecturally from that of other tribal people in the region. For one thing, it always had to be built near a river (source of water, but also mythical carrier of power), and running through the middle of the village was an imaginary line paralleling the river.

Bororo society was divided into two *moieties*—groups of exogamous relatives (i.e., members of one moiety were required to marry someone of the other moiety). Each side of the village was defined as the home of one of the moieties. Moreover (and not surprisingly in light of Lévi-Strauss' structural approach as outlined in chapter 5), each side of the village and each of the moieties was defined as either "natural" (i.e., concerned primarily with activities like hunting) while the other side was "cultural" (i.e., concerned primarily with things that assert power over nature, like shamanism). So pervasive was this division that it affected some of the most important aspects of Bororo life such as a marriage (which meant that a bride from one moiety had to cross the line to live with her husband's family on the other side) or a funeral (using culturally defined rituals to redress an imbalance in nature).

Most of these distinctions were not visible; in other words, the line bisecting the village was not painted on the ground or marked in any other way. But it was no less important to the people. In fact, when they were relocated by the government (with apparently good intentions), they were lost both physically and philosophically. Their new villages were supplied with piped in water, and the government planners were unconcerned about locating them near a river. Moreover, the new villages were laid out in an European pattern: main businesses arranged around a central square, with houses on streets running off in straight lines from the square. The Bororo were thus deprived of both the orienting symbol of the water, which made it impossible for them to figure out how to divide the village, and the overall structure of the circle. They were unable to reconstitute their moiety organization and despite the apparent material advantages of life in the new government settlements, they were depressed and unhappy to the point of falling ill. With the severance of the link between their concepts of the sacred and the physical space that represented those sacred ideas, the traditional Bororo culture could not survive.

Also doomed, but for different reasons, were the Caduveo. Most of the indigenous people of the South American forest have egalitarian social organizations—there is no marked division based on wealth or political power. But the Caduveo were a rare example of a ranked society; theirs was a rigid hierarchy with a small group of nobles ruling over warriors, laborers, and slaves (the latter taken in raids on other tribes). The nobles justified their position through mythology. All humans, they said, were drawn up out of a deep pit in the earth by the celestial spirits. As they came out, the spirits assigned them tasks to carry out. The nobles were the last to be drawn out, and by that time there were no tasks left except that of ruling over and benefiting from the labor of all the others. The Caduveo nobles believed it to be of special importance that they be seen as distinct as possible from ordinary humans.[3] To that end they shaved off all body hair. They denied that they partook of everyday bodily functions, including sex and childbirth; they did, in fact, have sex, but when a child was born, it was abandoned to be raised as a slave, and slave children would be adopted to be raised as nobles, all to preserve the fiction that the nobles themselves did not require the mundane mechanics of reproduction in order to perpetuate themselves.

Their most striking attempt at social differentiation was their use of face painting. Lévi-Strauss contends that while face-painting is a very widespread phenomenon, most people tend to treat the face as a kind of topographical map, bisected longitudinally by the nose and divided into horizontal thirds by the line of the eyes and the line of the lips. The forehead and chin are treated as balance points, as are the two ears. As a result, face-painting (or more permanent tattooing) involves balancing something done in one sector with something equivalent in another so that the end result is symmetrical. The Caduveo, by contrast, treat the face as if it were a flat piece of paper without natural features. They begin their design at any arbitrary point on that plane and create complex curvilinear designs that travel across the face according to the artist's whim, heedless of the supposed barriers of nose or lips. Lévi-Strauss claims that in this fashion, the Caduveo are expressing their political and philosophical creed in physical form. In effect, they are saying that their facial decoration, in which creative art overrides natural features, mirrors their "cultural" concept of rank and stratification, which takes precedence over the "natural" order of humanity (i.e., all people are the same).

So convinced were they of their own superiority that the Caduveo underestimated the powers of the European settlers ("men with hairy faces just like dogs," the Caduveo sneered) and they were wiped out. Before they met their fate, however, the Caduveo were apparently successful in creating a physical environment that expressed the abstract philosophical concerns of their religious tradition. The Bororo created "sacred space" on the ground; the Caduveo did it on their own bodies.

THE INTERSECTION OF SACRED AND PROFANE

People in various cultures look to the natural environment to find evidence of the supernatural in features like mountains, rivers, and deserts. They also create architectural forms or use other expressive arts to carve out a domain of the sacred. Nonetheless, for most believers (with the possible exception of the most advanced mystics), daily life can never be lived in a hermetically sealed bubble of sacredness. Although some religious groups (known as **communitarian societies**) try to create separate social worlds for themselves, the world as it is perceived through the eyes of faith is almost always bumping against the world of mundane reality.[4] The material world certainly imposes limits on the practice of religion. For example, economic conditions will determine the quality and extent of paraphernalia available for sacrifices or other ritual actions. Political factors will determine who gets to practice religion under which circumstances. Family obligations may dictate the practice of certain religious forms and make it difficult for individuals to explore their own consciences. Natural conditions (e.g., terrain, climate) will constrain the ways in which people can congregate for worship or other manifestations of religious activity.

By the same token, religion can have a strong influence on the material world. For example, religions may determine the eligibility of potential mates, and they may influence choices about whom to associate with in other social settings. Religion may make demands about diet or personal hygiene or the intimate sharing of food, clothing, or other objects (e.g., masks) that have a direct bearing on people's health. Religions that emphasize pilgrimage may require the movement of peoples in ways that may otherwise seem irrational for economic or political reasons. In sum, religion in all its forms in all the world's cultures has something to say about physical existence, the way people may and may not behave. It is intimately concerned with all the major life cycle transitions. Religion speaks to the way people are conceived, born, fed, cleaned, dressed, have sex, and are buried, and as a result, we can draw biological anthropology into our holistic understanding of religion.

KEY CONCEPTS

Be sure you can define the following terms, and give at least one illustrative example of each:

- aniconic tradition
- communitarian societies
- henotheistic
- representation
- sacrament

RESEARCH EXPLORATIONS

1. Visit a place of worship of any religious tradition other than your own. Do so at a time when no services are being held. Make one visit during which you observe and make notes on your own. Describe everything that you can perceive through your own five senses. (Do your best to take nothing for granted.) Then make a return visit in the company of some knowledgeable person and perceive that same place through the eyes of faith. Compare and contrast your own impressions with those that result from having seen the place with the aid of an insider. Write up a report, or prepare an in-class presentation of your findings. Be sure to include visual aids—sketches, photos, videos (with the permission of the proper authorities). Make very sure that the people you are dealing with understand that this is a class project and that you are not at this point interested in being converted. If they will not grant you access unless you promise to consider conversion, respect their position but find another site. Be very sure to check with your instructor about your university's norms regarding the signing of "informed consent" forms for projects of this nature.

2. Visit a public place that is supposedly secular in orientation, but that seems to have taken on sacred/mythic connotations. It might be a place of mainly local interest (e.g., a Revolutionary or Civil War battlefield), or it might be a place of national significance (e.g., Arlington National Cemetery; Ground Zero). It could be a place of pop cultural importance (e.g., Graceland) or scientific interest (e.g., Thomas Edison's laboratory). Observe the demeanor and actions of people as they interact with their physical surroundings. Write up your findings—supplemented, if feasible, by sketches, photos, or video—for an in-class presentation.

3. Conduct a critical review of the architecture (which would include both the buildings and the landscaping) of your university's campus. In what ways does it express the ideals embodied in your school's statement of mission? In what ways does it seem at variance with those ideals? Do you think that the physical space lends itself to the creation of a sense of emotional commitment to the university? If not, what recommendations might you give to your university's president with regard to "sacralizing" campus space so that people felt more of an emotional and spiritual attachment to the school? Present your plan to the class.

Notes

[1] For a seafaring people like the Greeks, the sea could be a metaphor for divinity; it was a force that had to be dealt with cautiously, but it was not something to be avoided. By contrast, a desert people like the ancient Hebrews thought of the sea as a distant and utterly terrifying thing, the symbol of the chaos that the divine power alone can bring under control.

2 Lévi-Strauss, Claude. 1967. *Tristes Tropiques: An Anthropological Study of Primitive Societies in Brazil*, tr. John Russell. New York: Atheneum (parts V and VI).

3 Lévi-Strauss always seems to find his nature/culture binary; nonstructuralists are skeptical about the universality of that distinction.

4 The United States, with its history of cultural pluralism, has a rich tradition of fostering communitarian groups who choose to live in isolation from the mainstream so as avoid corruption by the majority. The Amish are perhaps the best known of these groups; but it should be kept in mind that one of the ways the Amish are able to survive in the modern world is to open up their communities to tourists. They manage to keep visitors on the fringes of their everyday lives, but they can hardly be said to be living in splendid isolation.

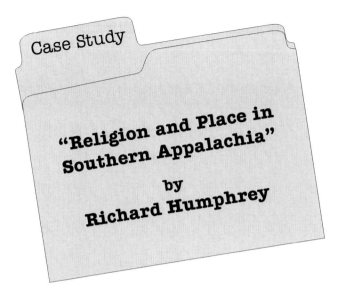

Case Study

"Religion and Place in Southern Appalachia"
by
Richard Humphrey

Humphrey explores the proposition that there is an intimate connection between religious consciousness and physical space through several examples from Appalachia. He compares and contrasts three Appalachian religious traditions. One group, the Religion of Zion, teaches that its members are God's chosen ones and that the land is God's chosen land. They are dependent on the cycles of the earth for their farming practices and believe that their personal health is dependent on the maintenance of the natural cycles of the earth. In their view, heaven and earth become one. Evangelical Christians, by contrast, view the land as wilderness needing to be subdued. This religious tradition focuses on individual rebirth from sin. Earth, unlike heaven, is only temporary. The third group, Mainstream Christianity, explains reality by breaking the whole into parts so that it can be analyzed rationally. Doctrine and laws—principles essentially external to the land itself—figure prominently in Mainstream Christianity, the only one of the three traditions that could be practiced anywhere.

Our Place, our identity, our roots is where someone close to us, our family, has been born and saved and died and been buried in the old churchyard. You ain't got no home unless you have birthed, reared, suffered, healed, sweated and laughed in a place.

—"Granny" Bunton, personal communication, 1978

Human land-use practices are strongly influenced by the ways in which people perceive their natural surroundings and their attitudes toward them. As Lynn White (1967) has observed, these perceptions and attitudes frequently have a religious

Reprinted by permission of the Southern Anthropological Society from *Cultural Adaptation to Mountain Environments,* ed. Patricia D. Beaver and Burton L. Purrington (Proceedings #17, 1984), pp. 122–141.

basis. In the Southern Appalachians the sense of place articulated by different religious groups is highly variable. A sense of place has helped form the religious consciousness of people in Appalachia and, in turn, has implications for their land-use practices. This [essay] will attempt to examine the interrelatedness between religious consciousness and place in Southern Appalachia.

In Southern Appalachia three distinct forms of religious consciousness relate to three different ways of interpreting people's relationships to the world around them. These three forms are the Religion of Zion, the evangelical, and mainstream Christian. These distinct religious worldviews have often gone unnoticed in studies of Appalachian religion because scholars have often divided Appalachian religion into traditional and mainstream, lumping all forms of traditional religion together. Statistical surveys and oral history interviews alike have investigated attitudes toward religious doctrine, economics, and political and social concerns. While this interest reflects mainstream interest, it only gives a partial picture of traditional religion in Southern Appalachia. Many people who have written about the region fail to make a distinction between the Religion of Zion and the evangelical; they lump the revivalists and antirevivalists together—those who do not use musical instruments in worship with those who play electric guitars.

Southern Appalachian people have an understanding of their place that is greatly influenced by their religious consciousness. The concept of "my place" constantly appears in conversations, whether people are educated or "just folks." However, there are differences in human relationships to the environment that are manifested in the three types of religious worldviews. The concept of place both informs and is formed by the religious consciousness of the people of Southern Appalachia. Whether the concept of place is related to self-identity, to heaven or hell, or to land, home, family, kin, community, church, and graveyard is determined by an individual's religious consciousness.

THE RELIGION OF ZION

The southern mountaineers who are tied closely to farming and a direct dependence on the land for their livelihood find that Christian Scripture offers the promise of continuity and stability in a potentially unstable world. For mountain farmers there is a definite pattern of both natural and sacred events that takes place according to each season, and a continuity among generations of families in their place. God assures mankind of the annual cycles of nature, and gives to mankind continuity through time. According to Scripture, mankind has the moon and the stars to plant by (Gen. 1:14) and the seasons of the year to plant and to pluck up by, to laugh and weep, to be sick and to heal. There is an appropriate season for everything (Eccles. 3:1). As God gave people plants and animals to eat (Gen. 1.29, 9:2–4), hard-working farmers are the first to receive crops (2 Tim. 2:6), and those who work the earth are blessed of God by the herbs that grow (Heb. 6:7). In turn, mankind must celebrate these cycles through the traditions of Christmas, Easter, the protracted meeting, conversion, creek baptism, the annual communion–foot washin' service, the flower service, the memorial service and funerals, Sunday worship, the singings, and the homecoming until Christ returns. These traditional sacred events reflect both the repetitive pattern of the annual seasons of nature by which humans work to make a living and the assurance of continuity in the Christian experience through the generations. The Religion of Zion is dependent upon the vision of Southern Appalachia as God's promised land.

The "hope and promise of the gospel" surrounds believers with the mountains of the Lord, as God surrounds them with the beauty of land, water, sky, plants, animals, and people. "My place" in the religion of Zion includes land, home, family, kin, community, and, for many, church and graveyard. This relationship to the land is expressed in the reminiscence of Mrs. Ida Presnell of Ashe County, North Carolina: "The Methodists said consolidation was good so they sold our church to the Baptists. We fooled them. They thought they could sell our church and graveyard. We're Baptist now" (personal communication, 1977). Rather than go to the larger church following consolidation of several small Methodist county churches, Mrs. Presnell and her neighbors kept their affiliation with the building and grounds of the old family church and became Baptists.

It is the experience with plants, animals, people, and seasons of the year that make all of this "my place." There is a sacred bond to one's geographic place. An older woman from Watauga County, North Carolina, powerfully described this hold the land has on people when she said:

> Our people are attached to the valleys and mountains all around surrounding us. It's been home for generations. They have the land, the place . . . probably more than the cities . . . How can people keep from having faith if they see this—you see God all around us . . . God put this here for us to live on, not destroy it. He wants us to keep it beautiful. People offer money for our land but we don't want to sell it. You just don't want to be cut off from the sacredness of your home and land. [1]

In turn, the book of Psalms is cited as reference to the sacred nature of mountainous places: "I will lift up mine eyes unto the hills from whence cometh my help. My help cometh from the Lord which made heaven and earth" (Ps. 121:1–2).

In Southern Appalachia churches with the names Zion, Old Zion, New Zion, Zion Hill, Zionville, Little Zion, Zion Valley, Zion Falls, Mount Zion, and Zion View are abundant. In these churches reference is frequently made to scriptural identification of Zion and God's assurance of peace: "For the Lord shall comfort Zion; he will comfort all her waste places; and he will make her wilderness like Eden, and her desert like the garden of the Lord; joy and gladness shall be found therein, thanksgiving and the voice of melody" (Isa. 51:3). The theme of the mountains is a common one, repeated at least thirty-one times in the Old Testament. The vision of Zion culminates in Revelation 14:1–3:

> And I looked, and lo, a lamb stood on the mount Zion and with him a hundred and forty-four thousand having his Father's name written on their foreheads. And I heard a voice from heaven, as the voice of many waters and as a voice of a great thunder: and I heard the voice of harpers harping with their harps and they sung as it were a new song.

This vision of Zion as a "favored" mountain landscape is found in hymns such as "Zion Stands with Hills Surrounded":

Zion stands with hills surrounded,
Zion kept by power divine;
All her foes shall be confounded
through the world in arms combine.

Refrain:
Happy Zion, what a favored lot is thine!
Happy Zion, what a favored lot is thine!

(*Broadman Hymnal* 1940:364)

The theme of Zion as a mountainous place of great beauty and eternal peace, in contrast to man's trials in the valley below, is found in the old favorite hymn popularly called "Beulah Land":

I am dwelling on the mountain
Where the golden sunlight gleams
O'er a land whose wondrous beauty
Far exceeds my fondest dream
Where the air is pure ethereal
Laden with the breath of flowers
They are blooming by the fountain,
'Neath the Amaranthine bow'rs.
I can see far down the mountain,
Where I wandered weary years,
Often hindered in my journey
By the ghosts of doubts and fears;
Broken vows and disappointments
Thickly sprinkled all the way,
But the Spirit led, unerring,
To the land I hold today.

Refrain:
Is not this the land of Beulah
Blessed, blessed land of light
Where the flowers bloom forever,
And the sun is always bright.

(*Calvary Songs* 1944:159)

Ambiguity characterizes the theology of the Religion of Zion. Adherents speak of Beulah Land and Zion as both here on earth and awaiting in heaven. However, many believers remind us that the end of the book of Revelation tells of a new heaven and a new earth to be established in these hills. For the people of the Religion of Zion their land, their place, is a gift from God, who has given them many passages of Scripture as evidence of the favored status of the land and the promise of eternity to come—in this place. The present mountain landscape has been assimilated to the geography of the Bible, to the geography of the new creation in Christ.

The testimony of the Old Regular Baptists demonstrates the view that they live in the time of the original creation—the time of Christ's creative divine acts. Elder Fugate, from Letcher County in Kentucky, speaking of the need to baptize in running water, explains that "Jordan is a mighty swift stream." With great reverence, church members took me to see their baptism hole in the creek and one member proclaimed, "We'uns have always baptized here. My Grandpa was saved in the church and he was baptized here goin' on fifty years ago." A layman rejoiced that the songs continue to ring through the mountains.

The Old Regulars wash feet because Christ initiated the pattern by washing the feet of Peter. This is commanded for all (John 13:12–15). This is the age when sin and death are real but "the kingdom of God is at hand." In the interim age one lives by "the hope and the promise of the Gospel." Accordingly, the "old fashioned" or "foot washin' " Christians of the Appalachian mountains emphasize following Christ's ordinances until their hopes and promises are fulfilled in Christ; the Lord's Supper is important since it is explicitly defined in 1 Corinthians 11:25–26: "Do this, as often as you drink it, in remembrance of me. For as often as you eat this bread and drink this cup you proclaim the Lord's death until he comes."

The model of Christ's humility is central and is an overt characteristic of the foot-washing service, in which believers humble themselves before fellow believers. This same emphasis on Christ's humility and an adherence to the gospel is found in other ordinances followed by "foot washin' " Christians, including the flower service, anointing the sick, the kiss of peace, or observance of a memorial. Regardless of which ordinance is followed, the emphasis is on reestablishing the world of Jesus the Christ in the church community. Foot-washing Christians take Paul's words of 1 Corinthians 11:1–2 very seriously: "Be imitators of me, as I am of Christ. I commend you because you remember me in everything and maintain the traditions even as I have delivered them to you" (Humphrey 1979).

Some Religion of Zion churches still have memorials when the sarvis blooms in the spring. The sarvis is the serviceberry *(Amelanchier arborea)*, the first tree in the woods to bloom and historically coincided with the coming of the itinerant preacher. Memorials are a type of revival, and revivals are always held between the planting season and the plucking and gathering season (Humphrey 1980a, 1980b).

Christmas and Easter are the central events within the Christian church as they revolve around the life of Jesus Christ. Yet the celebration of these events is dependent upon the sun and the heavenly bodies. The star of Bethlehem, the "birth" of the sun, and the moon phases signal the appropriate times for all sacred events in the Christian year. Genesis 1:14 reads, "And God said, let there be lights in the firmament of heaven to divide the day from the night, and let them be for signs, and for seasons, and for days and for years." According to Reverend Everett Haney, pastor of a Missionary Baptist church in Alexander, North Carolina, lights in the firmament, including the sun, the moon, and the stars, are signs for the change of weather and time. Signs guide people through the year, and are fruitful and shine without fail in their season. In the past, God has used a star to guide people to Christ. Using the stars and the moon as signs and planting by them shows faith in God and faith in the signs he made.

The tradition of planting by the signs is usually passed down from generation to generation. Le Roy Embler, a farmer in Alexander, North Carolina, said, "Everybody in my family knew about plantin' by the signs since way back before I can remember." A frequent explanation for planting by the signs was, according to Ruby Embler, " 'cause the ole timers do it" or " 'cause it seems to work." Le Roy remembered his grandfather saying that he planted by the signs out of faith and that it was a sin not to plant by the signs. Mr. Embler and several other farmers cited Ecclesiastes 3:1–2 as pertinent to planting by the signs: "To everything there is a season and a time to every purpose under the heaven; a time to be born and a time to die, a time to plant, and a time to pluck up that which is planted. . . . " Mr. Embler and Reverend Haney said that this verse means that people can no more reverse the times and order of planting, of digging up, and of transplanting than they can alter the times fixed for their birth and death. Humans cannot assume they are greater than God and plant out of season.

Mr. Embler explained the two ways of calculating planting signs as follows: "People who plant by the signs plant by the phases of the moon and the signs of the zodiac. Old timers tend to plant by the zodiac signs while the younger folk plant by the moon phases. The phases of the moon are the easiest to keep track of. One needs to know the monthly lunar cycle." According to Mr. Embler, if one observes the moon signs, it follows that plants that grow underground, such as potatoes, turnips, onions, and others should be planted in the dark of the moon or they will "go to tops," that is, be very leafy on top and have very few roots.

The dark of the moon is the time from the full moon to the next new moon. As the moon shrinks it pulls downward, causing a greater growth beneath the ground. The greatest pull downward occurs directly on the full moon.

Mr. Embler says that beans, peas, tomatoes, and other plants that crop above the ground should be planted in the light of the moon. The light of the moon is the time from the new moon to the next full moon. As the moon grows bigger in the lunar cycle, it pulls upward, causing a greater growth above the ground. The greatest upward pull occurs directly on the new moon.

Planting by the zodiac signs is a little more complicated than the moon phase method. One must have basic knowledge of astrology and familiarity with the twelve constellations that encircle the earth. During particular times of the year, certain constellations appear in the sky, designating specific planting times. For example, one plants seeds under the signs of Cancer, Scorpio, or Pisces because they are times indicative of moisture, productivity, and feminine receptivity (American Almanac Planting Calendar).

Reverend Haney and Ruby Embler cited several other verses in the Bible that pertain to planting by the signs. Psalms 104:19 reads, "He appointed the moon for seasons, the sun knoweth his going down." They explained that God provides and adapts to people's needs the appointed seasons. The sun and moon are gifts for people to use. However, God does not want us to worship the stars and the moon, since God spoke to Moses and told him that his people should not make idols out of animals or the stars in the heavens (Deut. 4:19).

Ecclesiastes 11:4 reads, "He that observeth the wind shall not sow, and he that regardeth the clouds shall not reap." In this verse the wind and the clouds represent earthly and unstable signs. To plant by the weather, or earthly signs, is wrong and this will not yield a good crop. Man should not look for his own signs in earthly things, but look for God's signs.

Farmers should rotate their crops every seven years, like Leviticus 25:3 commands. Ecclesiastes 11:6 reads, "In the morning sow thy seed." Most farmers will plant in the morning hour rather than in the heat of the day. The list of specific guidelines for planting, cultivating, and harvesting, using scriptural reference, is extensive.

Some signs to plant by are based on the model of Christ's death and passion. One must plant on Good Friday. The death of Jesus and the death of the old natural order coincide in the production of a new creation. As Jesus dies and overcomes death, following the lunar pattern of disappearing into the darkness of the underworld for three days, farmers plant seed in anticipation of the new cosmic situation produced by his resurrection.

According to the followers of the Religion of Zion, their sacred relationship to the earth and plants is not just confined to production of food. For mountain herbalists, understanding the sacred nature of the earth and plants is important for curing illness and maintaining good health. Clarence Gray[2] believes that God called him not simply to be a Christian but also to carry on his family's herbal tradition. A member of the Church of Christ in New Martinsville, West Virginia, Catfish uses his knowledge of herbs, his prayer, and his belief in faith healing to cure and heal people. He also believes that most illness is in the mind and is due to sinful living. He stands in a long line of Indian, Afro-American, and German herb doctors in Southern Appalachia, many of whom see a direct connection between religion, land, and plants. Catfish believes, as do most herbalists in Southern Appalachia, that the earth has everything humans need. God's creation is good. Evil is due to human abuses (Green 1978).

The Religion of Zion consciousness views all the people in a given place as sharing community because of their assumed kinship and their shared history and values. Their religious world view also fashions the concept of "place," so that being of a place includes visiting the sick and those in prison, feeding the hungry, giving hospitality, "pounding" preachers and the needy, and taking care of orphans and widows (Humphrey 1980a, 1980b). Pounding here refers to the giving of a pound of coffee, a pound of flour, etc., by members of the church to persons in need. When one combines this emphasis of "taking care of our own" with the church's practice of church discipline (excommunicating members for improper behavior) in accordance with Matthew 18:15–20, the concept of "my place" takes on a network of community mores, morals, and laws to abide by in the church. No one wishes to go through the disgrace of being brought before the church on some charge of moral turpitude or to be actually "churched" and written up in the official church records.

Foot washing has a dual emphasis on humility and service to one's neighbors. It has a tremendous therapeutic effect in healing hurt feelings and in bringing about a deeper sense of community. The flower service is observed annually in early September in several churches in Watauga County, North Carolina, and has a similar effect. On the appointed Sunday morning, church members bring flowers to church and place them on the altar. After the minister preaches, reminding the congregation of "Christian love, of forgiving one's neighbors," the worshippers exchange flowers, confess wrongdoings, ask forgiveness, bless one another, and embrace. The community achieves a sense of cleansing, reconciliation, and renewal.

"My place" in Zion is land and extended family; it includes the family church, which provides structure and justification for its members' way of life here on earth and prepares them for the life to come. This support system empowers them as individuals to become involved in local social movements that attack the evils of strip mining and other types of misuse of the environment. Their bodies at death will return to the earth in the church graveyard with their kin and friends who have gone on before them; they live with the knowledge that they all will be reunited on the day of the general resurrection, and will live forever in these hills in the new heaven and earth.

EVANGELICAL RELIGION

The dominant theology in Southern Appalachia is based upon the evangelical consciousness. Represented among the evangelicals are churches of the major denominations found in rural and small-town Appalachia such as the rural United Methodists and Southern Baptists, the Cumberland Presbyterians, Free Will Baptists, Church of Christ, Christian Church, Independent and Missionary Baptists, and the numerous churches of the Holiness and Pentecostal movement. For the evangelical, the land is not seen as Zion but as a wilderness that has to be subdued and controlled. If people live by nature, which sin controls, they would be damned (Gen. 3:17; Rom. 6:8). The mountains, the seasons, the Indians, the wild animals, and the poisonous plants are all seen as evil and man was put here to have dominion over them (Gen. 1:23). Believers see themselves as alienated from nature.

Since the Great Revival of 1787 to 1805, evangelical preachers have reminded listeners that they are alienated from God. If people do not learn to subdue nature, it is at the expense of their eternal souls (Rom. 8:14–19). Nature, even human nature, is controlled by sin. If believers wish to live right, they must be convicted of sin, repent of their sins, and humble themselves at the feet of Christ. Then God will save them through his son Jesus Christ's gracious and vicarious sacrifice. Jesus—"faith in Jesus"—is the way to salvation, the way from this place of the filth of sin and death to one's real home, one's heavenly home, "to life eternal." "Ye must be born again" (John 3:7).

The natural patterns and signs by which the children of Zion see God continually work through his creation are replaced by the evangelical emphasis on the evils of nature and on sin, repentance, faith, and new birth (Rom. 5:8). This rebirth frees believers from nature, sin, and death and makes them new creatures in Christ, ones who will live eternally with God and his kin in a new home—heaven (John 3:1–5; Matt. 25:34; Heb. 11:13–16).

The evangelical faith offers believers an escape from the terrors and insecurities of modern life. The emphasis is not on community or place but upon the individual. One is saved through *personal* repentance, faith, and regeneration. People are not dependent upon the natural order; they are free of it. The future course of the natural world does not affect their ultimate destiny (Gal. 5).

The evangelical religious consciousness places emphasis on the individual in need of salvation, and preaching focuses on the conversion of the individual. The theology of John Calvin, with its emphasis on a slow and often agonizing pilgrimage from sin to repentance to living the Christian life in community is replaced by an emphasis on the individual and instant conversion. The evangelical theology in Southern Appalachia is not based upon the Christian pilgrimage and a systematic interpretation of Scripture. Evangelical preachers emphasize that religion is not taught or nurtured in this world; their theology emphasizes a personal conversion experience. One is judged to be a Christian not by one's correct doctrine or one's life-style but by attesting to one's conversion experience. Evangelical mountain preaching is considered successful if it is exhortative and brings people to conversion. A common saying is, "Religion is caught, not taught."

Revivals, like their predecessor the camp meeting, are seen as primary for the life of the evangelical Christian, and all forms of worship focus on bringing the individual sinner to salvation. The exhortative style of preaching, the prayers, the gospel songs, baptism, the Lord's Supper, and even funerals become the means through which individuals might be saved. Believers must climb on board the "Gloryland Train" if they are to leave the filth and corruption of this world and put on "the Holy raiment" waiting for them in heaven. For believers this world and its sinful relationships have already been destroyed. Their real personal life is heaven (Boles 1972; Humphrey 1974, 1978).

This vision of eternity is vividly and powerfully proclaimed in gospel hymns like "When the Roll Is Called up Yonder":

> When the trumpet of the Lord shall sound,
> and time shall be no more,
> and the morning breaks eternal bright and fair;
> When the saved of earth shall gather over
> on the other shore,
> and the roll is called up yonder, I'll be there.
>
> (*New Songs of Inspiration, Number Nine* 1973:87)

The sin of the world and the search for heaven is seen in many songs such as "Looking for a City":

> Here among the shadows (living) in a lonely land,
> With strangers we're a band of pilgrims on the move;
> Through dangers burdened down with sorrows,
> and we're shunned on every hand,
> But we are looking for a city, built above.
> Looking for a city, where we'll never die,
> There with all the millions, never say goodby,
> There we'll meet our Savior, and our loved ones too
> Come O holy Spirit, all our hopes renew.
>
> (*Best Loved Songs and Hymns* 1961:193)

In "I'm Going Home," the earth is a prison to be endured until one enters the heavenly mansion, the promised home for believers:

> My heavenly home is bright and fair;
> Nor pain, nor death can enter there,
> Its glittering towers the sun outside,
> That heav'nly mansion shall be mine.
>
> My Father's house is built on high;
> Far, far above the starry sky;
> When from this earthly prison free,
> That Heavenly mansion shall be mine.
>
> Let others seek a home below,
> Which flames devour or waves o'er flow,

Be mine a happier lot to own
A heavenly mansion near the Throne.

Refrain:
I'm going home, I'm going home,
I'm going home, to die no more,
to die no more, to die no more,
I'm going home to die no more.

(*Best Loved Songs and Hymns* 1961:345)

For the evangelical, the hardships and insecurities of mountain life are only temporary. Eventually the suffering and death, the unpredictable seasons and weather will be replaced by the celestial city, where no pain and sorrow or night and day or any of the other contingencies of the natural order exist.

Following the Civil War and its disruptive and tragic effects upon land, family, community, and church, the evangelical consciousness found concrete expression in the birth of the Holiness–Pentecostal movement in Monroe County, Tennessee, and Cherokee County, North Carolina (Conn 1977). Through the second blessing one could actually go on to perfection in this life and become holy. Also one could find evidence of and bear witness to one's faith through the gifts of the Spirit described by the Apostle Paul in 1 Corinthians 12 and 14. Prophecy, speaking in tongues, interpreting tongues, and faith healing transcended the bonds of nature. As early as 1909, especially in areas near textile mills and coal-mining sections of the region, others found the command in Mark 16:17 to take up serpents as further evidence of God's power over the natural order. God truly could create anew. Through the power of the Holy Spirit, man's imperfections, sin, and illnesses could be overcome. The Spirit had power over the serpent that had beguiled Adam and Eve, the first man and the first woman, into sin. The serpent was now under God's power and could not harm the true convert of Jesus Christ. The Christians not only could be free of their natural bondage, but, through the power of the Holy Spirit, they bore witness of Jesus Christ's victory over nature, sin, and death.

The evangelical consciousness, with its views of nature and its conversion theology, had great appeal to the mountain people who found the land, the climate, and other people a burden and to those who were forced by economic necessity to leave the rural agricultural life in traditional communities for work in the burgeoning mill villages at the mountain fringe or in the coal camps of central Appalachia. It provided rationale for selling, leaving, changing, or destroying one's land and home place.

The evangelical Christian is caught in a place that is evil, a future death, and ultimate destruction of the world. But through this theology a person can become a new creature and thus become one who is alien to nature, who is a citizen of heaven and the world to come (Rom. 12:1–2). Through repentance the "saved" enter the Kingdom of God at the present moment. Their entire life is a foretaste of "glory divine." The evangelical consciousness offers people an escape from the terrors of everyday life through *personal* repentance, *personal* faith, and *personal* regeneration. Believers are not dependent on nature; they are freed of it. Its future course does not affect their own ultimate destiny.

The evangelical consciousness is found among Methodists, Southern Baptists, Presbyterians, the Church of God, the Assembly of God, and numerous Holiness sects in Southern Appalachia. Because of an otherworldly focus, adherents do not believe that religion should be mixed with politics or with social and economic issues or problems. For the evangelicals, "my place" is not in this world but in that other place; heaven is "up yonder."

MAINSTREAM CHRISTIANITY

The third form of religious consciousness began to make its presence known in Southern Appalachia in the 1880s and 1890s when both the southern and northern missionaries of mainline Christianity rediscovered mountain life. The mainline churches are United Methodist, American Baptist, Southern Baptist, Lutheran, Presbyterian, Episcopal, Christian, and Roman Catholic.

Mainstream Christian denominations are grounded in a critical consciousness, whose goal is to apprehend reality by breaking wholes into parts. This analysis occurs through the use of sensory experience and reason, skills that are universally available to human beings. From medieval Christianity this consciousness received a passion for doctrine, logic, and systems. From the Enlightenment and René Descartes, practitioners gained confidence in the use of reason, and from John Locke they knew sense data could be relied upon. Thus the Christians in mainstream Christianity have a religious consciousness based upon a system of rational doctrines, in which philosophical and religious truths are one and the same. Their faith lies in a reality that is apprehended by principle, law, or theory. Personal involvement—the subjective—is to be avoided. Fact and the gathering of data or "proof" are important. Doctrine is more abstract principle or theory than it is a story of image or representation of reality. Experience must be proven in the public domain by logic and/or the scientific method. Scripture, for mainstream Christianity, should not conflict with reason. In fact, believers study about the Scriptures and various ways of interpreting the Scriptures as much as they read the Scriptures. For many, the Scriptures are seen as an anthology of literature, as a history of man's understanding of his relationship to God or, in the tradition of Thomas Jefferson, as a moral guide for our lives.

Accordingly, the scientific-historical consciousness is hostile to or embarrassed by the truth claims of the stories and experiences presented by the Religion of Zion and the evangelical religion because they are personal and subjective and because they are not based upon historical fact, provable logic, or scientific data, theory, law, and principle. Mainstream Christianity has been most antagonistic to the very things the people of Southern Appalachia hold most dear—their religion and their place.

Mainline Christians for almost a century have developed caricatures of the Southern Appalachian region. One image is the "hard shell," ignorant Baptists, with their hellfire and damnation preaching and their old-fashioned ways. Scholars have referred to the traditional Christians as fundamentalist sectarians, as fatalistic with a puritan ethic (Ford 1967:22–23). Simultaneously they describe the mountaineer preachers as emotional and the worshippers as "holy rollers" or "snake handlers." Whether hard shell or holy rollers, traditional churches are seen as pagan, quaint, and peculiar.

The churches of mainstream America today dominate the county seats and larger cities of Southern Appalachia. The membership is largely made up of professional people (those who have "made it" by mainstream standards). Church members are often from outside the region or are people who have left their place in Southern Appalachia both geographically and psychologically. Worship services are more formal, are in "good taste," and have proper decorum. Their services follow a printed bulletin, they have educated clergy, and their choirs wear robes, as do most clergymen. Services use modern hymns (no shaped notes or lining of hymns), have a "logical" sermon, an anthem by the choir, and take up a collection. They spend a great deal of money on church buildings and Sunday school literature and tend to become involved in personal morality issues. Some Methodists, Roman Catholics, Episcopalians, and Presbyterians—mainly professional people from towns and cities—also become involved in social issues that affect Appalachia (e.g., strip mining, zoning, development, etc.) and in national issues (e.g., peace movements, abortion, prison reform, welfare, etc.).[3]

More important on the local level, members of these churches form the local elite and thus make decisions that influence the economic development of the region. The coal-mining executives, agency officials, school administrators, developers, bankers, tourist promoters, doctors, merchants, and professional people in general are members of mainline churches. They have in many cases uncritically accepted the premise that progress and modernity are necessarily good for the development of the region. This is reflected in their belief that more jobs, good roads, and consolidated schools will overcome Southern Appalachian people's "backwardness." Many accept the "culture of poverty" model of Appalachia and with great paternalism want to make things "better" for the poor of the region. They have come to believe that the traditional mountain religion keeps people living in yesterday's world (Weller 1965:121–133). These churches are still trying to "save" the other Christians of Southern Appalachia. In fact, they are either hostile to or embarrassed by the Religion of Zion and feel uncomfortable among the evangelicals. As Loyal Jones wrote: "No group in the country, in my estimation, has aroused more suspicion and alarm among mainstream Christians, than have Appalachian Christians and never have so many Christian missionaries been sent to save so many Christians than is the case in this region" (Jones 1977:120).

For mainline Christianity, a belief in progress and an optimistic attitude toward science and industry foster a continuing attack upon traditional Appalachian people's religion and place. Professionals in Kentucky, Virginia, and West Virginia still defend strip mining and through their control of local politics are destroying that which the traditional Appalachian people value most. In Tennessee, Georgia, and North Carolina tourism is proclaimed as a quick way to bring prosperity and progress to the people.

For mainline Christianity land is a commodity; it is no longer "place." The individuals whose identities reside within themselves now replace the emphasis on the otherworldly individuals of the evangelical. "This is my space. Don't intrude on my space" is the equivalent of moving one's place from the mountains and the "celestial city" to one's own body. This may not even be a totally conscious act. Yet with the modern emphasis on mobility for jobs, promotions, and economic development, progress, consumerism, and economic development all lead one away from a sacred and personal relationship to the land, the people, and the culture.

Mainstream belief systems have promoted a sense of alienation from the land. Organizationally the emphasis is placed upon national interest and concerns, and programs do not relate to local concerns. Ministers are educated for service in mainstream society, not for a particular region or subculture, and, like other middle-class Americans, are expected to move to other churches periodically. The Sunday school literature comes from a national publishing house and consequently focuses on mainstream issues and interests.

Mainstream Christians, with their scientific historical consciousness, their national organizations, programs, literature, and educated clergy see their culture and their religion as more advanced and thus better than that of their ancestors. For them, land is for economic development and a better way of life.

Conclusion

In Southern Appalachia, land and the place of the people are radically changing. While all mountain Christians recognize this change, Christians interpret it differently within the region. The Old Regulars and other "foot washin'" Christians (Religion of Zion) are trying to hold their own in the mountains and attribute their problems to pressure on people to be modern, to leave the home place. Mainstream consciousness views the Religion of Zion experience as alien to and as a threat to progress and a better way of life; hence those who profess traditional Christian values are labeled sectarian. As the children of traditional Christians go off to school and assimilate the scholarly consciousness, or as people move toward town and assimilate its urban consciousness, their loyalty to the home place is destroyed or tested (however, not all of them succumb). Their new external consciousness demands a different type of religious consciousness. This is provided by the churches whose values are more in line with that of modern society such as Presbyterian, United Methodist, and Southern Baptist.

A few of the adherents to the Religion of Zion and the evangelical world views are moving together, especially in their appreciation of the land as God's gift. Also some professionals in mainstream Christianity are realizing that the beauty and many of the values of the traditional culture of Southern Appalachia should be preserved and affirmed.

Religion and place have a strong influence on the people of the Southern Appalachian region whether they view the land as a gift of God or a commodity to be bought and sold. In the face of radical change, adherents of the Religion of Zion, the evangelical traditional, and mainstream churches are beginning to share environmental concerns. While the churches of the Religion of Zion and the evangelical will not officially take a stand on these issues, individuals, especially among the Religion of Zion churches, have been in the forefront of many local social movements. As environmental issues become more critical, this sensitivity to the environment—water, air, land, plants, animals, and even people may—lead to more cooperation and support between the traditional and the mainstream churches. The reverence for the land that is inherent in the Religion of Zion could inform both the evangelical and mainstream Christians' consciousness and lead all Christians of Southern Appalachia to articulate more responsible approaches to ecological systems.

Notes

[1] Statement made by an unidentified Watauga County, North Carolina, woman in the film *Region in Change,* University of Georgia, 1972.

[2] Clarence Gray is best known as "Catfish, Man of the Woods," as portrayed in the 1975 Appalshop film of that title.

[3] See Max E. Glenn's *Appalachia in Transition* (St. Louis: The Bethany Press, 1970). Mr. Glenn was executive director of the Commission of Religion in Appalachia (CORA). This book is written by leaders of the various denominations who are involved in CORA. The book illustrates their concerns with the issues in Southern Appalachia and also the tendencies toward paternalism. The most powerful statement addressing the issues dealing with the people and land in Southern Appalachia is "This Land Is Home to Me—A Pastoral Letter on Powerlessness in Appalachia by the Catholic Bishops of the Region," published by the Catholic Committee of Appalachia, *Richlands News Press,* Prestonsburg, Kentucky, July 3, 1974. The sad commentary is that the insights and concerns of these letters are not widespread within the local churches in the region.

QUESTIONS FOR DISCUSSION

1. How do Humphrey's Appalachian examples relate to data from other parts of the world? Is the relation between land and faith unique to Appalachia?

2. Consider the three Appalachian traditions. Do you think that the architecture of each of the three churches in any way reflects their different relations to the natural land? If so, how?

3. How might attitudes toward the land impact people's ideas about gender, family, and social relations?

SUGGESTED READINGS OR OTHER RESOURCES

General Works

Hostetler, John A. 1974. *Communitarian Societies.* New York: Holt, Rinehart and Winston.

Reynolds, Vernon and Ralph Tanner. 1995. *The Social Ecology of Religion.* New York: Oxford University Press.

Selected Case Studies

Molloy, Michael. 1999. Islam and the Arts. In *Experiencing the World's Religions* by Michael Molloy. Mountain View, CA: Mayfield (pp. 438–444).

Reichel-Dolmatoff, G. 1976. Cosmology as Ecological Analysis: A View from the Rain Forest. *Man* 11:307–318.

Videos

Amish and Us (Insight Media) is a 57-minute tour of the Amish community in Lancaster County, Pennsylvania, highlighting the interactions between the Amish and their visitors in its exploration of the dynamics of a deliberately segregated culture.

Trip to Awareness: A Jain Pilgrimage to India (Insight Media) is a 30-minute visit to four important Jain temples; philosophical principles of Jainism are discussed in relationship to these sacred sites.

8

Religion in an Age of Globalization

featuring

"Civil Religion Redux"
by Michael V. Angrosino

Most social philosophers of the nineteenth century assumed that religion would disappear as science replaced faith as a basis for knowing the world and as new technology gave humans an enhanced sense of mastery over their environment. Some of them looked forward eagerly to the new, religion-free world, believing that religion had been a force for ignorance and reaction. Karl Marx famously called religion the "opiate" of the people—a means by which those in power kept the oppressed masses from understanding their predicament and taking decisive action for change. Freud saw religion as a set of "illusions," a collective neurosis that, like any neurotic belief or behavior, needed to be exposed and thus disposed of.

As we have seen throughout our tour of the domain of the sacred, science itself, not to mention large, quasi-scientific belief systems like Marxism and Freudianism, can itself be seen as "religion." In effect, "religion" did not die in the twentieth century. Instead, it simply shifted away from the traditional, formalized religious institutions of the past and toward *other* systems of symbols that also act to establish powerful, pervasive, and long-lasting moods and motivations in people by creating conceptions of a general order of existence and clothing those conceptions in such an aura of factuality that they come to seem uniquely realistic. But we hardly need to be reminded that even in the new millennium the traditional, formalized religious institutions are far from dead. Fundamentalist and revivalistic movements have swept most of the great world religions, including Christianity, Islam, and Hinduism, and religion continues to be deeply intertwined with the political and social concerns of nations large and small.

The context in which religion flourishes has, however, changed dramatically over the past century. Advances in communication and transportation have brought a kind of global community into being, a world in which the old physical boundaries are increasingly less meaningful. With greater movement of people and ideas, religions no longer exist as autonomous isolates that can be studied as if they were closed systems. Anthropology developed as an academic discipline devoted to the study of small, traditional cultures, and its perspective on religion was shaped by its study of such cultures. So what does anthropology have to tell us about religion in an age of **globalization**?

RELIGION AND SOCIOCULTURAL CHANGE

Culture as a whole is a set of beliefs, behaviors, and material products that help a people adapt to its natural and social environment. As part of the system of culture, religion must also be thought of as an element in the process of human adaptation, and hence in the evolution of human culture. As environments constantly change, the means by which human groups adapt must also change. This evolutionary process is usually gradual—almost imperceptible—although it is possible to see any number of crisis points (wars, natural disasters, epidemics, and so forth) in the histories of many societies at which the process was necessarily speeded up. What seems to be different in the modern world is that the *pace* of change seems to be accelerating. Whether that acceleration is something that can be empirically measured is not the point; if people *perceive* it to be so, then their perception has consequences for how they respond to the world. Moreover, the *intensity* of change seems to have increased; no longer restricted to isolated historical moments of conflict and crisis, change seems to be pushing at us relentlessly. If people in the West—with their ideology of the desirability of progress—are sometimes rattled by the pace and intensity of change, such that they express a nostalgic longing for "the good old days," how much more will these perceptions impact people from smaller, more traditional societies whose cultures have not generally embraced change as a positive good?

People in such traditional societies may well feel that a continuity with a cherished past is now threatened. Even if that past wasn't as idyllic as people would like to remember it, its virtues seem to glow the more they are threatened by external influences whose meaning and ramifications are unclear and unsettling. Since religion is one way that people have to assert control over a world that threatens to spin into chaos, it is not surprising that one response to this perception of threat is to return to the "old-time religion." It is not always possible to do so: remember the Bororo and Caduveo discussed in chapter 7, and how rapid changes in their sociocultural environments led to their extinction before they ever had a chance to reflect on their plight and take steps to deal with it. But in larger societies with more institutional resources (e.g., economic or political institutions that can survive threats, at least in the short term), it is possible to rally the populace to action (or *re*action, as the case may be). One possible response might be one of the revitalization movements discussed in chapter 4. As we have seen, some revitalizations operate on the assumption that it is necessary to accommodate the old and the new, while others take the tack of complete rejection of the new and total reliance on the old. In either case, the adherence to whatever type of revitalization is chosen tends to be more "ecstatic" than adherence to religion in the period to the crisis. In the crisis period, the sense of threat touches not only the religion itself but the entire identity of the people, which was, at least in part, wrapped up in that religion. But if once they could take their religion for granted and go about their business, their beliefs and practices must be marked by special fervor if they are to be successful in helping people adapt to severe new challenges.

RELIGION IN PLURALISTIC, SECULAR SOCIETIES

A somewhat different set of challenges confronts people in the societies in the urbanized, industrialized world. If people in traditional societies may be said to suffer from **absolute deprivation** in the sense that they feel their entire way of life is threatened with extinction, people in "modern" societies may suffer from **relative deprivation**—the feeling that things, while not absolutely bad, are still considerably worse than they need to be. People suffering from a sense of absolute deprivation may be driven to extremes since it seems as if they have few viable options. Those suffering from relative deprivation may be no less depressed or frustrated, but they do have a variety of options. As such they tend to become "seekers," hopping from one promising path of enlightenment to another, always in the hope of finding the most satisfying answer. They rarely become iron-clad "true believers" who make their commitment only when the options are belief or death.

Many Westerners have lived in **pluralistic societies** for decades. They are home to people from many different cultural/religious traditions who have emigrated in hopes of economic opportunities or political freedom—and, perhaps as a corollary, are highly secular. Pluralistic societies have not, in general, been able to survive if they seem to give preference to religion, for to be partial to one could be construed as discrimination against the rest. In the United States, for example, the "separation of church and state" is considered one of the foundational points of our democratic system (although, of course, the exact meaning of that phrase is endlessly reinterpreted). Religion in such societies does not disappear, but it operates in an environment that encourages its withdrawal from the public arena. Religious bodies in such societies can and do speak out on major public policy issues, but by and large any citizen has the right to affiliate with any religious body—or with none at all—as he/she sees fit. In the United States, we cherish the compromise: "I won't push my beliefs on you if you don't push yours on me."

The right to individual expression is a very important value in U.S. culture. Even though Americans, like other people, seek out the fellowship of like-minded individuals, they do not like to feel that their own ideas and opinions are any less valuable than those that derive from the consensus of the group. Social scientists thus refer to the **privatization** of religion: people develop their religious ideas and carry out their religious practices in ways that do not infringe on their other duties and activities as citizens of a secular society. In an earlier era, U.S. religious leaders sometimes spoke of establishing a "city on a hill"—a new kind of society in which religious values would be proclaimed and cultivated as the basis for an idealized civic order. The "church" (using that term generically to refer to any formal religious institution) has not exactly gone underground, but few people expect, or want, it to be the guiding light for all the affairs of the entire nation. Indeed, the "church" has become for many in the United States a haven *from* the world rather than a beacon *for* the world.

The privatization of religion in a pluralistic secular society like the United States has led to a proliferation of "New Age" spiritualities. Americans like to distinguish between "religion" (by which they mean the traditional, institutionalized churches, synagogues, mosques, and so forth) and **spirituality** (by which they mean a concern with transcendent matters and the almost infinite variety of beliefs and behaviors associated with that concern). Although the United States still has by far the highest percentage of affiliated "church" members of any of the Western, industrial, urban democracies, an increasing number of Americans are opting to characterize themselves as "spiritual" rather than "religious," leading some scholars of American religion to characterize the typical American ideology as a kind of **pantheistic mysticism**—a belief that there is a bit of the divine in all things and that there are many ways (meditation, use of crystals, aromatherapy, and so forth and so on) to get in touch with that divine essence. Pantheistic mysticism may, in fact, be the modern urbanite's way of getting in touch with the animist roots of religion.

Perhaps the most explicit example of an animist-inflected revitalization in modern society is *Wicca*, said to be a revival of ancient witchcraft. Christianity spread in the West during the days of the Roman Empire, but traditional pre-Christian forms of worship (including a reverence for nature) undoubtedly survived in rural areas, away from political control. The rural folk were known to the urban elites as "pagani" and hence the old religion was referred to as "paganism." In the eyes of the Christians, any religion that failed to affirm Christian beliefs had to be the work of the devil, and hence paganism came to be associated in the minds of its opponents with the worship of Satan. Its practitioners—witches and warlocks—were probably well versed in the traditional arts of sorcery and were undoubtedly consulted by the common people for a wide variety of ailments and natural events such as childbirth. But they were castigated by the authorities as agents of Satan, were driven underground, and acquired the evil reputation that has clung to them throughout the centuries. Severely persecuted in Europe and North America until the eighteenth century, practitioners of witchcraft have experienced a remarkable revival in the more tolerant modern era.[1] Contemporary Wiccans celebrate the cycles of nature, and some of them have developed an elaborate belief system based on the centrality of a goddess figure, making Wicca an attractive alternative religion for some feminists and environmentalists.

From the standpoint of religion, one of the advantages of a pluralistic, secularized society is that it is tolerant of separatist **communitarian societies** that are free to hold whatever beliefs they please and to engage in whatever activities suit them, as long as they do so in ways that are physically removed from the mainstream and as long as they do not make nuisances of themselves. Some such groups, like the Quakers, came to America in the face of persecution. The Quakers began as dissenters from the established churches of Europe, but they eventually became a respectable denomination in their own right once free of constraint by the civil authorities. One American-born separatist movement, the Church of Jesus Christ of Latter Day Saints (the Mormons), began as a small group of people willing to trek far into the wilderness in order to practice their religion in peace. They have grown into a hugely successful (and now international) institutional organization. The United Society of Believers in Christ's Second Appearing (better known as the "Shakers") developed in a similar way throughout the nineteenth century, although their ranks are now very much depleted; they are now known mainly for their furniture and their distinctive singing style. Other, much smaller groups are made up of the descendants of people who came to America fleeing religious persecution; given the immensity of the land in the eighteenth and nineteenth centuries, they were able to stake out communities that flourished just beyond the margins of mainstream society. Groups like the Amish, the Hutterites, and the Mennonites continue to hang on to their traditional ways; they are generally viewed with favor by other Americans because they are believed to be peaceable, hardworking, and virtuous, and because they do not aggressively seek out converts. Indeed, a number of such communities are popular tourist attractions for hard-pressed Americans eager for a glimpse of homey, old-fashioned peace and quiet (although few of them would choose to live in such a community on a permanent basis).

A somewhat different kind of traditional community is that of the Pentecostalist serpent-handlers who have maintained their special identity in rural and out-of-the-way places for more than a century. The worship services of such groups feature dancing with venomous snakes and swallowing poisons in an attempt to prove that they are in the power of the Holy Spirit and, as such, can overcome all the works of the devil. The serpent-handlers do not enjoy the apple-pie-and-family-outing image of the Amish, and from time to time they have been persecuted for encouraging dangerous practices. But since they do not seek converts from outside their isolated communities (they do not, for example, show up to preach at busy shopping malls while carrying their snakes) they are generally treated with a sort of bemused contempt by the outside world, which sees them as an example of bizarre "local color" on the American landscape.

Considerably more controversial are the separatist communities that *are* perceived as nuisances at best and as pernicious influences at worst. They are usually referred to as **cults**, a label that implies that they have less than legitimate status even within the tolerant, pluralistic framework of American religion. The non-mainstream ideologies of such groups, as well as their propensity to evangelize and aggressively seek out new converts, have given them a reputation as "destructive" forces. The tragic ends of the Branch Davidians, the People's Temple (Jonestown), and the Heaven's Gate group have been taken as parables of the dangers of extremism in the name of religion. The failures of such groups are usually attributed to the malign influence of their charismatic leaders. Those leaders tend to be characterized in the popular media as demagogues and megalomaniacs (and probably sexual deviants to boot) who have somehow brainwashed their pathetic followers into madness. As usual, anthropologists prefer to avoid making value judgments about the beliefs and activities of other people, but it should be pointed out that the people who are attracted to such "cults" are probably motivated by the same fears and concerns that drive people in more traditional societies into fundamentalist revitalizations. They feel themselves to be cast adrift in a world out of control, and they gravitate to groups that give them stability, to leaders who promise them firm guidance, and to beliefs that seem to explain even the most horrible circumstances in terms that are spiritually and emotionally satisfying.

Another way in which people in a pluralistic, secularized society activate their religious sense is by adherence to a **civil religion**. More than simple patriotism, a civil religion imbues the institutions and traditions of the civil society with transcendent significance. The American version of civil religion is reviewed and analyzed in the case study article accompanying this chapter.

CONFRONTING THE CHALLENGES OF THE MODERN WORLD

Let us briefly consider a few examples of religious movements in the modern world that illustrate the nature of the perceived threats inherent in that world and the ways in which people in various cultures have responded to them.

From the 1970s through the early 1990s, the conservative religious/political movement known as the **Christian Right** was a prominent feature of the U.S. landscape. Rooted in evangelical Protestantism, the Christian Right offered a direct challenge to the historical U.S. separation of church and state; its explicit aim was to establish traditional Christianity as a dominant force throughout society, including the legal, educational, economic, and political spheres of activity. The Christian Right brought together the forces of institutionalized religion in order to increase the influence of religion on public life. Those forces included traditional means (the organizational clout of the established churches) and several new methods (televangelism, direct mail campaigns).

The Christian Right was strongly nationalistic, seeing the United States as the embodiment of good in a cosmic battle against the forces of evil. But, of course, the United States could only be an effective force for good if it embraced the values of the old-time religion. The leaders of this movement were part of a conservative response to the perceived threats of globalization and the consequent relativization of values. The Christian Right claimed that this nation and this religion had an effective monopoly on truth and that any infringement on those absolute values by other ideologies (or even by the complacent toleration of those other ideologies—a point of view condemned as "relativism" in its worst form) could not be taken lightly. The globalization taking place in the late twentieth century was, of course, propelled by U.S. economic, political, and military power. But the Christian Rightists felt that it had gotten out of hand; rather than ending up with the world meekly submitting to U.S. values and institutions, globalization had only succeeded in watering down those values and compromising those institutions. Like other revitalizations discussed above, the Christian Right movement was a kind of protest against a world seemingly spinning out of control.

The Christian Right declined in part because it functioned within the very sort of pluralistic society it derided. Unlike the fundamentalist movements of more homogeneous societies, the Christian Right always had to compete with other groups in the marketplace of ideas. In effect, there was nothing the Christian Right could do to mobilize its forces that other interest groups could not also do. Moreover, even Americans who were inclined to accept the conservative political philosophy of the Christian Right were a little skeptical of the way in which that philosophy was steeped in avowedly religious principles—always a touchy matter in a proudly secularized nation. The Christian Right also faltered with the collapse of international communism; the supposedly awesome "evil empire" that embodied all that was detestable in the world was gone, almost overnight. Deprived of its "evil" foil, the forces of "good" had little left to stand against.

Globalization has been, as we have seen, a problem for the United States, even though in some respects the U.S. has been in control of that process. The problem is much more severe, however, in those parts of the world (the "Third World" or the "developing countries" as labeled by the popular media) that have been swept up in the new market economy and the international political and financial structures that accompany it. One important religious response to this threat has been the emergence of the liberation theological movement, particularly in Latin America. **Liberation theology** puts a kind of Marxist spin on Christian theology, seeing Jesus Christ as a liberator in the economic, political, and social senses, and not just in the spiritual sense. Jesus, who came into the world as a poor man in an oppressed, occupied society, embodies God's solidarity with the poor and the oppressed. The goal of Christianity should therefore be to work for the liberation of the downtrodden masses. The organized churches of Latin America have, alas, all too often been on the side of the oppressive elites; liberation must therefore flow from "base communities" of concerned Christians who take the study of theology away from the elites and make it an instrument for the betterment of the poor.

Liberation theology had a brief flowering in the 1970s when the Vatican, in a flush of enthusiasm following its reforming council of the 1960s, expressed the Roman Catholic church's "preferential option for the poor." But the Vatican later threw cold water on the movement, mistrusting Liberation theology's affinities with Marxism. The movement still has some appeal to the oppressed, particularly in Latin America, but it has not made much headway against the entrenched political and economic forces of the various Latin American states, let alone against the forces of global capitalism. It is nonetheless an interesting example of how religion, often stereotyped as a conservative factor in society, can also be mobilized for radical, even revolutionary purposes in the face of very severe challenges to the well-being of large numbers of otherwise powerless people.

Catholicism was also deeply involved in the political and economic evolution of Poland in the late-communist and early post-communist era. The Solidarity Movement, which began the wave of organized protests against the Soviet system in Eastern Europe, succeeded at least in part because Catholicism had long been the Poles' bulwark against oppression. For much of its modern history Poland has not even existed as a nation, as it was invaded and carved up repeatedly by its more militarily powerful neighbors. But adherence to the Catholic church (in the face of either Protestant Germans or Orthodox, and later atheistic, Russians) gave the Poles an identity they could cling to. When it came time to mount a protest against the communist system, it was only the church that had the organizational strength and the moral authority to mobilize the people. The relationship between the church and the reform movement was cemented by the fact that the reigning pope was himself a Pole who openly embraced the aims and methods of the Solidarity Movement. Liberation theology faltered in part because it set itself against an "establishment" that the institutional church was part of; Polish Solidarity succeeded because it countered an "establishment" that the church considered an enemy.

The **Islamic revolution** in Iran is perhaps the most conspicuous example of religion as a political force in the modern world. It is, indeed, the prototype of the "political Islam" (sometimes referred to as "fundamentalist Islam") that has become such a major force in our own time. The Iranian revolution was a true revolution in the sense that it swept away the national political and economic institutions that had been in place for centuries (as opposed to a "coup," which simply replaces the rulers without really changing the underlying system). The revolution replaced those institutions with ones that were explicitly Islamic in nature. All authority was vested in the clergy, the accepted interpreters of the precepts of Islam. Under the regime of the Shah, Iran had achieved a measure of prosperity and international influence based on its oil riches. But the prosperity was not equitably distributed, and the international influence was always subject to that of the greater political and military powers. Ordinary Iranians saw their society corrupted by oil wealth; the shameless values of the West were sweeping the educated upper and middle classes while the lower classes continued to suffer in poverty. It is no wonder that a return to the "fundamentals" of Islam was seen as a reasonable and desirable alternative, a way to stem the slide into depravity, poverty, and subservience. Islam, after all, has always had an explicitly political side; it is one of those religious systems that has a great deal to say about economic, political, and social matters in the here-and-now in addition to its beliefs about the transcendent and eternal realms. And Shi'ite Islam (the version to which the majority of Iranians adhere) has a long tradition of being a voice of the oppressed and of making political common cause with those who suffer and are victimized. That Shi'ite Islam could once again be a vehicle of political and social expression is not all that surprising. It may be argued that the Islamic revolutionaries in Iran accomplished what the Christian Right would like to have seen in the United States—the official, formal establishment of one religious creed that subsumes all other institutions of the society.

HOW RELIGION ENDURES[2]

Religion is never a static phenomenon. It is deeply involved in the process of ongoing adaptation—the evolution of human culture. But the process of religious change is probably cyclical rather than linear, since dominant and established religions can lose their influence over time as they seem no longer as relevant as they once were in light of changing circumstances. They are replaced by completely new religions, by the emergence of once minority religions, or by syncretisms or revivals of one sort or another. These alternative forms grow and become dominant, but they in turn reach a peak and then decline. As they are challenged and give way, the cycle is repeated.

But it is central to the argument of this book that religion per se does not disappear, even if it takes on new forms that may make it unrecognizable to those who are accustomed to thinking of religion only in terms of one established tradition. Humanity will always have the same needs: for comfort, belonging, explanation of the mysterious, authentication of the significance and importance of experience. And these are precisely the needs that religion, regardless of the form it takes, continues to address.

KEY CONCEPTS

Be sure you can define the following terms, and give at least one illustrative example of each:

- absolute deprivation
- Christian Right
- civil religion
- communitarian societies
- cults
- globalization
- Islamic revolution

- liberation theology
- pantheistic mysticism
- pluralistic societies
- privatization
- relative deprivation
- spirituality

RESEARCH EXPLORATIONS

1. Access current national census reports and prepare a summary of trends in religious identification and affiliation.

2. Conduct an on-campus survey of religious identification and affiliation. (You should consult with your instructor regarding methods of survey construction. You should also find out about your university's regulations regarding informed consent in studies such as this one.) Which tra-

ditions are most prominent? Can you explain why? (Remember that "no affiliation" or "atheist" or "noninstitutional spirituality" are respectable answers as well as those identifying traditional faith traditions.) Do there seem to be any patterns of religious identification and affiliation correlated with race/ethnicity? With gender? With age category?

3. Select any one of the following classics in the social scientific study of religion. Discuss the work in the context of the historical period in which it was written. Comment on its continuing relevance. How does it illuminate concepts discussed in this text? Not all these works are by anthropologists; if you have chosen a work by a nonanthropologist, how does it relate to material discussed in this text? Does it enhance it? contradict it? Does it help you make any predictions about the future course of religion in the modern, globalized world? Write up your ideas in an analytical essay. Choose from among:

   • Émile Durkheim, *The Elementary Forms of the Religious Life*
   • Mircea Eliade, *The Sacred and the Profane*
   • Sigmund Freud, *Totem and Taboo*
   • William James, *The Varieties of Religious Experience*
   • Ninian Smart, *Dimensions of the Sacred*
   • Anthony F. C. Wallace, *Religion: An Anthropological view*
   • Max Weber, *The Protestant Ethic and the Spirit of Capitalism*

Notes

[1] See, for example, Orion, Loretta. 1995. *Never Again the Burning Ties: Paganism Revived.* Prospect Heights, IL: Waveland Press.

[2] The following remarks are based on an analysis developed in: Duke, James T. and Barry L. Johnson. 1989. Religious Transformation and Social Conditions: A Macrosociological Analysis. In *Religious Politics in Global and Comparative Perspective*, ed. William H. Swatos. New York: Greenwood Press.

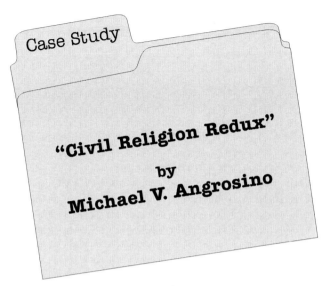

Case Study

"Civil Religion Redux"
by
Michael V. Angrosino

The author reviews the concept of "civil religion" and explores its renewed relevance to an understanding of U.S. culture and history in the wake of the events of September 11, 2001.

The events of September 11, 2001, have led to a public display of unity unseen for nearly four decades in fractious, pluralistic America. The response could be dismissed as simple reactive patriotism at a moment of crisis, and given the nebulous and attenuated nature of any likely "war on terrorism," one might guess that the fervor will be difficult to sustain at the level apparent at this moment. But American patriotism has always been a more complex matter than the stereotype of unthinking, jingoistic flag-waving might suggest. According to the political historian Richard Reeves, writing in the *New York Times* on October 1, 2001, "We are a self-created nation driven to defend our own masterwork. Being an American is not a matter of geography or bloodlines. America is a matter of ideas, the rejection of an Old World standards we thought corrupt." He cites De Tocqueville, who wrote that Americans "have been repeatedly and constantly told that they are the only religious, enlightened, and free people," and as a result, they "have an immensely high opinion of themselves." This attitude has been contextualized by a variety of social scientists within the concept of an enduring American "civil religion."

It might be argued that American civil religion became something of a joke in the era of political cynicism associated with Vietnam and Watergate (although it was revived very briefly during the Bicentennial). (See Jorstad 1990 for a more complete analysis of the transformation of the traditional American pieties into what he calls the "awakening to peace and justice" issues in the 1970s.) It certainly has not been a conspicuous element in the national consciousness during the subsequent decades of

Reprinted by permission of The Institute for Ethnographic Research from *Anthropological Quarterly* 75(2): 239–67 [2002].

increasingly bitter interest-group politics. Social scientists, heir to the positivist traditions of Comte and Marx, accepted as a given the trend of modern societies toward "secularization," and hence have grown increasingly impatient with the notion that religion—even a "civil" one—has any place in a modern polity (Wilson 1998). Nevertheless, troubled people in a secular society may seek meaning and solace in a civil religion in response to the same motives, emotions, and associations that lead people in traditional societies to the standard sacred religions. The historian Joanne Freeman (2001: B6) has noted that "in a way no one ever wanted or imagined, the events of this month [September 2001] have taken us back to the mindset of an earlier time, when the American nation was newly formed." It was a time when "only a deep and abiding loyalty to the nation's founding principles of governance prevented the early Republic from dissolving into civil war." Another historian, Richard Slotkin, reminds us that a society experiencing trauma may come to believe that a certain shocking event upsets its fundamental ideas about what can and should happen. Such a challenge to the authority of its basic values leads people to "look to their myths for precedents, employing past experience embodied in their myths—as a way of getting a handle on crisis" (2001: B11). This process, regardless of the form it might take in secularized societies, is a fundamental process of any religious system in any culture.

Culture is, after all, more than simple behavior (e.g., patriotic flag-waving). Behavior always flows from a complex of attitudes, beliefs, and values that derive from a common historical tradition. The concept of a civil religion allows us to interpret current behavior—which may appear superficially to be transitory and shallow—in light of historical tradition and values that have historically held meaning in American culture. At the same time, the concept allows for the analysis of particular values and behaviors in the larger context of cross-culturally salient categories of ideology, ritual, and myth making. For anthropologists trying to get a grip on a huge and somewhat amorphous entity like "American culture," the concept of civil religion may be a reasonable point of entree, particularly at a moment in history when the residual commonalities of the culture loom larger than its otherwise more prominent divisions.

It is, however, no easy task to deal with civil religion; as an analytical concept that attempts to make sense of a great diversity of social and political behaviors, civil religion seems to give a coherent reality to a set of attitudes and behaviors that some observers would prefer to treat as separate (and hence less meaningful). Moreover, even those who accept the possibility of that coherent reality have used the term "civil religion" in such diverse ways that the concept has come to seem impossibly vague. This paper aims to clarify the concept by reviewing its philosophical roots and historical applications; the paper also explores the reasons civil religion might remain salient in a multicultural society that, on the surface, would seem to be infertile ground for its (temporary?) resurgence. Social scientists may well hesitate to adopt American civil religion in any of its extant forms as a value system to which they personally wish to pledge allegiance. I hope, however, that this essay will at least convince them that the concept of civil religion is a useful analytical tool by means of which a number of sociopolitical trends can be put into cultural and historical context. It is certainly possible to use the insights of Marxist analysis to aid in understanding the relationship between economic forces and sociopolitical trends without thereby endorsing the applications of Marxist philosophy to structures of governance. It should therefore also be possible to use the insights of civil religion theorists to aid in understanding the relationship between religious ideals and sociopolitical trends without thereby endorsing that religion as a personal creed.

American civil religion is an institutionalized set of beliefs about the nation, including a faith in a transcendent deity who will protect and guide the United States as long as its people and government abide by his laws. The virtues of liberty, justice, charity, and personal integrity are all pillars of this religion and lend a moral dimension to its public decision-making processes quite different from the *realpolitik* that presumably underlies the calculations of states not equally favored by divine providence. American civil religion is clearly an offshoot of the Judeo-Christian tradition, but it is not confined to conventional denominational categories. And while the concept of divine providence implicitly stands behind American civil religion, its character is, by definition, secular—it functions through such institutions as the branches of government, patriotic organizations (e.g., the Daughters of the American Revolution, Veterans of Foreign Wars), and outlets of popular culture (e.g., music, movies). American civil religion is thus best understood in light of Geertz's position that a religion is any "system of symbols which acts to establish powerful, pervasive, and long-lasting moods and motivations in [a people] by formulating conceptions of a general order of existence and clothing these conceptions with such an aura of factuality that the moods and motivations seem uniquely realistic" (1973: 90). This definition, which also underlies Jorstad's detailed analysis of religion and politics in the modern U.S. (1990: xv), explicitly avoids concepts of the supernatural, so important in other theorists' views of religion, in favor of a framework for studying how people are made to feel and understand, and then to act on their feelings and understandings. What makes American civil religion "religious" is not that it is always, or even necessarily, conducted in the context of the institutions or philosophical assumptions of any organized religious body, but that it, like other religions, creates potent, compelling, and "uniquely realistic" moods and motivations in its adherents.

In recent decades, theologians and social scientists have grappled with the problem of organized religion (or of more generalized spiritual faith) in the modern, secular state. On the one hand, it is patently obvious that the doctrine of the separation of church and state imposes certain limitations on the ways in which religious voices can contribute to the public discourse, as well as on the topics they can legitimately address. As Hammond (1999: 30) has noted, "the public square does not rule out religious words and motives; it simply does not accord them authority until they are translated [into terms readily understandable even by the non-religious]." On the other hand, it is equally obvious that for all its secular materialism, the United States still struggles to define a moral dimension when formulating public policy. And despite their outer show of cynicism, Americans seem to feel that their political and social institutions are doing the "right" thing, and not simply the expedient thing. It may be presumptuous to assume that we know what Americans feel, but it might be possible to gauge those feelings by comparing the positive responses to a "righteous" call to war (the War on Terrorism as an act of self-defense) with the ultimately negative responses to an ambiguous war (Vietnam, which came to be seen as an expression of an outmoded, Cold War ideology rather than as a virtuous act of self-protection or as a way to help other people lead better lives). If this sense of American idealism must necessarily be divorced from specifically sectarian roots, how can we explain its enduring hold on the political imagination of the nation? And how is it possible for a set of professedly secular institutions to assume the character of a church?

The concept of civil religion provides a set of criteria, as well as an analytical vocabulary that has made it possible to deal with these questions. Interest in civil religion as a way to come to grips with the interface between divinely inspired morality and the sociopolitical realm peaked in both theology and the social sciences (especially sociology, and, to a lesser extent, political science and cultural anthropology) during the 1970s, around the time of the American Bicentennial. But it has been argued (by Williams 1999, among many others) that the particularly American form of civil religion is too exclusivist/elitist. It has been seen as an offshoot of Judeo-Christian theology and as the preserve of a presumed WASP establishment even as the United States has become a multicultural, religiously pluralistic society. Like many handy labels, it has also come to be applied to far too many disparate referents; American civil religion is sometimes seen as too diffuse an entity to make any real difference in American public life. Its generality has meant that it cannot be pinned down in such a way as to permit the formulation of hypotheses that might help us predict the further evolution of those trends. It has been charged that it cannot even help us understand who among us are actually believers or, more to the point, how (of even if) those believers will translate their faith into action for social justice.

Nevertheless, well before President George W. Bush declared a War on Terrorism, the philosopher Leroy S. Rouner (1999: 4), in a series of lectures delivered in his capacity as a Phi Beta Kappa Visiting Scholar in 1998–99, suggested that American civil religion had not, in fact, lost its salience, and that it might be an opportune time for scholars to pay attention to it once again. It has become commonplace, he claims, to decry the ascendancy of "special interest" influence in American life even as the political system seems increasingly to operate in a context of fragmentation in which all policy decisions must be made in the interest of one group or another, there being no real common ground on which to stand. The gist of Rouner's argument is that there continues to be an American civil religion that undergirds a persistent collective identity even in the face of the increasing heterogeneity of the body politic. He notes that critics have scorned the very concept of American civil religion because in the past it has been misused as a way of promoting a mindless "Americanism" as a club to beat us all into conformity. But as he points out, it is a grave mistake (and an ethnocentric judgment to boot) to condemn any religion because of its misapplication by misguided adherents. And in this specific case it is an even more serious error to assume that the capacity of a religious tradition (most assuredly including a civil religious tradition) to stake out "common ground" is somehow incompatible with the maintenance of a proud multiculturalism.

CIVIL RELIGION: A BRIEF ORIENTATION

The sociologist Robert N. Bellah is perhaps the most prominent analyst of American civil religion. His seminal 1967 article on the concept inaugurated the contemporary exploration of this theme. In a later work (1975: ix) he explained that:

... [A]ny coherent and viable society rests on a common set of moral under-standings about good and bad, right and wrong, in the realm of individual and social action. It is almost as widely held that these common moral understand-ings must also in turn rest upon a common set of religious understandings that provide a picture of the universe in terms of which the moral understandings make sense. Such moral and religious understandings produce both a basic cultural legitimization for a society which is viewed as at least approximately in accord with them, and a standard of judgment for the criticism of a society that is seen as deviating too far from them.

In other words, social policy is a statement about the good/desirable/feasible. Expedient self-interest is certainly one way to judge what is good/desirable/feasible; but there are usually broader, more transcendent values that help a political system (certainly any democratic one) arrive at such judgments. The notion of civil religion provides a context for understanding how such broader values shape the decisions that lead to policy. To the extent that social policy is developed by, with, and/or for "the American people," it behooves us to understand what motivates that large, abstract, somewhat amorphous mass. To the extent that such policy seeks ultimately to bind the nation together rather than drive it further into corners of self-interest, it becomes necessary to deal with the qualities and characteristics that constitute the admittedly shrunken patch of common ground. For Bellah (1999: 66), there remains a "deep inner core" of American culture, one that is "ultimately religious: the sacred-ness of the conscience of every individual." This author does not in any way mean to suggest that the concept of civil religion explains everything about American social policy, let alone defines some sort of monolithic American character; but it may be seen to provide some fruitful leads as we seek to understand the directions of such pol-icy as we cope with the present crisis and perhaps even look beyond it to the coming, presumably multicultural, millennium.

THE CONCEPT OF CIVIL RELIGION

The concept of civil religion entered modern political thought via Jean-Jacques Rousseau's discourse on republican government in his essay *The Social Contract*. Rous-seau's argument was intended as a challenge to the Platonic idea of a "civic religion." Plato saw the latter as a means by which the *polis* freed itself from factions and saw to the right development of character, goals with which Rousseau generally agreed. But Plato's civic religion was based on strict state control and explicit dogma (Rouner 1999: 4) whereas Rousseau argued for a polity based on the sovereignty of the general will of the people and the necessity for the voluntary agreement of individuals to the conditions of the social contract. Religion was a key element in that social order, although Rousseau was certainly no advocate of the traditional organized religions, which, he believed, had led only to division, strife, and oppression. He preferred a purely civil religious faith that would support the social order, and he advocated a sys-tem of religious sentiments, convictions, and commitments that could only emerge from the separation of church and state. The doctrines of such a civil faith would, of necessity, be "few, simple, and clearly stated" (Chidester 1988: 82).

More specifically, Rousseau's ideal civil faith should affirm the existence of a powerful, intelligent, and good divinity, who should be regarded as exercising foresight and providence in the destiny of the community. Rousseau also believed that this faith should also include a belief in the survival of the soul after death, as a belief in the ultimate happiness of the just and punishment for the wicked would provide necessary supernatural sanctions for a just social order. Moreover, a civil faith should be committed to the sanctity of the social contract and the laws of the land. In this civil religion, the social contract is sacralized (i.e., infused with religious power because its authority derives ultimately from the Divinity). These very general doctrines notwithstanding, Rousseau believed that the civil religion should be tolerant of the diversity of private religious opinions, as long as they were not allowed to disrupt the unifying sentiments generated by the "faith" of the entire polity.

Echoes of Rousseau's ideas have appeared in various formulations of the role of religion in modern, secular society, such as Martin Marty's concept of "religion-in-general" (1959) and Sidney Mead's exploration of the "religion of the republic" (1963). But by general agreement, the most significant theoretical and descriptive work on the concept of civil religion has been that of the sociologist Robert Bellah, whose 1967 article, "Civil Religion in America" appeared at the height of the Vietnam War in an atmosphere of anguished national reappraisal. As such, it struck responsive chords among theologians and social scientists alike. As Rouner interprets Bellah:

> American civil religion is not what we believe in our heart of hearts about the destiny of our immortal souls. It is, rather, the beliefs we share with our fellow citizens about our national purpose and about the destiny of our national enterprise. Vague and visceral it may be, but there is an American creed, and to be an American is to believe the creed. America is, in this sense, a religious venture (Rouner 1999: 3).

But, of course, the religion at the core of the venture is Rousseau's brand of civil faith.

TYPES OF CIVIL RELIGION

Three major strands of thought have emerged in the analysis of civil religion: (1) civil religion as culture religion, (2) civil religion as religious nationalism, and (3) civil religion as transcendent religion. There is considerable conceptual overlap among these three, and it may well be that the different aspects of the American civil religion have recombined with one another, producing distinctive constellations at different points in the nation's history. Nevertheless, it is possible to distinguish the three trends for purposes of this overview discussion. *Civil religion as culture religion is* a position that derives from classical French sociology and its insistence on viewing society itself as a set of collective representations symbolizing a common identity. The symbols of a culture religion are independent of church and state, but their symbolic resonance permeates both religion and politics. This diffuse set of collective representations can be described, interpreted, and analyzed in the same way that a cultural anthropologist might try to reconstruct the religious perspective that gives a certain coherence to a traditional folk or tribal society. Culture religion theorists (see, e.g., Williams 1951) contend that every functioning society has its own religion insofar as it possesses a common set of rituals, ideas, and symbols that supply an overarching sense of unity even in a society riddled with conflicts. Particularly in a society with the potential for fracture, the common culture religion can provide a more or less systematic vocabulary of sacred symbols, allowing for a degree of cooperation, integration, and solidarity.

This point of view is predicated on religion being understood to be the meaningful inner core of culture, and on culture being the outer manifestation of religion, an idea developed extensively by the theologian Paul Tillich (1959). Religion, for Tillich, is the ultimate power that drives the shared, common life of a community. That power need not be identified exclusively with organized religious institutions, however, since it is an inherent force that finds expression in the basic patterns of a culture—as likely to be revealed in the activities surrounding economic exchange or family life or artistic endeavor as in formal religion per se. In this respect, culture religion is the "invisible religion" of a community (Luckmann 1967), which is manifested in its shared symbols, values, and ideals.

Culture religion can be analyzed in terms of its interrelated aspects of belief, practice, and experience—or, in other terms, its myth, doctrine, and ritual. There is, in addition, a strong ethical component to the culture religion, in the sense that it fosters a more or less systematic set of standards for ordinary action. These standards must ultimately be translated into "meaningful" experience—i.e., those experiences that can be communicated and shared, as opposed to those that are purely mystical and interior. The most common meaningful experience in culture religion is patriotism, which in this sense is more than simple adherence to a body of laws and a respect for certain institutions. It is, rather, "a dynamic power, energy, and enthusiasm awakened through personal involvement" with the culture (Chidester 1988: 91). Military service, jury duty, and voting are all activities that make "patriotism" meaningful in the experience of most citizens; those experiences can then be symbolized by such things as flags, certificates, or membership cards that serve to remind people of their mutual bonds.

The second strand of thinking is that of civil *religion as religious nationalism*, a perspective that draws from the German, rather than the French school of sociological theory. This viewpoint focuses on the power of religion to legitimize the state, to the extent that the state itself came to be defined by its sacred power. In modernizing societies, traditional religious institutions lose their force. As Bellah and Hammond (1980: 77) put it, "religion declines as power coalesces in the institutions of the state." But religious feelings are not eliminated—they are simply displaced to the state. Such a tendency was a feature of the "state Shinto" of Japan in the first several decades of this century (Kitagawa 1987), although it took its most extreme form in the Soviet Union, and, perhaps even more self-consciously, Nazi Germany. At such extremes, religious nationalism can become "the idolatrous worship of national identity purposes, and destiny" (Chidester 1988: 84), although it can more benignly be a way to mobilize symbolic resources to legitimize the aims, goals, and purposes pursued by the nation.

Finally, it is possible to view civil *religion as transcendent religion.* When civil religion involves what Bellah calls a "genuine apprehension of universal and transcendent religious reality as seen in, or . . . as revealed through the experience of the . . . people" (Bellah 1979: 179), then the historical experience of the society provides the context for the relationship between God and the world. In such a transcendent religion, the nation's history takes on the character of a sacred myth and is expressed in terms of powerful religious values and sacred ideals. The collective experience of that nation therefore "stands under transcendent judgment and has value only insofar as it realizes, partially and fragmentarily at best, a 'higher law'" (Bellah 1970: 255). In the transcendent religion, religious and political spheres interpenetrate in the formation of collective symbols that do not only evoke certain moods in people, but also actually motivate them or impel them to action (see, e.g., Geertz 1973). Transcendent religion is distinguished from religious nationalism, which it superficially resembles, insofar as it is less a form of national self-worship and more the subordination of the nation to ethical principles that transcend it and in terms of which it should be evaluated (Bellah 1970: 168).

CIVIL RELIGION IN AMERICA: CONCEPT IN ACTION

The American prototype of Rousseau's image of civil religion was provided by Ben Franklin, in whose *Autobiography* we find the following avowal:

> I never was without some religious principles. I never doubted, for instance, the existence of the Deity; that he made the world, and govern'd it by his Providence; that the most acceptable service of God was the doing of good to man; that our souls are immortal; and that all crime will be punished, and virtues rewarded, either here or hereafter. These I esteem'd the essentials of every religion (in Wentz 1998: 53).

Franklin considered these elements of a general religiosity to be necessary to the creation of a unified social order. Religious doctrines supporting morality, virtues, and dedication to public service were deemed to be necessary for the unity of the republic (LeBeau 2000: 68). As Wentz notes, "There is a story to tell [about the translation of Franklin's vision into the fabric of the American polity] that sheds light on the origins of the American people" (Wentz 1998: 53), and it is certainly no accident that the American Bicentennial of 1976 was the "golden age" of civil religion inquiry (Mathison 1989: 130), with Bellah's own reassessment, *The Broken Covenant,* as its centerpiece.

Civil religion in America has displayed persistent elements of theism and even theocracy, in the sense that the government was, in a way, held to be divinely ordained, and given a role as protector and arbiter of morality that Europeans even today find perplexing (Novak 2000: 165). It has nurtured a sense of a unique American destiny and a type of civil millenarianism that leads Americans to view the nation as the focus of God's work in human history.

Moreover, American civil religion has been based on the elevation of the democratic system to a sacred status. In treating democratic principles, institutions, and the voice of the people as sacred elements in an overarching religious faith, civil religion in America has infused the democratic system with an aura not shared by most other civil polities. It has also made it difficult for Americans to understand how people of good will and intelligence could choose to be anything but democratic. Non-democratic states have typically been held to be, at best, the products of uncritical adherence to tradition and, at worst, the results of systematic brainwashing.

American Civil Religion as Culture Religion

If we define a myth as the imaginative truths by means of which people construct their lives and order their thinking, then there is a foundational myth that tells the story of who the American people are, why they came to the New World, and what they stand for. John Locke, the British philosopher, consciously used Biblical imagery in his famous statement, "in the beginning, all the world was America." His point was that America, for Europeans at least, has traditionally been the pure Eden, a place of innocence and fresh starts. The myths behind American civil religion all speak to this presumed primordial condition. The story includes an event similar to the Exodus (the migration of people from oppression in tradition-bound societies to freedom in the New World). There has always been a sense that those who came to America were a new kind of people—freer, larger in spirit, more open, more honest, more pure than those made small and bitter by tyranny. Lincoln's Gettysburg Address spoke of the bringing forth on this continent a "new nation" that was explicitly trying to forge a union out of a multiplicity of peoples and religions. To be sure, this mythology applies only to those who migrated voluntarily. The involuntary migration of the slaves has been conveniently ignored in the foundation narratives of American civil religion. The American story begins with the "discovery" by Europeans—another convenient lapse of historical memory common to the myth-making process, for just as the slaves were excluded from the great narrative of Exodus, so the Native Americans were excised from the process of the "discovery" of the New World Eden. In any event, the Europeans (both the Catholic Spaniards and French and the Protestant English) often acted as if they were divinely commissioned in their quest. In finding a "new world," they established the physical context in which a "new people" could flourish. In such a context, there was no room to acknowledge the presence of an ancient people with a very different outlook on life.

The process by which myth becomes a civil religion also includes processes of investing symbols with transcendent significance, translating ordinary people into heroic legends, and creating rituals that encourage the celebration of those symbols and people.

In some contexts, "myth" connotes a fanciful, unhistorical—and hence irrelevant—belief (see, e.g., Swift 1998: 262). But anthropologists certainly do not underestimate the power of myths to create their own reality. Myths are formed by symbols, and also give rise to new symbols. Every nation symbolizes itself in a flag, but the United States has compounded that symbol by choosing as its national anthem a song about the defense of one particular flag that was in physical danger. It is probably no accident that "The Star-Spangled Banner" became the national anthem, despite being notoriously difficult for untrained singers to perform. Both "God Bless America" and "America the Beautiful" (the latter with its invocation, "God shed his grace on thee") have been far more popular as songs, and both have figured prominently in public expressions of national solidarity since September 11, 2001. But in a civil religion, a totemic figure such as the national flag is a safer and more unifying symbol than God, who is, after all, subject to so many different sectarian interpretations. (During the recent crisis, people in my southern state have been writing letters to the editor and besieging call-in talk shows with requests that folks put away their Confederate flags—in calmer times defended in some quarters as symbols of "heritage"—for the duration, as a sign of national unity.) It is a measure of the intensity of the current crisis that God is once again a rallying cry and not a cause of division. We should, however, keep in mind that the God of Irving Berlin is not any recognized sectarian deity, but more akin to the principle of Divine Providence as it might have been understood by the American founders (or Rousseau, for that matter).

America has been particularly rich in the symbolism entailed in the legendary embroidering on the lives of actual historical people, places, and events that are believed to embody the story of the national identity. George Washington is conventionally referred to, without apparent irony, as the "Father of the Country," and his presumed qualities of courage, dedication, and honor stand for the typical American virtues. Washington's role as both symbol and secular saint is as important as his actual historical role as a military and political leader. In the stories enveloping other the other Founding Fathers (like John Adams and Thomas Jefferson, who died within hours of each other on the Fourth of July, 1826, the fiftieth anniversary of the signing of the Declaration of Independence), as well as later heroes like Lincoln, we can see the ideas basic to the civil religious tradition. We can see that Americans believe in equality, and that they constitute a leveling society in which citizenship is valued for its ingenuity, native intelligence, effort, and private initiative (Albanese 1976).

There are also, to be sure, written texts analogous to sacred scriptures that embody and preserve those teachings that construct the American worldview and its sense of what is ultimately meaningful. We revere, for example, the Declaration of Independence, the Constitution, the Federalist Papers, and the orations of the great patriots. It is interesting to note that in his "I Have a Dream" speech, Dr. Martin Luther King, Jr. used the Declaration as a homiletic text, much as he might have used the Bible when preaching in his church. The rhetorical pattern of the "Dream" speech is rooted in the language of the Declaration as much as it is in the cadences of the African American Baptist sermon (Wills 1978:175; see also Raboteau 1990; Spillers 1998). But King's use of the Declaration also echoed Lincoln's use of that same document in his Gettysburg Address, where it stood for the moral underpinning of his vision of the renewed nation. Any religious tradition, after all, builds through a process of accretion and cross-referenced allusions across the generations.

The mythologizing of Washington is illustrated by a story that involves the Marquis de Lafayette, the French aristocrat who fought in the American Revolution. In 1824, the elderly Marquis returned to the United States for a triumphal farewell visit. While he was paying his respects at Washington's tomb, an eagle was spotted soaring on high—the traditional symbol of the apotheosis of the Roman emperors. And then about a decade later, Washington's remains were placed in a new marble coffin; it was widely reported (and widely believed) that although the great man had been dead for nearly forty years, there was no bodily corruption or odor. "The wholeness of Washington's body seemed a sign of the wholeness of America grounded on its past" (Albanese 1981: 302).

If Washington is the quasi-divine embodiment of American virtue, Lincoln may well be the American Christ figure. Assassinated on Good Friday, he was a sacrificial victim who in death succeeded in a way he never had as a living politician—in helping to heal the wounds of civil strife. He died so that there might be a Union, a compact among diverse peoples who had torn the nation apart for the sake of their unrestrained self-interest. Lincoln's blood was shed for his people, sanctifying the very ground that had so recently been saturated with the blood of fratricides.

Like any people, Americans needed to translate their myths into rituals through which they continually celebrated, and thus reaffirmed, their common values. In their various ways, the Fourth of July, Memorial Day, Thanksgiving, and the birthdays of great presidents and patriots, all are occasions for acting out what it means to belong to America. Many holidays have been detached from their original historical meanings, but even if young people have to be constantly reminded of why it is important to celebrate such days, the fact remains that these celebrations of the national identity continue to figure prominently on our annual calendar of remembrances. Moreover, social institutions, such as the public schools, have historically functioned to instill a general, shared religious commitment to a common national identity. Public institutions (and even some private enterprises) for example, typically are closed for business on such holidays, which is usually not the case for strictly sectarian religious days of observance, such as the Feast of the Assumption, or Divali, or Rosh Hashanah. Believers may be granted days off for such observances, but the enterprise as a whole does not shut down. At its core Christmas is, of course, a sectarian observance. But it has been translated into a major public holiday through celebration of the generalized civic virtues of "peace and good will."

G. K. Chesterton once quipped that "America is the only nation in the world that is founded on a creed," a creed shaped by two major sources of religious belief: the Enlightenment ideals embodied in the Declaration of Independence, and the persistent, residual traces of a Puritan covenant theology. According to Chesterton (in Mead 1975: 20):

> The creed is set forth with dogmatic and even theological lucidity in the Declaration of Independence. It enunciates that all men are equal in their claim to justice, and that governments exist to give them that justice, and that their authority is for that reason just. It certainly does condemn anarchism, and it does also by inference condemn atheism, since it clearly names the Creator as the ultimate authority from whom these equal rights are derived.

The principles of equality, liberty, and justice thus take their place with the traditional Scriptural "theological virtues" of faith, hope, and charity, because they are all believed to derive from the authority of a divine Creator. Doctrines of divine election, special providence, and manifest destiny reflected the influence of Puritan covenant theology. These elements do not, to be sure, form a systematic formulary of belief, but they have been of enormous influence in shaping American self-understanding as a nation. These elements "create a theological vocabulary for achieving ideological consensus and for conducting ideological conflicts in American culture religion" (Chidester 1988: 88). In an important sense, the philosophical and theological constructs of Puritanism were transformed by the architects of the American civil religion, who believed that "the whole society, not merely some of its parts [i.e., its specifically religious institutions], constituted the bedrock of the future" (LeBeau 2000: 67).

This American ideological vocabulary has been encapsulated in the term "utilitarian individualism" (Bellah and Hammond 1980: 170). This orientation to personal and social ethics in American society reflects a generally practical set of standards, suggesting that things are to be used and people are to be useful. Utilitarian individualism looks beyond any presumed intrinsic value in people and things, and instead finds value in the measurement of their usefulness as resources. This practical orientation has been certainly been abused—there has been a longstanding tendency to "objectify" the human that is clearly at variance with the tendency of Judeo-Christian anthropology. Nevertheless, utilitarian individualism has obliquely contributed to the establishment of an ethical dimension in American collective life. The organized conception of how things ought to be, or how people ought to act and interact, may be defined as the *ethos* of a culture. The distinctive *ethos* of American civil religion has been shaped by the cultural forces of pragmatism, materialism, and an abiding faith in human progress through technological development. The result of American pragmatism is that any religious value must ultimately be measured and justified in terms of its practical consequences. Bellah has come to identify the tendency to calculate such consequences in narrowly, selfishly individualistic terms as a perversion of this orientation. "Utilitarian individualism" in its best sense allows the individual to understand that his/her best individual interest lies in upholding the common good. In America, "religion" can only be tolerated to the extent that it is capable of cultivating both individual self-improvement and civic virtue.

In a culture religion, civic virtue is ultimately embodied in a sense of patriotism, which in America, as elsewhere, also has a negative side, in that it can be used to inflame sectarian interests. In the United States, "the mantle of patriotism . . . has periodically been claimed as the exclusive privilege of particular social, political, and religious interest groups" (Chidester 1988: 92). Bellah and Hammond (1980: xiii) have noted "a pull toward archaic regression in the American civil religion," the tendency to identify a particular constellation of Americans (traditionally white, Protestant, Anglo-Saxons) as the exclusive representatives of a uniquely American community of righteousness; patriotism thus became a call to adhere to the standards of the elite. But American civil religion is more complex than that image might suggest, because an important element in American self-identity is the tradition of righteous dissent and the obligation to speak out against mindless homogenization. Thoreau's civil disobedience in the face of unacceptable national policies represented a view that the "true America" was a notion open to different interpretations. The elite conservators of American patriotic civic virtue have certainly not always been kind to dissenters, but the right of people to dissent has never been expunged from the list of cherished American values, no matter how seriously it has been curtailed in practice. Wilson (1990), for example, argues that there have always been regional subvarieties of the national civil religion, and Bellah (1999: 57) has pointed out that the sectarianism that has always characterized religion in the United States is a kind of template for a modern sense of multiculturalism. For these reasons, it would be incorrect to see American cultural religion as the homogeneous creation and tool of the elite; its expression also includes the "others" who have historically been "invisible" (Long 1974: 220). In effect, the tensions in American culture in general are also tensions in American civil religion. The incorporation of those tensions into the set of expectations encompassed by the civil religion is what gives the concept its evolving dynamism as a way to come to terms with the emerging multicultural society.

It is therefore clear that the personal experiences of Native Americans, African Americans, immigrants, and women have revealed basic tensions in American culture religion. Although the overarching symbols of a civil faith provide the potential for a unifying, all-inclusive religious devotion to America, many have felt excluded by those very symbols. The voting booth was the great symbol of the triumph of democracy—but certainly not to the freed slaves who faced harshly discriminatory policies when they tried to exercise their new franchise. But because voting rights became a centerpiece of the early phase of the Civil Rights Movement, the voting booth was reclaimed as a potent symbol of American democracy. The symbol was not jettisoned—it simply expanded to include a greater diversity of American meanings, as a result of organized dissent conducted within the general parameters of the democratic process. The ability to continue to accommodate "otherness" within a unified culture religion is perhaps the greatest challenge facing American civil religion, although its historical tendency to do so provides grounds for hope that it may continue to be a vehicle for the nurturance of diversity without fragmentation.

American Civil Religion as Religious Nationalism

Although the United States has avoided the excesses of religious nationalism seen in totalitarian states, certain tendencies in that direction certainly exist. Bob Dylan's caustic Vietnam-era protest song, "With God on Our Side," is perhaps the most famous pop cultural critique of the attitude that the institutions of the state were not, in fact, expansive systems of symbols (as the above discussion suggests) but actually embodiments of a divine will that could not be challenged. Those who have claimed to speak for the United States adopted an aura of sacredness relatively early in the history of the nation—long before it became a global military and economic power—and such voices continue to represent the U.S. in terms of a unique national destiny and as a locus of God's interaction with the world. The founding of the Republic was couched in terms of a chosen people and their millennial destiny. LeBeau (2000: 67), for example, contends that the Founding Fathers and most of their contemporaries accepted the idea that a successful republican society and government depended on a virtuous people, such that one of the functions of government was to inculcate those virtues in the populace. The impulse of religious nationalism has continued to be a powerful force in shaping American history; examples include the "manifest destiny" creed that fueled our westward expansion, and the intimations of fulfilling a divine plan that underscored a host of wars and imperial adventures. It even, for an unconscionably long time, buttressed both the maintenance of the institution of slavery and the genocide perpetrated on Native Americans. Closer to our own time, religious nationalism has found expression in the rhetoric of the Cold War and its "evil empire" imagery (Jorstad 1990: 1). The September 11 crisis has been explicitly cast as a battle of "good vs. evil"—moral, rather than political or diplomatic principles are at stake. The White House often refers to Osama bin-Laden as "The Evil One"—not merely a man who commits evil acts, but the very embodiment of evil, so transcendent in nature as to be literally unutterable. As the historian Elwyn Smith (1971: 155) has noted, "The Republic—both its morals and its unity, and therefore its power to survive—rested on a pervasive religious and moral consensus."

An important stream of American religious nationalism has been the "republican theocracy" (Smith 1971: 168) associated with Calvinist theologians of the nineteenth century (Timothy Dwight, Nathaniel W. Taylor, and Lyman Beecher among them). Rousseau's classic model of the civil religion had explicitly excluded Christianity, since to him it was just one more "sect" that tended to divide rather than uphold the civil order. But the American Calvinists were interested in salvaging both Christianity and the sacred state, and so came to the conclusion that God exercises moral government over the state, although divine moral government in America is carried out by awakening "the voluntary energies of the nation itself" (Beecher in Chidester 1988: 96). As such, the democratic order was interpreted as God's theocratic order. God's divine laws for human government were said to be embodied in the Constitution. "With a sophisticated theological precision, Lyman Beecher and the other republican theocrats affirmed a residual Puritan heritage in the notion of America as a chosen people with a unique destiny under the moral government of God" (Chidester 1988: 96).

The Civil War was a grave challenge to American religious nationalism, since two separate polities, both claiming the mantle of the divinely ordained state, were contending for power. The New England-based republican theocrats looked upon the secession of the Confederacy as a "cosmic disruption of the sacred order represented by national union. As the divine governor of that union, God could only be expected to restore order" (Chidester 1988: 96). But the southern preachers yielded to no one in their ability to cloak their cause in Biblical imagery. Particularly popular among the secessionists was the image of the Exodus—ironic in light of the fact that the descendants of the southern slaves were to use that same image in the course of their later struggle for civil rights. The southerners argued that the federal constitution had betrayed its mission by avoiding mention of God—an oversight corrected by the constitution of the Confederacy, which became the new embodiment of the chosen people. Strange as it may seem in our own time, when public religious rhetoric (if not religious feeling) has been considerably toned down, Abraham Lincoln was but the most prominent political figure of that era to spend a great deal of time in anguished effort to discern God's will in the midst of the political and military conflict. Lincoln has been described as the "greatest American civil theologian" (Rouner 1999: 5), and in his second inaugural address, he stated:

> If we shall suppose that American slavery is one of those offenses which, in the providence of God, must needs come, but which, having continued through His appointed time, He now wills to remove, and that He gives to both North and South this terrible war as the woe due to those by whom the offense came, shall we discern therein any departure from those divine attributes which the believers in a living God always ascribe to Him? Fondly do we hope, fervently do we pray, that this mighty scourge of war may speedily pass away. Yet, if God wills that it continue until all the wealth piled by the bondsman's two hundred and fifty years of unrequited toil shall be sunk, and until every drop of blood drawn with the lash shall be paid by another drawn with the sword, as was said three thousand years ago, so still it must be said, "The judgments of the Lord are true and righteous altogether."

American Civil Religion as Transcendent Religion

American civil religion has been described as a concatenation of the ultimate and universal principles of a republican form of polity, embodied in Enlightenment religious and political ideals as expressed by the Founding Fathers, with the character of biblical prophecy (Mead 1975: 65). Moreover, American transcendent religion is the "moral architecture" of the nation; the legal separation of church and state, combined with a vital, dynamic pluralism in American society, has supported a civil religion devoted to putting basic moral principles of republican government into practice (Bellah and Hammond 1980: 142). In effect, the overweening power of the state—the ugly potential end product of religious nationalism—is always constrained by the recognition that there are principles that transcend the state, to which even the officers of government must bow. This principle was invoked to counter the so-called "Nuremberg defense."

For political interests to establish themselves in or near the center of the American political arena, they are obliged to make some claims to transcendent symbols. In recent times, such diverse "religiopolitical" figures as Jerry Falwell and Jesse Jackson have "quoted in prophetic tones from the Bible, and claimed special access to the inner significance of transcendent civil religious principles of American government" (Chidester 1988: 105). Even politicians who lack official clerical status know how to invoke those symbols. Henry Kissinger, for example, that master of *realpolitik,* claimed that the only justification he could think of for the NATO intervention in Yugoslavia was in order to demonstrate that NATO was still a viable organization. But President Clinton knew better than to try to rally support for his policy with such a self-serving argument. Instead, he focused on the humanitarian catastrophe, implying that a failure on our part to act decisively would allow a wicked dictator and his morally bankrupt henchmen to continue to perpetrate evils unknown in Europe since the end of the Second World War. The image of the western democracies' craven appeasement of Hitler looms large in the moral vocabulary of our times. Although a historian might logically point out numerous flaws in the presumed analogy between the Nazis and the Serbs, the fact that such an analogy had widespread resonance made it possible for the NATO response to be tolerated (albeit grudgingly) by public opinion. This is hardly the place to debate the merits of American policy in the Balkans; the point is that once that policy had been decided, it could only be successfully "sold" in the loftiest moral terms, on the assumption that Americans (and the people of the other western democracies who have begun to adopt American attitudes toward "foreign" policy) would be unwilling to think of themselves as people who commit the ultimate violence of war in anything but the most transcendently unambiguous terms of good confronting evil.

By the same token, Slotkin (2001: B11) points out that one of the myths evoked since September 11 is that of Pearl Harbor—the ultimate justification of the "good war." Since the enemy in both cases could, in the shock of the moment, be dehumanized as the very embodiment of treachery and evil, America-the-victim by contrast must therefore be the embodiment of good, or else why would the powers of evil hate it so?

To be sure, one person's transcendence can be regarded by another as oppression, illusion, or heresy. Consider, for example, the public policy debate on abortion; the dread word itself rarely appears, supplanted by the imagery of either "choice" or "life," both values that transcend ordinary political discourse (and, for that matter, the ordinary discourse of medical procedure) in their appeal to higher moral concerns of which the American state is expected to be the defender.

Former Senator and presidential candidate George McGovern (1977: 34) has clearly expressed the relationship between transcendence and political experience in the American context:

> The study of [Hegel and Marx] forced me to think seriously about the political process, but neither of them captured my interest with anything approaching the enthusiasm I experienced in discovering "The Social Gospel." This effort to find in the New Testament and the Hebrew prophets an ethical imperative for a just social order strongly appealed to me. To know that long years of familiarity with the Bible and the idealism nurtured in my public-school years were resources that I could direct to humane political and economic ends was a satisfying discovery. Religion was more than a search for personal salvation, more than an instantaneous expression of God's grace; it could be the essential moral underpinning for a life devoted to the service of one's time. Indeed, one's own salvation depended upon service to others.

American Civil Religion: The Current Status of the Concept

According to Wentz (1998: 57), American civil religion is "that cluster of ideas and convictions, the special practices, and the sense of peoplehood that belong to America." American civil religion emerged from a many-faceted world of ideas and practices that had to be reconciled with each other in a land with no provision for the legal establishment of religion. As a result, the principles of government have been couched in terms suggestive of transcendent, rather than sectarian religious doctrine. The democratic social contract has become a civil religious contract that embodies sacred principles to be enacted in the political order. The civil religion is sometimes difficult to apprehend because it is like a church with no buildings or membership statistics; moreover, it has appropriated so many of the symbols of Christianity and Biblical Judaism that it is sometimes easy to forget that in the United States the image conjured up by the phrase "a land flowing with milk and honey" refers not so much to ancient Canaan as to America itself. Moreover, "civil religion in America . . . may be considered as a religiopolitical system, independent of both organized religions and the institutions of government, which represents a set of collective religious symbols, a sacralized national identity, and a system of transcendent, quasi-religious principles of political order" (Chidester 1988: 83).

Civil religion in America can be analyzed in at least three dimensions: as the folk religion of a people; as the religious legitimization of a nation; and as a set of transcendent ideals against which the American people and nation have been assessed. These aspects of the civil religion have in their own ways affected the distribution of power in the United States. The plurality of civil religions should not disguise the fact that these systems of power in America have often achieved a relatively unified consensus by excluding "others" from full participation, even as they have incorporated the professed ideal of legitimate dissent into the creed.

Detailed sociological research has tended to confirm Bellah's insight that civil religion is a distinct cultural component within American society that is not captured either by party politics or by denominational religiosity. Americans do, indeed, affirm civil religious beliefs, even though most of them would not recognize the label. Surveys summarized by Wimberley and Swatos (1998: 95) indicate that Americans generally endorse such sentiments as, "America is God's chosen nation today," or "Holidays like the Fourth of July are religious as well as patriotic," or even "Social justice cannot only be based on laws; it must also come from religion." Studies have also found, however, that adherence to the civil religious norms varies across the population. In general, college graduates and those identifying themselves as political liberals appear to be less imbued with civil religious principles than others. Members of several religious bodies having denominational roots within the United States (e.g., Mormons, Adventists, Pentecostalists) are the most apt to identify with civil religious values, while Jews, Unitarians, and those with no religious preference are the least apt to do so. Wimberley and Swatos (1998: 96) conclude that the extant research demonstrates that "religious beliefs do exist in people's minds, that these beliefs are widely shared and provide a basis for pluralistic social integration across the society, and that a civil religious beliefs may be a relatively important factor in making a difference in public preference for presidential candidates and social policies." Fowler, Hertzke, and Olson (1999: 260) lend cautious support to this conclusion, admitting that the civil religious concept "does tell us something about what may still bind many Americans politically," although they are not confident that this binding effect will survive in the face of the strength of cultural pluralism and "political cynicism." They are downright skeptical of the utility of the concept in helping us understand such specific aspects of political life as voting patterns or the agenda setting of various interest groups. In a similar vein, Wuthnow notes that "America's secular legitimating myths" have been in the ascendancy during times of American supremacy in the world; Americans lose faith as the nation's position declines (Wuthnow 1988*)*. Writing in a period of economic uncertainty and the last phase of the Cold War, Wuthnow implied that Americans no longer believed that our system and its values could solve all problems. Subsequent economic, political, and military successes—and the image of a nation supposedly besieged by the force of unreasoning evil—may well have reversed this trend, leading to a renewed salience of the civil religious faith of the nation.

REFLECTIONS ON AMERICAN POLITICAL THEOLOGY

There is an extensive literature in which the impact of specific denominational bodies on public policy is documented and interpreted. But the tendency to view religious organizations in the United States as essentially a subspecies of the more general special-interest category can obscure the possibility that some responses to policy initiatives are better understood in reference to a civil religious creed that transcends denominational special interest. As Bellah (1978: 21) has noted, "every movement to make America more fully realize its professed values has grown out of some form of public theology." Those values, as the previous discussion has shown, are not denomination-specific, and the "public theology" of which Bellah writes is not sectarian doctrinalism but the civil religion—admittedly amorphous, but still highly influential.

Bellah and Hammond (1980) argue that every society must deal with the tension between religion and politics. In forms of society they label "archaic," the problem is solved by a fusion of the two sectors (theocracy). In "historic" or "early modern" societies, the two spheres are differentiated, but not separated (e.g., the "established churches" of post-Reformation Europe). But civil religion proper comes into existence only in "modern" society, where church and state are separated as well as differenti- ated. In other words, "a civil religion that is differentiated from *both* church and state is possible only in a modern society" (Yamane 1998: 49).

But how does public theology in Bellah's sense really affect American politics? The literature suggests that the influence actually arises out of a constant and creative tension between conservative and liberal brands of civil religion (Wuthnow 1983: 1989; see also Reichley 1985). Conservative political theology is predicated on the assumption that the Bible should be the foundation of all law and that therefore any law contrary to Biblical teaching should be considered unconstitutional; in other words, the Constitution is tantamount to the Word of God. Liberal political theology, by contrast, does not assume that God stopped speaking to America in 1789; the Con- stitution is not the final revelation, but a work in progress. Liberal public theology tends to place a greater emphasis on human agency in the larger plan of God than does the conservative branch. For example, it has been pointed out that conservative theologians have been relatively uninterested in the attempt to halt nuclear prolifera- tion, but not because they are inherently militaristic or unconcerned with the destruc- tion of the planet. Rather, they look on God as sovereign, such that nuclear catastrophe could happen only if God allows it. Liberals, who preserve a role for human action within God's plan, are more prone to foster political or diplomatic efforts to halt or limit the spread of nuclear weaponry (Dunn 1984).

In the course of American history, the conservative type of civil religious theology thrived in the agrarian context, while liberal public theology has been influential in the urban, industrial sector. Conservative theology, however, periodically comes to the fore even though our nation is now predominantly urban/industrial. It happens when a stable and healthy economy allows conservative moral issues to be considered appropriate topics for public scrutiny, a point that has recently been advanced to explain why we were able to afford the "luxury" of the Clinton-Lewinsky debacle—a spectacle we might have been spared had there been more pressing (i.e., economically dire) things for us to worry about. Unstable economic conditions, by contrast, usually lead to demands for a larger role for government and for the strengthening of the national over the local governments, an atmosphere in which liberal theology has tra- ditionally flourished.

A case might therefore be made that although the current revival of American civil religion, albeit clothed in symbols traditionally appropriated by the political right wing, is actually a manifestation of the theological left wing, since the rhetoric is all about people doing their part, pitching in, and contributing to the war effort. God may be on our side, but Americans are being called to step up and be the active agents of God's will.

Throughout American history, religious values have moved to the foreground as an impetus to political mobilization when a group falling outside the prevailing con- sensus assumes a highly visible role. In such a situation, religious values often are reaf- firmed in public discourse as a means of defending a way of life that suddenly may seem threatened. The American civil religion was thus a source of the anti-immigrant fervor of the nineteenth and early twentieth century. But immigrants are not the only possible out-groups who provoke such a response. In the 1950s, the specter of communism occasioned the formation of groups such as the Christian Anti-Communist Crusade and the John Birch Society, both of which moved the political discourse in the direction of apocalyptic rhetoric, with international events often interpreted through the theological prism of the Book of Revelation. The atheism of communism came to be seen as a flaw just as heinous as communism's economic theories or its association with totalitarian political structures (Swift 1998: 261). In the 1960s and 1970s, conservative religious sentiment was mobilized by "lifestyle" issues, often in reaction to "countercultural" emphases on drug use, sexual permissiveness, feminism, abortion, and gay rights. There is currently a danger that the religious discourse may be mobilized to exclude American Muslims, as Islam has been widely stereotyped as an ideology that is inherently anti-democratic, irrational, and prone to violence. (It is ironic that conservative political commentators—in other times no friends of women's rights—have been pointing with horror at the Taliban's wretched treatment of women as evidence of the moral depravity of fundamentalist Islam.) On the other hand, national leaders have taken pains to distinguish law-abiding American Muslims from the crazed, evil terrorists who presume to speak for all of Islam. In other words, the current rhetoric insists that one can be a devout Muslim but still be a good American—a worshiper, as it were, in the church of the civil religion, expanded to accommodate a no-longer strictly Judeo-Christian nation.

It would be incorrect, therefore, to think of American civil religion as simply the vehicle for reaction against dissent or progressive initiatives. Sometimes the values implicit in civil religion can be invoked to call the citizenry to an enhanced vision of issues that have traditionally been very narrowly conceived. For example, some elements in the "pro-life" movement have adopted the rhetoric of the late Cardinal Bernardin; moving away from their almost exclusive focus on abortion, they have become more inclined to see "life issues" as a "seamless garment" encompassing such matters as opposition to the death penalty, criticism of welfare "reform," and support for environmental protection, gun control, health care reform, and immigration rights. The term "right to life" is admittedly ambiguous, but it is language that is without dispute part of the "sacred writings" of our foundational national creed. In this case, the values said to be part of that creed can move public discourse in new, expansive, and creative directions, just as they have so often in the past been used to oppose change.

The threat of religious particularism to the agenda of public theology/civil religion led Ralph Reed, until 1997 the Executive Director of the Christian Coalition and still a visible and influential spokesman for the "Christian right," to a pragmatic compromise. To the extent that specifically doctrinal values are potentially divisive, they should be kept in the sphere of private devotion, off-limits to public debate. Instead, Reed has offered a "new ecumenism" in which people of different religious traditions can work together for public policies designed to protect and enhance "family values." The latter term carries unfortunate political baggage that has prevented Reed's initiative from getting very far. But in the wake of September 11, there is a certain appeal to the idea of setting aside theoretical and ideological points of division and looking for common ground, particularly when it comes to morally approved actions like relief efforts or interfaith dialogue forums. (Johnston [1986] has argued that in fact the New Christian Right has always been a much more diverse group than it appears; it is perforce a coalition, since a tiny core of homogeneous "true believers" could never attain much political clout.) Such a strategy brings us full circle to Rousseau's original analysis of civil religion—the avoidance of sectarian disputation in favor of the unifying values around which a stable . . . society could coalesce.

CONCLUSIONS

Bellah himself grew disillusioned with American civil religion in the midst of the post-Vietnam and Watergate malaise. In 1975, he declared it to be "an empty and broken shell" and apparently did not see that it had a continuing relevance in a changing American culture. Nevertheless, he continues to express the hope that the "biblical and republican" traditions of the United States can reassert themselves. Even if one does not share his faith in the phenomenon of American civil religion per se, one can certainly see the utility of the concept of civil religion as a way of understanding the relationships among a number of salient points in American history and culture.

For Bellah, a public focus on commitment to the common good, as opposed to the excesses of utilitarian and expressive individualism is possible if the once-dominant cultural language of that biblical and republican tradition (relegated for the past several decades to the status of "second language" but revived with much rhetorical fanfare after September 11) is reappropriated by citizens actively pursuing a semblance of the moral order. There are formidable obstacles to forging a national community based on common moral understandings drawn from the traditions of the American civil religion, although the obstacles seem to drop away as crisis makes it once more fashionable to "stand together." By the same token, there is a real danger in allowing these sentiments to slide into triumphalist, unthinking "America first"-ism. Bellah, who was strongly influenced by the theology of Paul Tillich, therefore sees the role of social science as that of facilitator of an evolving dialogue between discipleship and citizenship. American civil religion, as both a social movement and an analytical concept, is probably only salient in the current situation if it provides a moral basis for establishing a new coalition of interests grounded in the traditional values.

According to Novak (2000: 178):

> Judaism and Christianity provided a great deal more than meets the eye . . . to the American founding. They reinforced in men's minds the role of reason in human affairs; the idea of progress in history (as opposed to a wheel of endless rotation); the centrality of personal dignity and personal liberty in human destiny; and the idea of a cosmic process conceived, created, and governed (even in its tiniest details) by a benevolent Deity: Lawgiver, Governor, Judge, gentle and caring Providence. This Deity would one day ask of each human an accounting for his thoughts and deeds. In other words, liberty is no trifling matter. How humans use this liberty matters infinitely. Liberty, so to speak, is the purpose for which the sun and the stars are made. In that respect, America's experiment in liberty is especially dear to Providence.

Richard Mouw (2001: B17), an evangelical Christian theologian, says that September 11 ushered in a "very important time for self-examination." He dismisses the statements of fellow evangelicals Jerry Falwell and Pat Robertson, both of whom claimed that the attacks in New York and Washington had occurred because God had withdrawn his protective shield in anger at America's moral lapses. Mouw prefers to see "every church service, every synagogue service, every mosque service" calling people to "look into their own hearts and lives" and to respond to a "religious call to self-examination." That religious call is therefore clearly not based in denominations or on specific faith traditions; the religion of which Mouw speaks can only be that which unites America—the old civil religion. It is interesting to note how rapidly and thoroughly both Falwell and Robertson were ridiculed and marginalized, despite their prior claim to speak for America's "moral majority." The crisis situation made it clear to a great many Americans that their brand of narrow-minded religiosity is not, after all, the "American way."

REFERENCES CITED

Albanese, Catherine L. 1976. *Sons of the Fathers: The Civil Religion of the American Revolution.* Philadelphia: Temple University Press.

———. 1981. *America: Religions and Religion.* Belmont, CA: Wadsworth.

Bellah, Robert N. 1967. "Civil religion in America." *Daedalus* 96: 1–21.

———. 1970. *Beyond Belief: Essays on Religion in a Post-Traditional World.* New York: Harper.

———. 1975. *The Broken Covenant: American Civil Religion in Time of Trial.* New York: Seabury.

———. 1978. "Religion and Legitimation in the American Republic." *Transaction* 15: 15–22.

———. 1999. "Is There a Common American Culture? Diversity, Identity and Morality in American Public Life." In *The Power of Religious Publics: Staking Claims in American Society,* ed. William H. Swatos and James K. Wellman, 53–68. Westport, CT: Praeger.

Bellah, Robert N., and Phillip E. Hammond. 1980. *Varieties of Civil Religion.* Berkeley: University of California Press.

Chidester, David. 1988. *Patterns of Power. Religion and Politics in American Culture.* Englewood Cliffs, NJ: Prentice-Hall.

Dunn, Charles W. 1984. *American Political Theology: Historical Perspectives and Theoretical Analysis.* New York: Praeger.

Fowler, Robert B., Allen D. Hertzke, and Laura R. Olson. 1999. *Religion and Politics in America: Faith, Culture, and Strategic Choices, 2nd ed.* Boulder, CO: Westview.

Freeman, Joanne B. 2001. "The American Republic, Past and Present." *Chronicle of Higher Education* 48 (5): B6.

Geertz, Clifford. 1966. "Religion as a Cultural System." In *The Interpretation of Cultures,* ed. Clifford Geertz, 87–125. New York: Basic Books.

Hammond, Phillip. 1999. "Can Religion Be Religious in Public?" In *The Power of Religious Publics: Staking Claims in American Society,* ed. William H. Swatos and James K. Wellman, 19–31. Westport, CT: Praeger.

Johnston, Michael. 1986. "The "New Christian Right" in American politics." In *The Political Role of Religion in the United States,* ed. Stephen D. Johnson and Joseph B. Tamney, 125–45. Boulder, CO: Westview.

Jorstad, Erling. 1990. *Holding Fast/Pressing On: Religion in America in the 1980s.* New York: Greenwood.

Kitagawa, Joseph. 1987. *On Understanding Japanese Religion.* Princeton, NJ: Princeton University Press.

LeBeau, Bryan F. 2000. *Religion in America to 1865.* New York: New York University Press.

Long, Charles H. 1974. "Civil Rights—Civil Religion: Visible People and Invisible Religion." In *American Civil Religion,* ed. R. E. Richey and D. G. Jones, 211–21. New York: Harper and Row.

Luckmann, Thomas. 1967. *The Invisible Religion: The Problem of Religion in Modern Society.* New York: Macmillan.

Marty, Martin E. 1959. *The New Shape of American Religion.* New York: Harper.

Mathison, J. A. 1989. "Twenty Years After Bellah." *Sociological Analysis* 50: 129–46.

McGovern, George. 1977. *Grassroots.* New York: Random House.

Mead, Sidney E. 1963. *The Lively Experiment.* New York: Harper.

———. 1975. The nation with the soul of a church. New York: Harper and Row.

Mouw, Richard. 2001. "A Time for Self-Examination." *Chronicle of Higher Education* 48(5): B17.

Novak, Michael. 2000. "The Influence of Judaism and Christianity on the American Founding." In *Religion and the New Republic: Faith in the Founding of America,* ed. James H. Hutson, 159–185. Lanham, MD: Rowman and Littlefield.

Raboteau, Albert J. 1990. "Martin Luther King, Jr. and the Tradition of Black Religious Protest." In *Religion and the Life of the Nation: American Recoveries,* ed. Rowland Sherrill, 46–63. Urbana: University of Illinois Press.

Reeves, Richard. 2001. "Patriotism Calls Out the Censor." *New York Times* on the Web October 1. http:www.nytimes.com.

Reichley, A. James. 1985. *Religion in American Public Life.* Washington, DC: Brookings Institution.

Rouner, Leroy S. 1999. "Civil Religion, Cultural Diversity, and American Civilization." *The Key Reporter* 64(3): 1–6.

Slotkin, Richard. 2001. "Our myths of choice." *Chronicle of Higher Education* 48(5): B11.

Smith, Elwyn A. 1971. "The Voluntary Establishment of Religion." In *The Religion of the Republic,* ed. Elwyn A. Smith, 145–60. Philadelphia: Fortress.

Spillers, Hortense J. 1998. "Martin Luther King and the Style of the Black Sermon." In *Religion in American History,* ed. Jon Butler and Harry S. Stout, 469–85. New York: Oxford University Press.

Swift, Donald C. 1998. *Religion and the American Experience: A Social and Cultural History,* 1765–1997. Armonk, NY: M. E. Sharpe.

Tillich, Paul. 1959. *The Theology of Culture.* New York: Oxford University Press.

Wentz, Richard E. 1998. *The Culture of Religious Pluralism.* Boulder, CO: Westview.

Williams, Rhys H. 1999. "Public Religion and Hegemony: Contesting the Language of the Common Good." In *The Power of Religious Publics: Staking Claims in American Society,* ed. William H. Swatos and James K. Wellman, 169–86. Westport, CT: Praeger.

Williams, Robin M. 1951. *American Society: A Sociological Interpretation.* New York: Knopf.

Wills, Gary. 1978. *Inventing America.* Garden City, NY: Doubleday.

Wilson, Bryan. 1998. "Secularization: The Inherited Model." In *Religion in American History,* ed. Jon Butler and Harry S. Stout, 336–44. New York: Oxford University Press.

Wilson, Charles Reagan. 1990. "God's Project": The Southern Civil Religion, 1920–1980." In *Religion and the Life of the Nation: American Recoveries,* ed. Rowland Sherrill, 64–83. Urbana: University of Illinois Press.

Wimberley, Ronald C., and William H. Swatos. 1998. "Civil religion." In *Encyclopedia of Religion and Society,* ed. William H. Swatos, 94–6. Walnut Creek, CA: AltaMira.

Wuthnow, Robert. 1983. *The New Christian Right: Mobilization and Legitimation.* Hawthorne, NY: Aldine.

———. 1988. *The Restructuring of American Religion: Society and Faith since World War II.* Princeton, NJ: Princeton University Press.

———. 1989. *The Struggle for America's Soul.* Grand Rapids, MI: Eerdmans.

Yamane, David. 1998. "Robert Bellah." In *Encyclopedia of Religion and Society,* ed. William H. Swatos, 48–51. Walnut Creek, CA: AltaMira.

QUESTIONS FOR DISCUSSION

1. What are the three main forms of civil religion, and how have they been expressed in U.S. history?

2. Discuss elements of belief, ritual, and mythology in American civil religion.

3. What does the author have to say about the future prospects of American civil religion? What is your opinion?

SUGGESTED READINGS OR OTHER RESOURCES

General Works

Baumann, Gerd. 1999. *The Multicultural Riddle: Rethinking National, Ethnic, and Religious Identities*. New York: Routledge.

Beyer, Peter. 1994. *Religion and Globalization*. London: Sage.

Johnstone, Ronald L. 1997. *Religion in Society*. 5th ed. Upper Saddle River, NJ: Prentice Hall.

Selected Case Studies

Bakhash, Shaul. 1990. *The Reign of the Ayatollahs: Iran and the Islamic Revolution*, rev. ed. New York: Basic Books.

Bellah, Robert N., Richard Madsen, William M. Sullivan, Ann Swidler, and Steven M. Tipton. 1996. *Habits of the Heart: Individualism and Commitment in American Life*. Berkeley: University of California Press.

Gutiérrez, Gustavo. 1988. *A Theology of Liberation*, trans. C. Inda and J. Eagleson. Maryknoll, NY: Orbis.

Jorstad, Erling. 1987. *The New Christian Right*. Lewiston, NY: Edwin Mellen.

Videos

Civil Religion (Insight Media) is a 60-minute look at civil religion as a symbol-filled form of myth that validates the social order. It considers various types of symbolic activity that characterize civil religion and poses questions about American myths and the cycle of American holidays.

Community of Praise (Insight Media) is a 60-minute examination of faith working in the lives of a fundamentalist family in the U.S.

The Journey: From Faith to Action in Brazil (Insight Media) is a 29-minute case study of liberation theology in practice.

Popular Religion: New Age (Insight Media) is a 60-minute examination of key themes in modern religion, including universalism, illuminism, and millennialism. It includes a clip of an eco-feminist Wiccan full moon harvest ritual and an interview with the group's spiritual leader.

Appendix
Questions for Review

$$\mathrm{T}$$he following chapter-by-chapter questions are designed to help you review the material covered in the text.

CHAPTER ONE: OVERVIEW AND BASIC CONCEPTS

1. What three things are said to be "universal" elements of human culture? What do anthropologists mean when they speak of cultural universals?

2. Who were the Tasaday and what does their case tell us about religion in cultural perspective?

3. What was Tylor's definition of "culture"? Why has it remained the basis for the anthropological understanding of culture?

4. What is implied by the phrase "complex whole" and how does it apply to the study of culture?

5. What is Geertz's definition of "religion"? Why is it of particular use to the contemporary anthropological student of religion?

6. When we speak of the domain of the "sacred," what cultural elements are involved?

7. In what ways do the four subfields of anthropology contribute to a holistic understanding of religion?

8. Explain how the following disciplines differ from anthropology in their study of religion: theology, philosophy, psychology, sociology, comparative religion.

9. In what ways does Nathans' study of a southern black community after slavery help us understand the general principles integrating religion and culture?

CHAPTER TWO: PREHISTORIC RELIGION

1. In what ways is the contemporary anthropological study of prehistoric religion different from the ways it was studied by anthropologists of the nineteenth century?

2. What are some of the main differences between the ways archaeologists and cultural anthropologists study religion as an element of culture?

3. Discuss the role of inference and analogy in the archaeological reconstruction of prehistoric religion.

4. What are some of the material items that might be of interest to an archaeologist studying prehistoric religion?

5. What does the controversy surrounding the interpretation of Machu Picchu, the presumed sacred center of the Incas, tell us about the nature of archaeological research on religion in cultures without written history?

6. What can we know about the culture of prehistoric peoples? In what ways might their subsistence strategies have been involved with their religious practices?

7. What kind of evidence might support the argument that Homo erectus had religious beliefs? Why are we cautious about affirming such an argument?

8. What kind of evidence might support the argument that the Neanderthals had religious beliefs? Why are we cautious about affirming such an argument?

9. What kind of evidence might support the argument that Homo sapiens populations of the Late Stone Age had religious beliefs? Why do we feel that such an interpretation is more likely to be upheld than those dealing with earlier populations?

10. What is "magic," and how might it have been involved in prehistoric religion? What role might it play in modern religions?

11. What is "animism," and why did Tylor think it was the basic form of human religion?

12. Can we say for sure whether animism or animatism came first? Does it matter?

13. How does LeCount's discussion of Mayan feasting help us understand the methods of archaeological reconstruction? How does she make us aware of the limitations of such reconstruction?

CHAPTER THREE: THE IDEOLOGICAL COMPONENT OF THE SACRED

1. What are the three main elements in any belief system? Give examples of each.

2. What is "cosmology," and what types of cosmologies do we find in the world's religions?

3. What are the major types of supernatural beings found in the world's religions? Give examples of each.

4. What does the Hindu concept of *dharma* demonstrate about the ways in which a belief system addresses supernatural, natural, and social orders of existence? Which Hindu sacred book most vividly expresses the concept of *dharma*? How does it do so?

5. Why did the Aztec and Maya engage in human sacrifice?

6. What are the four ways in which someone might become a believer in a given belief system? Give an example of each.

7. What are the five dimensions or levels of belief? Given an example of each.

8. What are the four types of religious experience? Give an example of each.

9. In Turner's article, how do the beliefs of the anthropologist and the community she is studying intersect? In what ways were they the same? How were they different? How did the anthropologist's own beliefs affect her analysis of the culture she was studying?

CHAPTER FOUR: THE RITUAL COMPONENT OF THE SACRED

1. What are the main elements in a definition of "ritual"?

2. Why is ritual so important to religion? How did Rappaport interpret the role of ritual in religion in particular and in culture in general?

3. What are the five major things an anthropologist will look for when studying ritual? Give an example of each.

4. What are the five main types of ritual? Give an example of each.

5. Why is "divination" usually part of a process of healing?

6. What are some examples of divination?

7. What are the five main categories of disease/misfortune causation? Give an example of each.

8. What are the main differences between male and female puberty/initiation rites of passage?

9. How do rites of passage differ from rites of intensification?

10. What was the "vision quest"? Who were the "berdaches" and how does their situation help us understand the importance of the vision quest?

11. What sort of rite of intensification did Durkheim analyze, and why did he think it had cross-cultural significance?

12. What is the difference between salvationary and revitalization rituals?

13. Why do participants in salvationary rituals so often seek to be possessed by the spirits? Which syncretic religious tradition that revolves around spirit possession has been intensively studied?

14. What were some of the main differences between the Handsome Lake and Ghost Dance revitalizations?

15. What was the aim of the cargo cult devotees?

16. What is Rastafarianism, and why is it a particularly interesting example of religion in the age of globalization?

17. What sorts of ritual practitioners are most commonly associated with literate religious traditions? Which ones are most commonly associated with nonliterate traditions?

18. What is the difference between a shaman and a sorcerer? How do they both differ from a witch?

19. What are some of the ways in which a person might be designated as a candidate to become a shaman?

20. Why might accusations of witchcraft be as socially important as the actual practice of witchcraft?

21. In what ways are elements specific to Iroquois culture reflected in Iroquois ritual, as discussed by Tooker? In what ways do Iroquois rituals conform to the general categories discussed in this chapter?

CHAPTER FIVE: THE MYTHOLOGICAL COMPONENT OF THE SACRED

1. What is a "myth"? What is a "mythology"?

2. Why do anthropologists study myths? Why do they not need to be concerned with the empirical truth of those myths?

3. What are some of the main functions of myth?

4. What are the five things an anthropologist will look for in analyzing a myth? Give an example of each.

5. What are the three main traditions associated with the analysis of the function of myth? Give an example of each.

6. Why did Malinowski reject psychoanalytic interpretations of myth? What sort of analysis did he prefer?

7. What are some of the differences between the Freudian interpretation of myth and non-Freudian psychological interpretations (e.g., Kluckhohn's)?

8. How does the concept of "archetype" help us understand Richardson's contrast between Christ and Gilgamesh?

CHAPTER SIX: THE ETHICAL AND MORAL COMPONENTS OF THE SACRED

1. What do we mean when we speak of the "moral code" of a society? What do we mean when we speak of the "ethics" of a given society?

2. How do "laws" differ from moral norms?

3. What are some of the major explanations given in various cultures for where morality comes from?

4. How do moral codes help minority populations in pluralistic societies maintain their identities?

5. Compare and contrast Buddhist, Jain, Christian, and Confucian ethical systems, particularly with regard to the specific "virtues" upheld by each.

6. What are some of the distinctive features of Jivaro ethics? In what ways are they similar to the systems associated with the "world" religions?

7. How does the Navaho conception of ethics differ from that of the white people with whom the Navaho must interact? In what ways are they similar?

Chapter Seven: The Environment of the Sacred

1. What is the difference between "representational" and "sacramental" ways of making the transcendent seem realistic? Give examples of each.

2. What is an "aniconic" religious tradition? Which major world religions are aniconic? In what material ways do they deal with the abstract and the transcendent?

3. What are some of the features of the natural environment that are commonly thought of as constituting "sacred space"?

4. Compare and contrast the architectural design of worship space among the Egyptians, Greeks, Buddhists, Hindus, Confucians, Jews, Muslims, Protestant Christians, Catholic Christians, and Orthodox Christians.

5. Why may some secular places come to be "sacred spaces"? Give some examples.

6. How do the cases of the Bororo and the Caduveo illustrate the interrelationship between the manipulation of material items and religious ideas?

7. How do "communitarian societies" carve out "sacred space" in the midst of pluralistic, secular societies? Give some examples.

8. What are some of the ways religion influences such physical matter as personal hygiene, mating, reproduction, and death? Give examples.

9. How do the three Christian groups in Appalachia studied by Humphrey illustrate the complex interrelationships between people and the land?

Chapter Eight: Religion in an Age of Globalization

1. Why did Freud and Marx look forward to the demise of religion as they understood it?

2. What are some of the main components of the religious response to rapid social change in traditional societies? Give some examples.

3. What are some of the main components of the religious response to social change in pluralistic, secular societies? Give some examples.

4. What are some of the consequences of the "privatization" of religion in modern society?

5. How does Wicca illustrate some of the processes of religious change in modern society?

6. Compare and contrast the Quakers, Mormons, and Shakers on the one hand and the Amish, Hutterites, and Mennonites on the other with regard to their response to the challenges of pluralistic, secular society.

7. What do the popular media usually mean when they speak of "cults"?

8. How does "civil religion" take the place of more traditional religions in modern society? In particular, what are the main dimensions of American civil religion?

9. Compare and contrast the American Christian Right, Liberation Theology, Solidarity, and the Iranian Islamic Revolution. How do they represent variants on a religious response to the challenges of the modern world?

Index[1]

ahimsa, 150
altars, 28
Amish, 205
aniconic religious traditions, 176
animatism, 32, 67
animism, 31, 67
anthropology
    as four-field discipline, 10
    holistic approach of, 10
    perspective on religion of, 10
    subject matter of, 3
archaeology
    analogies in, 28
    definition of, 10, 27
    inferences in, 27
archetypes, cowboys as mythic, 124–125
Arunta, 98
astrology, 96
augury, 96
Aztec, 69–70

baraka (*see mana*)
bear cult, 30
belief systems
    assumptions of, 65–66

beliefs of, specific, 66
consequential level of, 72
emotional level of, 72
facts in relation to, 66
ideological level of, 72
intellectual level of, 72
participation in myth and ritual as factors
    in, 71, 124
and personal experience, 70
and rituals, 94
berdaches, 98
Bhagavad-Gita, 69, 74f
biological anthropology (*see* physical
    anthropology)
body actions, divination by analysis of, 96
Bororo, 179–180, 202
Branch Davidians, 205
Buddhism, 150
burial places, 28

Caduveo, 180, 202
cannibalism
    and human sacrifice, 69, 74f
    ritual, 29
cargo cults, 101–102

---

[1] Featured articles are not included in the index.

Carnival, 99
caste, 68
chaos, primal, 67
charismatic leaders, 206
Christianity, 151, 176, 177, 201
Christian Right, 206–207
churches, 178
Church of Jesus Christ of Latter Day
     Saints, 149, 205
civil religion, 206
communitarian societies, 181, 183f, 204
compadrazco, 98–99
comparative religion, 11
Condomblé (*see* Vodun)
Confucianism, 148, 152
consciousness, altered state of, 104
cosmologies
     natural order of, 67
     social order of, 67
     supernatural order of, 67
cults, 205, 206
cultural anthropology, definition of, 10
cultural relativism, 9
culture
     as complex whole, 5
     concept of, 4, 10
     domain of, 9
     idefinition of, 4
     as learned behavior/ideas, 5
     as shared behavior/ideas, 5
     system of, 70
culture hero, 68
     Prometheus as example of, 68

deity, 67, 68
     as source of morality, 148
Delphi, oracle of, 104
deprivation
     absolute, 203
     relative, 203
dharma, 69, 74f, 148
divination, 96
dreams, 96
Duke, James T., 210f
Durkheim, Emile, 27, 98

equilibrium of nature, 67
essential order, 67
ethics, 147
ethnology (*see* cultural anthropology)
evil eye, 67

fetish, 67
fieldwork, 10, 95
filial piety, 149
folktales, 131f
Force, the, 67
Freud, Sigmund, 127, 201

Geertz, Clifford, 6, 9, 65
Genesis, Book of, 67, 129
genre (*see* myth, form of)
Ghost Dance, 101
ghosts, 68
globalization, 202, 206
grateful dead, 68
grave goods, 30
Ground Zero, 179

Handsome Lake, 100–101
haurispicy, 96
Heaven's Gate, 205
henotheism, 177
Hinduism, 67, 68, 150, 176, 201
Homeric epics, 125, 126, 129
Homo erectus, 29
human universals, 3
hunting and gathering societies, 28
Hutterites, 205

ideology (*see* belief)
Inca, 28
Incwala, 99
Iroquois, 100
Islam, 149, 176, 177, 201
     architectural features of, 178
Islamic Revolution (Iran), 208

Jainism, 148, 150
Jivaro, 152
Johnson, Barry L. (*see* Duke, James T.)
Jonestown (*see* People's Temple)
Judaism, 149, 176, 177
Jung, Carl, 128

karma, 69
Kluckhohn, Clyde, 128
kosher, laws of, 149

language
     of dolphins, 12f
     symbolic forms of, 3
Lascaux, 31, 33f

laws, 147
Lévi-Strauss, Claude, 129, 179
liberation theology, 207
linguistics, 10
lots, casting of, 96

Machu Picchu, 28
magic, 31
Mahavira, 150
Malinowski, Bronislaw, 127
mana, 67
Mardi Gras (*see* Carnival)
Marx, Karl, 201
    and liberation theology, 206
Maya, 67, 69
Mennonites, 205
metaphors, 126
morality, 147
Mormons (*see* Church of Jesus Christ of
    Latter Day Saints)
mosques, 178
mother goddess, 31
myth, 71, 123
    as charter, 124
    content of, 125
    context of, 126
    form of, 125
    function of, 126
    psychological, 127
    social, 127
    structural, 129
    provenience of, 125

Navaho (Navajo), 128, 131f
Neanderthals, 29
necromancy, 96
nirvana, 150

object intrusion, 96
offerings, 28
ordeals, 96
ouija boards, 96

Paiute, 101
Pentecostalism, 205
People's Temple, 205
philosophers, 10
physical anthropology, 10, 181
pillars, 28
pluralism, social, 203

Poseidon, 176
possession, supernatural, 96, 99
    cults of, 100
    and exorcism, 99
prayer, 103
presentiments, 96
priests (and priestesses), 102
privatization of religion, 203
psychologists, 10

Quakers (*see* Religious Society of Friends)

Rappaport, Roy, 94
Rastafarianism, 102
    reggae music and, 102
religion
    aura of factuality of, 8
    conceptions of general order in, 7, 71
    definition of, 6
    moods and motivations in, 7
    as system of symbols, 6
    uniquely realistic nature of, 8, 175
religious experience
    confirming, 73
    ecstatic, 73
    responsive, 73
    revelatory, 73
Religious Society of Friends, 205
religious studies (*see* comparative religion)
representation, 175
revitalization movements, 100–102, 202
rhythm of the seasons, 67
rites of ceremonial obligation, 98–99
rites of intensification, 98
rites of passage, 97–98
rites of reversal, 99
ritual
    active dimension of, 94
    definition of, 93
    human dimension of, 95
    ideological, 97
    material dimension of, 94
    mythological dimension of, 95, 124
    participation in, 71
    revitalization, 100
    salvationary, 99
    supernatural dimension of, 95
    technological, 95
    therapeutic, 96
Roman Catholicism, 176, 207, 208

sacrament, 176
sacred
    domains of, 65, 175, 181
    and profane, 9
    space, 94, 175, 16
    time, 175
soul loss, 97
souls (*see* ghosts)
spirit intrusion, 97
spirituality
    New Age, 204
    pantheistic mysticism, 204
Star Wars (*see* Force, the)
supernatural, 175
Swazi Kingdom, 99
symbols, 6, 126
synagogues, 178
syncretism, 100

taboo
    breach of, 97
    incest, 148
Tasaday, 3
temples
    Buddhist, 178
    Confucian, 178
    Egyptian, 177
    Greco-Roman, 178
    Hindu, 178
theologians, 10
tjurunga, 98
tools
    used by humans, 3
    used by nonhuman primates, 3
    used by other mammals, 3
tool traditions, 3, 29

trance (*see* consciousness, altered state of)
trickster, 68
    Anansi as example of, 68
    coyote as example of, 68
    Sphinx as example of, 68
Trobriand Islands, 127
Tylor, Edward
    definition of animism, 31
    definition of culture, 4

United Society of Believers in Christ's
    Second Appearing, 205

value
    system of, 147
varna (*see* caste)
Venus figurines, 30
virtues
    Buddhist, 149
    Christian, 151
    Confucian, 152
    Jain, 150
vision quest, 97–98
    medicine and, 97
visions, 96
Vodun, 100, 175

Wallace, Anthony, 100
Wicca, 204
witches (non-Western), 104
Wodziwob, 101
Wovoka, 101

Xango (*see* Vodun)

Zionism, 177